CONSULTATION IN COMMUNITY, SCHOOL, AND ORGANIZATIONAL PRACTICE

THE SERIES IN CLINICAL AND COMMUNITY PSYCHOLOGY

CONSULTING EDITORS
Charles D. Spielberger and Irwin G. Sarason

Auerbach and Stolberg Crisis Intervention with Children and Families
Burchfield Stress: Psychological and Physiological Interactions
Burstein and Loucks Rorschach's Test: Scoring and Interpretation
Diamant Male and Female Homosexuality: Psychological Approaches
Erchul Consultation in Community, School, and Organizational Practice: Gerald Caplan's
    Contributions to Professional Psychology
Fischer The Science of Psychotherapy
Hobfoll Stress, Social Support, and Women
Krohne and Laux Achievement, Stress, and Anxiety
London The Modes and Morals of Psychotherapy, Second Edition
Muñoz Depression Prevention: Research Directions
Olweus Aggression in the Schools: Bullies and Whipping Boys
Reisman A History of Clinical Psychology, Second Edition
Reitan and Davison Clinical Neuropsychology: Current Status and Applications
Rickel, Gerrard, and Iscoe Social and Psychological Problems of Women: Prevention and Crisis
    Intervention
Rofé Repression and Fear: A New Approach to the Crisis in Psychotherapy
Savin-Williams Gay and Lesbian Youth: Expressions of Identity
Spielberger and Diaz-Guerrero Cross-Cultural Anxiety, Volume 3
Spielberger, Diaz-Guerrero, and Strelau Cross-Cultural Anxiety, Volume 4
Suedfeld Psychology and Torture
Veiel and Baumann The Meaning and Measurement of Social Support
Williams and Westermeyer Refugee Mental Health in Resettlement Countries

IN PREPARATION

Auerbach Clinical Psychology in Transition
Diamant Homosexual Issues in the Workplace
Spielberger and Vagg The Assessment and Treatment of Test Anxiety

The Caplans—Ruth, Gerald, and Ann.

"It is fitting that this frontispiece should picture the three Caplans because not only are we a tightly knit and mutually supportive family unit, but over the past twenty years most of my books have been written as collaborative family projects. Ann, Ruth, and I have each made available our complementary abilities and skills to one another. Ruth is a historian of ideas who has focused on the 'borderland' between psychology and literature, and has developed specialized skills in analyzing the intricacies of personal and social relationships. I have made use of my clinical experience as a psychoanalyst and as a population-oriented child and family psychiatrist. Ann, a student of politics, has provided both of us with nurturant support and guidance on the cultural and sociopolitical implications of our work. This can be seen most clearly in our latest book, *Mental Health Consultation and Collaboration* (Caplan & Caplan, 1993). Some chapters were written primarily by Ruth, some primarily by me, and some as an integrated joint endeavor, so it is difficult to identify which of us developed the ideas and who wrote the final text."

CONSULTATION IN COMMUNITY, SCHOOL, AND ORGANIZATIONAL PRACTICE:

GERALD CAPLAN'S CONTRIBUTIONS TO PROFESSIONAL PSYCHOLOGY

Edited by

William P. Erchul, Ph.D.
North Carolina State University

 Taylor & Francis

USA	Publishing Office:	Taylor & Francis 1101 Vermont Avenue, N.W., Suite 200 Washington, DC 20005-3521 Tel: (202) 289-2174, Fax: (202) 289-3665
	Distribution Center:	Taylor & Francis Inc. 1900 Frost Road, Suite 101, Bristol PA 19007-1598 Tel: (215) 785-5800, Fax: (215) 785-5515
UK		Taylor & Francis Ltd. 4 John St., London WC1N 2ET Tel: 071 405 2237, Fax: 071 831 2035

CONSULTATION IN COMMUNITY, SCHOOL, AND ORGANIZATIONAL PRACTICE:
Gerald Caplan's Contributions to Professional Psychology

1 2 3 4 5 6 7 8 9 0   B R B R   9 8 7 6 5 4 3

This book was set in Times Roman by Taylor & Francis. The editors were Karen D. Taylor and Heather Jefferson; the production supervisor was Peggy M. Rote; and the typesetter was Phoebe Carter. Cover design by Michelle Fleitz. Cover photography by Michelle Fleitz. Printing and binding by Braun-Brumfield, Inc.

A CIP catalog record for this book is available from the British Library.

♾ The paper in this publication meets the requirements of the ANSI Standard 239.48-1984 (Permanence of paper).

Library of Congress Cataloging-in-Publication Data

Consultation in community, school, and organizational practice:
    Gerald Caplan's contributions to professional psychology / edited by
William P. Erchul.
        p. cm.—(The Series in clinical and community psychology)
    Includes bibliographical references and indexes.

    1. Community psychology. 2. Caplan, Gerald. 3. Mental health
consultation. 4. Community psychiatry. 5. Child mental health.
I. Erchul, William P. II. Series.
    [DNLM: 1. Caplan, Gerald. 2. Community Mental Health Services.
3. Community Psychiatry. 4. Models, Psychological. 5. Referral and
Consultation. 6. School Health Services. WM 30 C7582]
    RA790.95.C66   1993
    362.2′2—dc20
DNLM/DLC
for Library of Congress   92-48807
ISBN 1-56032-264-0   CIP
ISSN 0146-0846

Contents

Part One: The Ideas, Career, and Contributions of Gerald Caplan

Part Two: Caplan's Contributions to the Practice of Psychology

Part Three: Assessing the Present and Future Impact of Caplan's Contributions

Contributors

Thomas E. Backer, Ph.D., president, Human Interaction Research Institute, Los Angeles, CA; associate clinical professor of Medical Psychology, University of California-Los Angeles School of Medicine

George M. Batsche, Ed.D., associate professor, School Psychology Program, Department of Psychological and Social Foundations, University of South Florida, Tampa, FL

Donna Brent, Psy.D., adjunct assistant professor, Department of Psychology, Hartwick College, Oneonta, NY

Gerald Caplan, M.D., F.R.C.Psych., scientific director, Jerusalem Institute for the Study of Psychological Stress and Jerusalem Family Center, Jerusalem, Israel; professor emeritus of Psychiatry, Harvard University; professor emeritus of Child Psychiatry, Hebrew University of Jerusalem, Israel

Jane Close Conoley, Ph.D., professor and chair, Department of Educational Psychology, University of Nebraska-Lincoln, Lincoln, NE

William P. Erchul, Ph.D., associate professor, Department of Psychology, and director, School Psychology Program, North Carolina State University, Raleigh, NC

Ellen Faherty, C.A.S., adjunct faculty member, Alfred University, Alfred, NY

Ira Iscoe, Ph.D., Ashbel Smith professor of psychology, and director, Institute of Human Development and Family Studies, The University of Texas at Austin, Austin, TX

James G. Kelly, Ph.D., professor, Department of Psychology and School of Public Health, University of Illinois at Chicago, Chicago, IL

Howard M. Knoff, Ph.D., professor, School Psychology Program, Department of Psychological and Social Foundations, University of South Florida, Tampa, FL

Harry Levinson, Ph.D., chairman, The Levinson Institute, Belmont, MA; clinical professor of Psychology, Harvard University Medical School, Department of Psychiatry

Joel Meyers, Ph.D., professor, Department of Educational Psychology and Statistics, and director, Programs in School Psychology, University at Albany, State University of New York, Albany, NY

Christine Modafferi, C.A.S., school psychologist, Cairo-Durham Central Schools, Cairo, NY

Ann C. Schulte, Ph.D., associate professor, School of Education, University of North Carolina, Chapel Hill, NC

Charles D. Spielberger, Ph.D., Distinguished Research Professor and Director, Center for Research in Behavioral Medicine and Health Psychology, University of South Florida, Tampa, FL

Edison J. Trickett, Ph.D., professor, Department of Psychology, University of Maryland, College Park, MD

Carolyn Wright, M.S.Ed., director of program, Quality Living, Inc., Omaha, NE

Foreword

by Charles D. Spielberger

The impact of Gerald Caplan's work on the professional practice of psychology over the past three decades is unexcelled. In addition to the tremendous influence of his writings, especially his 1970 book, *The Theory and Practice of Mental Health Consultation*, he has personally and directly affected the professional careers and contributions of a number of distinguished psychologists who worked with him at Harvard, including the authors of several chapters in this volume.

The impetus for this book came from a most exciting symposium, in which I was privileged to participate, on Caplan's contributions to professional psychology. The symposium was held in Boston in August 1990 at the 98th Annual Convention of the American Psychological Association (APA). Organized by William Erchul and sponsored by the APA Division of School Psychology, this symposium celebrated the 20th anniversary of Caplan's classic book. It brought together prominent leaders in community, school, and organizational psychology who were asked to examine and assess the current and future impact of Caplan's ideas on the evolving practice of professional psychology.

This book, *Consultation in Community, School, and Organizational Prac-*

tice, provides a comprehensive and highly informative review of Caplan's contributions to community mental health and population-oriented psychiatry. His creative and highly original approaches to mental health consultation are described in detail from a number of different perspectives. Information is presented by the editor, on Caplan's highly productive career and the work settings in which his concepts and practices developed and evolved, providing a broad framework for understanding Caplan's work. Caplan's perspective on his own work, as reflected in his chapter and in the epilogue, and Erchul's sensitive interview with Caplan add a deeper and richer meaning to this understanding.

Given the origin of Caplan's pioneering work in providing mental health consultation to teachers in Israel, the special focus of this volume on consultation in school settings is most appropriate. Beginning in the late 1950s, my work in public school and community settings during the five years I served as a mental health consultant to the city of Wilmington and New Hanover County, North Carolina, was inspired by Caplan's writings, and I greatly benefited from the opportunity of sitting in on his seminars at the Harvard School of Public Health while I was a member of the Duke University faculty. Caplan's emphasis on detection and prevention of mental health problems, and on working with caregivers in helping children to cope with these problems, has continued to guide my consultation efforts in school and community settings.

In this volume, Iscoe and Meyers et al. report successful applications of Caplan's approach to mental health consultation in the schools, and Knoff and Batsche describe Project ACHIEVE—a comprehensive intervention program in a public school system guided by Caplan's consultation and organizational principles. Conoley and Wright examine some of the challenges that are likely to be encountered in future applications of Caplan's principles in the schools, and Kelly and Trickett describe applications of Caplan's principles and practices in clinical and community psychology. Backer extends the application of Caplan's organizational consultation principles to innovations that contribute to productive survival in public mental health organizations.

The current national debate on public school reform makes the timing of this volume critically important. The application of Caplan's principles of mental health consultation and community psychiatry by school psychologists in public school settings can contribute significantly to enhancing the effectiveness of teachers and the learning experiences of children. Its development during the centennial year of the American Psychological Association is especially pleasing to me, occurring during my 1991–1992 tenure as APA president in which I have endeavored to expand psychology's contributions to education.

Preface

While a first-semester Ph.D. student at the University of Texas in the late 1970s, Professor June Gallessich introduced me to a very thought-provoking and exceedingly well-written book. The book was *The Theory and Practice of Mental Health Consultation*, authored in 1970 by child and community psychiatrist Gerald Caplan. Although I was well acquainted with direct clinical services, Caplan's bold ideas of working in a preventive sense and serving far greater numbers of clients indirectly through consultation had an immediate and strong appeal. After reading the book, I knew I had encountered a framework that was to affect my development as a psychologist in a profound way.

Over a decade or so, I learned that many others shared my admiration for *The Theory and Practice of Mental Health Consultation*, because the book was a widely cited and influential reference in the professional psychology literature. As the 1990 convention program chair for the Division of School Psychology of the American Psychological Association, I invited Gerald Caplan to present an address that would commemorate the 20th anniversary of the publication of his important book.

This anniversary, plus the fact that the APA convention was to be held in Boston—Caplan's home for 26 years while he served as a professor at the Harvard School of Public Health and Harvard Medical School—suggested that a convention program honoring Caplan and his ideas was warranted. Caplan accepted the invitation to speak, and his address was scheduled. To round out this convention program, a symposium panel was formed consisting of prominent leaders in community psychology (Ira Iscoe, James G. Kelly, Charles D. Spielberger), school psychology (Joel Meyers), and consulting psychology (Thomas E. Backer). The charge given to panel members was to describe and assess the impact of Caplan's ideas on the practice of professional psychology. Caplan's address and the symposium panel were well received, judging from the very positive reactions of the many convention participants who attended these sessions.

The present volume, which emerged from that convention program, has two distinct purposes. The first is to describe and evaluate Caplan's approach to consultation and related activities with respect to the current and future practice of community, school, and organizational psychology. The second purpose is to pay tribute to Gerald Caplan, whose ideas relative to prevention, crisis theory and intervention, support systems, community mental health, community organization, mental health consultation, mental health collaboration, mediation, and population-oriented psychiatry have greatly influenced the practice of professional psychology and allied fields.

As editor, I have been very fortunate in securing the cooperation of a most distinguished group of contributors. Each senior author is a recognized national leader and scholar within community, school, and/or organizational psychology. Nearly all have served as president of one or more divisions of APA. Some have been presidents of state psychological associations; others have served as president of other national organizations, such as the National Association of School Psychologists. It has been my pleasure to work with each author in developing the chapters that comprise this volume.

The book consists of three major sections. Part One, "The Ideas, Career, and Contributions of Gerald Caplan," contains three chapters providing background information for the remainder of the volume. In Chapter 1, Ann Schulte and I describe Caplan's conceptual framework, which comprises four models (i.e., primary prevention, crisis, support systems, and population-oriented preventive models) and six methods for practice (i.e., community organization, crisis intervention, consultation, collaboration, support systems intervention, and mediation methods). In Chapter 2, Caplan looks back in evaluating aspects of consultation as well as the community mental health movement, and relates his more recent experiences in Jerusalem as a population-oriented psychiatrist. The interview with Caplan in Chapter 3 offers a personalized account of the development of many of his models and methods, with an emphasis on mental health consultation.

Part Two, "Caplan's Contributions to the Practice of Psychology," consists of five chapters that document Caplan's influence on the way psychology has been applied in various settings. Some of Caplan's less well-known but very important contributions are pointed out by Kelly (Chapter 4) and Iscoe (Chapter 5), two prominent community psychologists who were postdoctoral fellows under Caplan's direction at the Harvard School of Public Health. In Chapter 6,

Meyers and his associates offer a comprehensive review of Caplan's impact on the practice of psychology in the schools. In Chapter 7, Knoff and Batsche describe a current public school reform effort that makes extensive use of Caplan's ideas regarding prevention, consultation, and support systems. Part Two concludes with Chapter 8, in which Backer proposes the Caplan-inspired "survival mode innovation," an adaptive strategy for public mental health agencies to implement in times of decreased funding for services and increased stress among staff.

Part Three, "Assessing the Present and Future Impact of Caplan's Contributions," continues the line of inquiry begun in the previous section and adds to it a glimpse of the future. The three chapters by Trickett, Conoley and Wright, and Levinson evaluate the current and future influence of Caplan's ideas within community, school, and organizational psychology, respectively. In Chapter 12, Caplan has the final word as he reacts to themes presented in the preceding eleven chapters.

Over the course of this project, numerous individuals have offered considerable encouragement and assistance, for which I am grateful. In addition to the chapter authors, these people have included George Albee, Anthony Cancelli, Ruth Caplan, Marvin Fine, Denis Gray, Roy Martin, Walter Pryzwansky, Sylvia Rosenfield, Ann Schulte, and Alex Thomas. Also, Marie Killilea and Herbert C. Schulberg were especially helpful in arranging my initial contact with Gerald Caplan. I wish to acknowledge the financial support of the William T. Grant Foundation, whose Officers' Discretionary Grant #90133990 helped to fund Gerald Caplan's appearance at the 1990 APA convention. Ron Wilder and the editorial staff at Taylor & Francis have been very accommodating and responsive throughout the production process. I am also thankful to Charles D. Spielberger for his great commitment to and support of this book from its inception.

Although it goes without saying, this book could not have been produced without the active support and participation of Gerald Caplan. It has been an honor to have worked with him over the past three years, and I trust that the present volume succeeds in documenting Professor Caplan's outstanding professional achievements as well as conveying his seminal ideas to another generation of mental health and educational professionals.

These opening comments have been written in a very auspicious year. The year 1992 marks the 500th anniversary of Columbus's arrival in the Americas as well as the centennial of the American Psychological Association. Far less widely known, but relevant to the aims of the current volume, is that Gerald Caplan celebrated his 75th birthday in March of this year. I, for one, am gratified that the APA and Gerald Caplan have grown up together. Certainly the practice of psychology in communities, schools, and organizations would be much different today had Gerald Caplan not developed and shared his many insights with us through the years.

William P. Erchul

Part One

The Ideas, Career, and Contributions of Gerald Caplan

Gerald Caplan's Contributions to Professional Psychology: Conceptual Underpinnings

William P. Erchul
North Carolina State University

Ann C. Schulte
University of North Carolina at Chapel Hill

INTRODUCTION

> Consultation . . . denote[s] the process of interaction between two professional persons—the consultant, who is a specialist, and the consultee, who invokes his help in regard to a current work problem with which the latter is having some difficulty, and which he has decided is within the former's area of specialized competence. The work problem involves the management or treatment of one or more clients of the consultee, or the planning or implementation of a program to cater to such clients. (Caplan, 1963, p. 470)

With the advancement of this definition and approach to practice, the delivery of psychological services was forever changed. No longer was a psychologist restricted to a traditional role of conceptualizing a client's problems as the result of an internal pathology and then providing psychotherapy. Instead, the psychologist now was able to function at a higher systems level, helping clients by working with consultees and incorporating a new set of assumptions, models, and techniques to prevent the occurrence of psychological problems in the entire client population.

It seems difficult to overestimate the impact that child and community psychiatrist Dr. Gerald Caplan has had on the modern practice of psychology in communities, schools, and organizations. From creating methods of mental health consultation in the late 1940s, to adapting public health principles for the field of mental health in the 1950s, to training many future leaders of various helping professions from the 1950s on, to pioneering principles that propelled the community mental health movement in the 1960s, to refining social support system interventions in the 1970s, to maintaining and promoting a population-oriented approach throughout the 1980s and 1990s, Dr. Caplan has fashioned a remarkable career dedicated to prevention in its broadest sense. His many achievements have affected not only clinical, school, community, counseling, and organizational psychology, but psychiatry, social work, medicine, and nursing as well.

Many of Caplan's ideas have had and continue to have a forceful impact on the practice of professional psychology. Although the above quote, the title of this volume, and the content of many of its chapters suggest that consultation is Caplan's principal contribution, it is but one piece of a conceptual framework designed to prevent mental illness and promote mental health in the population at large. It is the goal of this chapter to acquaint the reader with the specific elements of this framework.

Following a synopsis of Caplan's career, we offer descriptions of four conceptual models (i.e., the population-oriented prevention, primary prevention, crisis, and support systems models) and six methods for practice (i.e., community organization, crisis intervention, consultation, collaboration, support systems intervention, and mediation) that are associated with Caplan. Figure 1 depicts these models and methods and, as such, serves as an advance organizer for the content of this chapter. The chapter concludes with an assessment of Caplan's impact on professional psychology.

THE AUTHORS' ASSUMPTIONS

Before proceeding further, we wish to make explicit four assumptions. First, although the above models and methods are intertwined and unable to be separated in practice, we have chosen to present each one individually in this chapter for the sake of clarity. Second, because each of the models and techniques merits greater attention than space permits, we present several lists of selected books to consult for additional information, and refer to other chapters in this volume that describe relevant content in greater detail. Although intended to be helpful, we realize the inherent limitations of this approach due, in part, to the vastness of the topics addressed. For example, a recent annotated bibliography (Trickett, Dahiyat, & Selby, in press) on the topic of primary prevention alone lists over 1,300 published articles from 1983 to 1991.

Conceptual Models

Population-Oriented Preventive Model	Primary Prevention Model	Crisis Model	Support Systems Model

Methods for Practice

Community Organization	Crisis Intervention	Mental Health Consultation	Mental Health Collaboration	Support Systems Interventions	Mediation

Figure 1 Gerald Caplan's conceptual models and methods for promoting mental health and preventing mental illness.

Third, Caplan's work may be best interpreted within the context of community mental health, but this is not the explicit focus of the present chapter and volume, which emphasize Caplan's impact on professional psychology generally, and community, school, and organizational psychology specifically. Interested readers are referred to Schulberg and Killilea's (1982) festschrift for a comprehensive treatment of Caplan's work specifically within the framework of community mental health.

Last, but perhaps most importantly, although we attempt to describe concepts associated with Caplan, it is essential to realize that Caplan has worked with many collaborators through the years, and many of the concepts have been developed and extended by individuals having no direct connection to Caplan. It is outside the scope of this chapter to specify precisely how others have contributed to the development of these ideas. Instead, we describe the four models and six methods for practice as revealed primarily through Caplan's writings. We apologize in advance for failing to acknowledge all other individuals who have contributed significantly to these models and methods, which, in the final analysis, go well beyond the thinking of one child and community psychiatrist.

THE CAREER OF GERALD CAPLAN[1]

The Early Years

Gerald Caplan was born in 1917 and was raised in Manchester, England, where he attended Manchester Grammar School. He later went on to Manchester University, from which he earned a special bachelor of science degree in anatomy and physiology in 1937, and his medical degree (MB, ChB) in 1940.

Caplan's first job out of medical school was as a house physician at Winson Green Mental Hospital in Birmingham, England. There, Caplan met and married Ann Siebenberg. In 1943, Caplan and his wife moved to Swansea, South Wales, where he assumed the position of deputy medical superintendent at the Cefn Coed Mental Hospital. While in Wales, Caplan developed and helped to market the "Caplan Electroconvulsive Apparatus," a lightweight electroconvulsive machine. His series of experiments on electroshock treatment formed the basis of a thesis for which he earned the advanced degree of MD from Manchester University.

From 1945 to 1948, Caplan trained in child psychiatry under John Bowlby's direction at the Tavistock Clinic in London. He also received training in psychoanalysis at the Psychoanalytic Institute. Kate Friedlander served as

---

[1]The chronology of events described here is taken from Dr. Ruth Caplan-Moskovich's (1982) excellent biographical chapter. Interested readers are urged to consult this reference for additional information.

Caplan's analyst during this training period, and Anna Freud was the control analyst for Caplan's first psychoanalytic treatment case.

From 1948 to 1952, Caplan lived in Israel, where he assisted in developing the fledgling Jewish state. Initially, he was put in charge of army psychiatry, and later undertook the job of senior advisor in mental health to the Ministry of Health. He also organized the first Department of Mental Health in the state of Israel. Due to a political reorganization, Caplan resigned from the ministry and accepted a position at the Hadassah Hebrew University Medical School. There he established the Lasker Mental Hygiene and Child Guidance Center during the years 1949–1952. At the Lasker Center, Caplan began to build a program of preventive child psychiatry. In particular, his method of "counseling the counselors" (known today as "consultation") enabled staff members to deal more effectively with the more than 1,000 disturbed children who were referred for treatment each year (Caplan, 1970; Rosenfeld & Caplan, 1954).

During a U.S. lecture tour in 1951, Caplan met Erich Lindemann of the Harvard School of Public Health. These two had been unaware of each other's work relative to methods of prevention, yet it was apparent that they were thinking along similar lines. These similar interests led Caplan to request a 1-year sabbatical with Lindemann at Harvard. However, Caplan's request for leave was denied by his superiors at Hadassah. If he were to leave, there would be no guarantee that his position would remain open for him should he return to Jerusalem. In 1952, Caplan left for Boston to begin what would turn out to be a 26-year career at Harvard. Interestingly, Caplan later remarked that, if his Hadassah position had been guaranteed, he would almost certainly have returned to Jerusalem at the end of his 1-year sabbatical (Caplan-Moskovich, 1982).

The Years 1953–1963

When Lindemann moved to the Harvard Medical School as head of the Department of Psychiatry at Massachusetts General in 1953, Caplan replaced him as head of the Community Mental Health Program at the Harvard School of Public Health, where he remained until 1964. During that time, Caplan was involved in many activities, some of which are listed below.

1   He learned about, modified, and applied conceptual models of public health for use in the mental health field (Caplan, 1961a, 1964). In particular, Caplan evolved a new model of prevention of mental disorders, incorporating the now familiar notions of primary, secondary, and tertiary prevention, and attempted to shift the focus of preventive efforts from individuals to populations.

2   At the Boston Psychoanalytic Institute, Caplan continued his training in psychoanalysis, which he completed in 1955. Until 1970, Caplan maintained a

clinical practice that included seeing several patients weekly for intensive individual psychoanalysis.[2]

3   Caplan, Lindemann, and others advanced the model of crisis as a central fulcrum for primary prevention. The emphasis was on the crisis period as one in which individuals are more open to outside influence, and, therefore, to short-term interventions by nonspecialist counselors.

4   Caplan developed, described, defined, and evaluated techniques of mental health consultation (Caplan, 1961a, 1963, 1964).[3]

5   Caplan headed a graduate training program in community mental health that produced more than 100 graduates, many of whom went on to leadership positions in psychology, psychiatry, medicine, public health, social work, and nursing. Two contributors to this volume, James G. Kelly (Chapter 4) and Ira Iscoe (Chapter 5), were postdoctoral fellows under Caplan's direction at the Harvard School of Public Health.

6   Caplan was influential in shaping mental health policy in the state of Massachusetts and the entire United States, as the Community Mental Health Centers Act, P.L. 88-164, became a reality in 1963. In his foreword to Caplan's (1964) *Principles of Preventive Psychiatry*, then Director of the National Institute of Mental Health Dr. Robert H. Felix termed the book a "bible" for community mental health workers.

The Years 1964–1977

In 1964, Caplan moved from the Harvard School of Public Health to the medical school. There his work continued, until his departure from Harvard in 1977. Caplan's significant professional accomplishments from this period are listed below.

1   Caplan refined techniques of mental health consultation, the definitive statement of which is contained in *The Theory and Practice of Mental Health Consultation* (Caplan, 1970). This book, considered a classic reference within professional psychology, is the most frequently cited book in articles that appeared in the *Journal of School Psychology* from 1963 to 1982 (Oakland, 1984).

2   Caplan organized a highly successful multidisciplinary staff seminar on Human Relations and the Law at Harvard Law School, which ran for 3 years (Caplan, 1989).

3   Continuing his lifelong commitment to Zionism, from 1969 to 1977 Caplan studied the intercommunity conflicts of Arabs and Jews in Jerusalem.

---

[2]These career developments help explain why Caplan's population-oriented-models and methods center on a psychoanalytic perspective. Both the more traditional, individual psychoanalytic orientation and Caplan's population-orientation attempt to promote mental health by understanding and genuinely appreciating individuals' personal needs and psychology (Caplan-Moskovich, 1982).

[3]A series of films depicting Caplan's approach to mental health consultation was produced during the mid-1960s. These films are still available for rental from: Audio-Visual Services, The Pennsylvania State University, Special Services Building, 1127 Fox Hill Road, University Park, PA 16803-1824.

This work centered on the community mental health aspects of these conflicts, with special emphasis on mediation (Caplan & Caplan, 1980).

4 Although the beginnings of support systems may be traced to Caplan's work in the early 1950s (Caplan-Moskovich, 1982), Caplan and his associates refined and documented support systems theory and practice during the mid-1970s (Caplan, 1974; Caplan & Killilea, 1976).

The Years 1977–the Present

In 1977, Professor Caplan took early retirement from Harvard and settled in Jerusalem, although little evidence has accumulated over the past 16 years to suggest he retired at all. From 1977 to 1985, Caplan directed a department of child and adolescent psychiatry in the Hadassah Hebrew University teaching hospitals in Jerusalem. During this period, he explored mental health collaboration and other professional partnerships (Caplan, 1981, 1982; Caplan, LeBow, Gavarin, & Stelzer, 1981).

Since 1985, Caplan has been working at the Jerusalem Institute for the study of Psychological Stress and the Jerusalem Family Center, centers that he helped to establish. There he has focused on developing a program to prevent psychological disturbance in the children of divorced and separated parents. He firmly believes that such children represent the largest and most important high-risk child population of our time (Caplan, 1989).

As a result of the warm reception he received at the 1990 convention of the American Psychological Association, and the realization that many of his books are now out of print, Caplan and his daughter Ruth have written a new book. *Mental Health Consultation and Collaboration* (Caplan & Caplan, 1993) provides a thorough, revised description of techniques shown to be useful to those professionals who endorse a population orientation.

To complement the foregoing biographical information, Chapter 3 of this volume contains Caplan's personal career reflections. Next, we present the conceptual models and methods for practice associated with Caplan and his colleagues.

CONCEPTUAL MODELS

Population-Oriented Preventive Model

As early as 1948, Caplan advocated the importance of a population-oriented preventive approach: "The fundamental object of Child Guidance is the promotion of mental health and the prevention of mental disorder both in childhood and in later adult life" (Caplan & Bowlby, 1948, p. 1). Through the years, Caplan elaborated on the population-oriented preventive model using at least three different terms: "community mental health" (Caplan, 1961a), "preventive psychiatry" (Caplan, 1964), and "population-oriented psychiatry" (Caplan, 1989). However it is labeled, this model may well serve as the cornerstone on which his other models and methods rest. Caplan's vision of providing for the psychological well-being of an entire population (vs. individual clients) was central to the launching of the community mental health movement, a point that is underscored and developed further by Trickett in Chapter 9. It is clear that Caplan's population-oriented perspective combined with his preventive orientation resulted in a major shift in how professionals viewed mental illness and its treatment.

The basis for the population-oriented preventive model is found in the field of public health. In the early 1950s, Caplan attended lectures on conceptual models within public health and epidemiology presented by Professor Hugh R. Leavell and other Harvard colleagues. In particular, Caplan has credited Leavell (Clark & Leavell, 1958) with the conceptual development of primary, secondary, and tertiary prevention within public health practice (G. Caplan, personal communication, May 10, 1991). Caplan (1961b, 1964) later evolved a new model of prevention in the mental health field that incorporated this typology of prevention. Although others (Cowen, 1973; Klein & Goldston, 1977) have modified the typology, Caplan's description remains the most well known.

Primary prevention refers to measures that reduce the incidence (i.e., rate of occurrence over time, or new cases) of a disorder by counteracting the harmful factors before they produce the disorder in the population. Within public health, primary prevention may be achieved through actions aimed at health promotion (e.g., education) or specific protection (e.g., vaccination) (Clark & Leavell, 1958). In adapting this concept for use in preventive psychiatry, Caplan (1964) noted that the primary prevention of mental disorders may be achieved through social action (including strategies to increase physical, psychosocial, and sociocultural supplies to the population) and interpersonal action (including strategies to maximize the mental health professional's benefit to the population). Caplan's primary prevention model has evolved to a point of much greater sophistication and utility (Caplan, 1986), and it is presented more extensively in the next section.

Secondary prevention refers to attempts to reduce the prevalence of a disorder, with prevalence denoting the percentage of the population that is afflicted with the disorder at a given time. Whereas primary prevention efforts tend to focus on the entire population, secondary prevention efforts typically focus on a "population at risk"—a portion of the entire population that, under proper conditions, may be very susceptible to a particular disorder. For instance, children of recently separated or divorced parents may constitute a population at risk for behavioral and emotional difficulties. Several well-known examples of secondary prevention efforts are the Primary Mental Health Project (Cowen & Hightower, 1990), the Head Start program, and the recently implemented P.L. 99-457, the Preschool Education of the Handicapped Act.

Tertiary prevention refers to actions that decrease the extent of impairment in the population currently afflicted (Caplan, 1964) and/or increase the extent of ongoing role functioning in the population that already has recovered (Caplan, 1989). Tertiary prevention may be achieved through rehabilitation or disability limitation efforts (Clark & Leavell, 1958). The goal of tertiary prevention is to return disordered individuals to their highest level of adaptive, productive functioning as quickly as possible (Caplan, 1964), such as providing job skills to a recently deinstitutionalized client. Although one may consider tertiary prevention to be synonymous with rehabilitation, Caplan (1964) has restricted use of the latter term to refer to individuals rather than to the population.

With regard to a second semantic issue, Caplan now prefers the term "population orientation" (as in population-oriented psychiatry) to "community" (as in community mental health). He believes it is misleading to refer to people residing in a particular geographic space (i.e., catchment area) as a "community," when in reality they frequently do not share a common history, feeling of identity, or source of stress. In Chapter 2, Caplan develops this point as a critical weakness of the community mental health center model.

Primary Prevention Model

As noted, Caplan's initial conceptual thinking regarding prevention focused on adapting accepted elements from the public health field for use in the mental health field. During the 1960s, his work in primary prevention centered on two major tasks: (a) identifying *biopsychosocial hazards*—stressful events and processes believed to increase the risk of later mental disorder in an exposed population (see Kornberg & Caplan's [1980] extensive review of these risk factors for children), and (b) analyzing *life crises*—brief periods of psychological disequilibrium that represent positive or negative turning points for the development of mental disorder (Caplan, 1964, 1986).

Caplan's further development of the primary prevention model during the 1970s led him to study two other influential factors. The first, *competence*, refers to an internal constitutional and acquired characteristic of individuals that allows them to withstand and master the effects of life's stressors. Competence encompasses the constructs of self-efficacy and invulnerability (Caplan, 1989). The second factor, *social support*, is an external mechanism that allows individuals to handle stressors and master their environment through contacts with significant individuals, groups, and community organizations (Caplan, 1974). Social support theory and intervention, as well as the crisis model and intervention, are topics that are presented in greater detail later in this chapter.

Caplan (1986) assembled these four elements (i.e., biopsychosocial hazards, life crises, competence, and social support) to form a comprehensive model of primary prevention, which he termed the "Recurring themes model of primary prevention." This model is depicted in Table 1.

Although Caplan and Bowlby (1948) were able to speak of prevention only in global terms, Caplan's (1986) "Recurring themes model of primary preven-

Table 1 Recurring Themes Model of Primary Prevention

Past Risk Factors	Intermediate Variables				Outcome
Biopsychosocial hazards (episodes or continuing)	Teaching of competence	Competence (constitutional and acquired)	Reaction to recent or current stress (crisis)	Social supports	
Examples Genetic defects Pregnancy problems Birth trauma Prematurity Congenital anomaly Developmental problems Accidents Illness Hospitalization Poverty Cultural deprivation School failure Family discord Family disruption Parental mental or physical illness Sibling illness	Parents and teachers provide opportunities for child to learn self-efficacy and problem-solving skills. Exposure to increasing stress while providing guidance, emotional support, and teaching skills.	Self-efficacy Quality of self-image and identity. Expect mastery by self and support by others. Tolerance of frustration and confusion. Problem-solving skills, social and material.	Biopsychosocial hazard Bodily damage. Current or recent life change events: loss, threat, or challenge. Adaptation by *Active Mastery* versus *Passive Surrender*. Hopeful perseverance despite cognitive erosion and fatigue. Containment of feelings. Enlisting support.	Cognitive, emotional, and material Supplement ego strength in problem solving. Validate identity. Maintain hope. Help with tasks. Contain feelings. Counteract fatigue.	Sense of well-being. Capacity to study, work, love, and play. Enhanced or eroded competence. Actual psychopathology (D.S.M. III)

Types of Intervention

Social action in health, education, welfare, and legal services Consultation collaboration, and education for professionals	Education of parents and child-care professionals	Education of children and parents	Crisis intervention by anticipatory guidance and preventive intervention	Promote supports Convene network. Convene mutual-help couple. Help mutual-help organizations. Support the supporters.

Preventive intervention to target populations (highest risk groups)

Note. From Caplan, G., "Recent Developments in Crisis Intervention and in the Promotion of Support Services." In M. Kessler and S. E. Goldston (Eds.), *A decade of progress in primary prevention*, p. 237. Copyright 1986 by the Vermont Conference on the Primary Prevention of Psychopathology. Reproduced by permission.

13

tion" offers a high level of specificity made possible only through decades of further study. In this model, past risk factors (i.e., biopsychosocial hazards) interact with intermediate variables (i.e., competence, reactions to crisis, and social supports) to produce outcomes of good or poor mental health. Interventions to aid primary prevention include community social action, consultation, collaboration, education, crisis intervention, and support systems intervention. It is the interaction of these many variables, or "reverberations" (p. 238), that gives the model its name (Caplan, 1986).

Many other authors have written about primary prevention, and Table 2 provides a selective listing of books on this topic. As mentioned in the beginning of this chapter, primary prevention continues to attract considerable attention in human service fields, with over 1,300 papers published on the topic from 1983 to 1991 (Trickett et al., in press).

Crisis Model

It seems paradoxical to talk of crisis as a time for preventive action, but an understanding of Caplan's view of the role of life crises in both mental health and illness resolves this paradox. At the time Caplan was formulating his ideas of how psychiatry and allied professions could prevent psychopathology, crises were seen as important both in normal personality development and the development of psychopathology. Erikson (1950, 1959) portrayed personality development as a series of successive phases, each of which culminated in a crisis and, beginning with Lindemann's (1944) landmark paper, adaptive and maladaptive coping in crises and the role of crises in the development of psychopathology had been topics of study by Caplan (1960, 1964) and others (Janis, 1958; Rapoport, 1963).

A *crisis* is a short period of psychological upset that occurs when a person faces important life problems that cannot be escaped and are not readily resolved with his or her usual problem-solving strategies (Caplan, 1974). These crises may be developmental, arising from the physiological and psychological changes that are part of normal growth, or they may be situational, arising from changes in a person's environment, social role, or health status. The most common example of a life crisis, and the one studied by Lindemann (1944), is the loss of a loved one.

A crisis begins as a situation that causes distress for an individual. When the person's habitual problem-solving responses do not resolve the problem, the individual becomes upset and distressed at both the continuance of the stressor and the inability to deal with it effectively. Usual patterns of functioning are disrupted, and the person experiences a range of negative emotions that can include fear, anxiety, frustration, or guilt.

This upset and tension becomes a stimulus for the individual to mobilize internal and external resources. He or she is more likely to seek the help and counsel of others and is more suggestible and open to new patterns of behavior

Table 2 A Selective Listing of Books/Monographs on Primary Prevention

Author(s)	Year published	Title
G. Caplan	1961	*An Approach to Community Mental Health*
G. Caplan	1961	*Prevention of Mental Disorders in Children*
G. Caplan	1964	*Principles of Preventive Psychiatry*
G. W. Albee & J. M. Joffe	1977	*Primary Prevention of Psychopathology Volume 1: The Issues*
D. C. Klein & S. E. Goldston	1977	*Primary Prevention: An Idea Whose Time Has Come*
D. G. Forgays	1978	*Primary Prevention of Psychopathology Volume 2: Environmental Influences*
R. H. Price, R. F. Ketterer, B. C. Bader, & J. Monahan	1980	*Prevention in Mental Health: Research, Policy, and Practice*
M. Bloom	1981	*Primary Prevention: The Possible Science*
R. D. Felner, L. A. Jason, J. N. Moritsugu, & S. S. Farber	1983	*Preventive Psychology: Theory, Research, and Practice*
M. C. Roberts & L. Peterson	1984	*Prevention of Problems in Childhood: Psychological Research and Applications*
B. A. Edelstein & L. Michelson	1986	*Handbook of Prevention*
M. Kessler & S. E. Goldston	1986	*A Decade of Progress in Primary Prevention*
R. K. Conyne	1987	*Primary Preventive Counseling: Empowering People and Systems*
L. A. Jason, R. Hess, R. Felner, & J. Moritsugu	1987	*Prevention: Toward a Multidisciplinary Approach*
J. Steinberg & M. Silverman	1987	*Preventing Mental Disorders: A Research Perspective*
N. D. Reppucci & J. Haugaard	1991	*Prevention in Community Mental Health Practice*

to resolve the problem or find relief. If these new ways of approaching the situation resolve the problem, the tension and upset abate and psychological equilibrium returns. However, if the problem continues, "major disorganization of the individual" (Caplan, 1964, p. 41) occurs.

How a crisis is resolved has implications for subsequent crises. If, during this period of rising tension, openness to others, and suggestibility, appropriate and adaptive coping strategies are learned, then these strategies are available for dealing with subsequent crises. Likewise, if the strategies that the individual adopts to deal with the crisis are ineffective or maladaptive, the person is left more vulnerable to psychopathology. Thus, in Caplan's words, every crisis ". . . presents both an opportunity for psychological growth and danger of psychological deterioration. It is a way station on a path leading away from or toward mental disorder" (Caplan, 1964, p. 53).

This formulation of crises and their effects on individuals has many implications for prevention. A crisis is a psychological reaction. Whether a particular event precipitates a crisis depends on an individual's perception of the event, available coping mechanisms, and resources to resolve the problem. Some events are likely to be seen as crises for large numbers of persons. By examining these events (i.e., biopsychosocial hazards), some crises can be prevented or lessened. For example, the transition from elementary school to junior high school, with its increased demands, greater number of teachers, and increased peer pressure, can be seen as a hazardous time for many children, precipitating crises in a percentage of students. Modifying the school environment to lessen this crisis, through adoption of a middle school model, can prevent or lessen crises at this transition point.

Crisis also presents an opportunity for prevention. Helping a person resolve a crisis adaptively can prevent a disorder from arising from less healthy coping mechanisms. For example, helping a bereaved widow to mobilize new sources of social support rather than fantasizing that her husband is still alive can help her cope adaptively with the present and leave her better prepared for future crises. Crises also are important from a preventive standpoint, because they are a time when intervention can be done efficiently. Because individuals in crisis generally seek out others and are more open to influence and change than individuals not in crisis, a relatively minor intervention can have significant and long-lasting effects (Caplan, 1964).

The crisis model described above has had a substantial impact on the fields of prevention and community mental health. In addition to giving rise to specific crisis intervention techniques, such as anticipatory guidance and preventive intervention (to be described in a subsequent section of this chapter), the crisis model is the basis for the support systems model, which has changed the field of prevention markedly. The notion that encounters with social institutions and their caregivers (e.g., teachers, nurses, police) during periods of crisis could buffer or exacerbate the effects of the crisis and play a role in their favorable resolution, became a critical foundation for mental health consultation (Caplan, 1970). For the field of community mental health, more generally, crisis theory led to an emphasis on a short time framework and immediacy in dealing with persons in crisis (Caplan, 1986), and signaled a shift in conceptualizing clients from sick persons to everyday persons in untenable circumstances (Auerbach, 1986).

Table 3 provides a selective listing of books on the crisis model and techniques of crisis intervention.

Table 3   A Selective Listing of Books/Monographs on the Crisis Model and Crisis Intervention

Author(s)	Year published	Title
G. Caplan	1961	*An Approach to Community Mental Health*
G. Caplan	1964	*Principles of Preventive Psychiatry*
H. J. Parad	1965	*Crisis Intervention: Selected Readings*
A. Simon, M. F. Lowenthal, & L. J. Epstein	1970	*Crisis and Intervention*
D. C. Aguilera & J. M. Messick	1970, 1986 (5th ed.)	*Crisis Intervention: Theory and Method*
L. Bellak & L. Small	1965, 1978 (2nd ed.)	*Emergency Psychotherapy and Brief Psychotherapy*
J. Lieb, I. I. Lipsitch, & A. E. Slaby	1973	*The Crisis Team: A Handbook for the Mental Health Professional*
R. K. McGee	1974	*Crisis Intervention in the Community*
L. L. Smith	1976	*Crisis Intervention Theory and Practice*
N. Golan	1978	*Treatment in Crisis Situations*
S. L. Dixon	1979	*Working with People in Crisis: Theory and Practice*
E. Lindemann	1979	*Beyond Grief: Studies in Crisis Intervention*
G. F. Jacobson	1980	*Crisis Intervention in the 1980's*
A. W. Burgess & B. A. Baldwin	1981	*Crisis Intervention Theory and Practice: A Clinical Handbook*
B. S. Dohrenwend & B. P. Dohrenwend	1981	*Stressful Life Events and Their Contexts*
K. France	1982	*Crisis Intervention: A Handbook of Immediate Person-to-Person Help*
B. Hafen, B. Peterson, & K. Frandsen	1982	*The Crisis Intervention Handbook*
H. A. Duggan	1984	*Crisis Intervention: Helping Individuals at Risk*
K. A. Slaikeu	1984, 1990 (2nd ed.)	*Crisis Intervention: A Handbook for Practice and Research*
S. M. Auerbach & A. L. Stolberg	1986	*Crisis Intervention with Children and Families*
H. L. Pruett & V. B. Brown	1990	*Crisis Intervention and Prevention*

Support Systems Model

Early in Caplan's writing on crisis intervention, he noted that the outcomes of crises were affected by the support provided to persons in crisis by family members, friends, other members of the community, and social institutions.

This finding, along with work growing out of consultation that emphasized peer rather than professional support and research on the effects of stress on animals and humans (Cassell, 1974), led Caplan (1974, 1976) to propose a much broader model to guide prevention efforts—the support systems model (Caplan, 1986; Caplan-Moskovich, 1982).

The basic premise underlying the support systems model is that social support plays an important health-promoting function and can lessen the risk of both physical and mental illness (Caplan, 1986). This simple premise has profound implications. For primary prevention, it implies that increasing the social supports available to a population can decrease the incidence of physical and psychological disorders. For secondary and tertiary prevention, it implies that individuals who have, or are provided with, social support in stressful situations will be more likely to experience positive outcomes.

Caplan (1974) defined social support as ". . . an enduring pattern of continuous or intermittent ties that play a significant part in maintaining the psychological and physical integrity of the individual over time" (p. 7). Characterizations of how social support accomplishes this effect have focused on the feedback others provide concerning the appropriateness of an individual's actions and interpretations of environmental cues. This feedback permits the individual to distinguish dangerous from safe situations. Without this feedback, the individual would be in a constant state of arousal, which would be so taxing that he or she would be left vulnerable to both physical and psychological disorders. Social supports also can: (a) help the individual mobilize psychological resources and master emotional burdens, (b) share tasks, and (c) provide additional supplies of resources such as money, materials, or skills (Caplan, 1974).

An understanding of the importance of social support in fostering an individual's optimal functioning, under high- and low-stress conditions, leads to many options for the mental health professional interested in prevention. The professional may function as a source of support, convene support for a target individual, promote the functioning of natural helpers in a community, or convene support groups or mutual help groups for individuals facing a common problem (Caplan, 1986). For more information, readers are advised to examine Table 4, which displays some books describing support systems theory and intervention methods.

Although researchers have struggled to precisely define social support systems and understand their effects (Gottlieb, 1983), there can be no doubt that Caplan's pioneering efforts in this field have changed the face of prevention. As medical researchers document links between stress and susceptibility to illness (Cohen, Tyrrell, & Smith, 1991), and loneliness and heart disease survival (Williams et al., 1992), Caplan's legacy is clear.

Table 4   A Selective Listing of Books/Monographs on Support Systems Theory and Intervention

Author(s)	Year published	Title
G. Caplan	1974	*Support Systems and Community Mental Health*
G. Caplan & M. Killilea	1976	*Support Systems and Mutual Help: Multidisciplinary Explorations*
A. H. Katz & E. I. Bender	1976	*The Strength in Us: Self-Help Groups in the Modern World*
A. Gartner & F. Riesmann	1977	*Self-Help in the Human Services*
M. A. Lieberman & L. D. Borman	1979	*Self-Help Groups for Coping with Crisis: Origins, Members, Processes, and Impact*
P. R. Silverman	1980	*Mutual Help Groups: Organization and Development*
B. H. Gottlieb	1981	*Social Networks and Social Support*
B. H. Gottlieb	1983	*Social Support Strategies*
R. E. Pearson	1990	*Counseling and Social Support: Perspectives and Practice*
B. R. Sarason, I. G. Sarason, & G. R. Pierce	1990	*Social Support: An Interactional View*

METHODS FOR PRACTICE

In the previous section, we presented four conceptual models that provide an overarching structure for Caplan's comprehensive approach to promoting mental health and preventing mental disorders. In this section, we describe the six methods for practice that undergird this structure. Examples illustrating the use of each method are included as appropriate.

Community Organization

Achieving the aims of population-oriented preventive psychiatry requires the mental health professional to leave his or her office and enter into the community and/or organizations within the community. Caplan anticipated that individuals within these social systems would have difficulty completely understanding or accepting the professional acting in this new role, and thus might not maximally benefit from the professional's services. As a result, Caplan (1970) spelled out issues surrounding the professional's entry into the community and its organizations to increase the latter's effectiveness. After entry has been achieved, the professional helps to organize community services with the intent of identifying and satisfying the needs of the population (Caplan & Caplan,

1980). *Community organization*, within a Caplanian framework, therefore refers to a set of considerations regarding both the professional's entry into community systems and the subsequent efforts to organize the community for social
action.

Before the professional enters the community to provide mental health services, a detailed assessment of the community must be completed. This analysis, often conducted with the community's support and input, may include an
examination of social, educational, physical health, and mental health needs, as
well as private and public professional resources currently available to meet
these needs. More generally, the community's demographic, political, and economic characteristics (especially when embedded within a historical context)
comprise other important information. Having such knowledge facilitates the
professional's efforts to tailor a mental health program to the community's
unique features (Caplan, 1970).

When this analysis is completed, the professional works with community
leaders to intervene through social action. The intervention component of community organization is illustrated in the book *Arab and Jew in Jerusalem* (Caplan & Caplan, 1980). Over an 8-year period, Caplan served as an assistant to
the mayor of Jerusalem and was charged with developing ways of satisfying the
needs of Jerusalem's Arab population for health, education, and welfare services. One specific project was Caplan's involvement in the development of a
program to improve the vocational education system for Arabs in East Jerusalem. Following several months of data collection (encompassing demographic,
cultural, socioeconomic, sociopolitical, psychosocial, and educational considerations), Caplan submitted an extensive report with detailed programmatic recommendations to influential leaders in education, industry, and government.
Because Caplan earlier had solicited extensive input on the recommendations
from these leaders, the overall plan for action was well received and its implementation widely endorsed. Unfortunately, logistical and budgetary factors pre-
cluded effective implementation of the plan.

It is critical to note that the achievement of community-wide change requires the active involvement and support of political leaders. Otherwise the
professional has no recognized sanction for his or her mission. Having the
support of the mayor of Jerusalem and other key leaders in the Arab and Israeli
communities no doubt contributed to the overall reported success of Caplan's
Jerusalem experience, if not the success of the described vocational education
program (Caplan & Caplan, 1980).

The ultimate goal of community organization is to develop the community's own problem-solving structure and ability (Caplan, 1974). Thus,

> If the community has a well-developed pattern of leaders and followers, good
> communications, an effective control system, and efficient ways of identifying
> problems and of mobilizing and deploying its resources to deal with them, as well

as a value system which accepts the importance of satisfying the human needs of its members, it is likely that the prevalence of mental disorder will be lower than in a similar population and ecological setting which manifests a less developed communal problem-solving structure. (p. 248).

Besides the larger community context, the professional is likely to work within a specific organization and thus must assess and understand its inner workings prior to intervening. Many significant issues regarding entry into an organization are detailed in Caplan's (1970, Ch. 4) description of the steps taken by a mental health consultant in building a relationship with a host (i.e., consultee) organization. Acknowledging that developing ties with the consultee institution can be a lengthy and complicated process, Caplan noted several key elements in building these relationships. For example, the consultant must seek sanction from the highest level administrator, but also inform and seek sanction for consultation at all levels of the organization, because lack of support from any source can impede consultation. (See Kelly's "Law No. 1" in Chapter 4.)

The consultant works initially to develop cordial relations with upper-level administrators and staff members, and to establish a reputation as competent, trustworthy, and willing to help, but remains respectful of the organization's and staff members' own prerogatives. The consultant also should strive to understand the organization's unique set of social norms governing issues such as formality, ways of making appointments, and punctuality. Finally, roles and responsibilities of both the consultant and the consultee institution are to be specified in a contract. Although not always a legally binding document, the contract should be written rather than verbal to avoid misunderstandings between parties and to facilitate later renegotiation if needed (Caplan, 1970).

Once the ground has been prepared through community organization, the professional then may proceed with a variety of services to include crisis intervention, consultation, collaboration, support systems intervention, and/or mediation. We present each of these methods in turn.

Crisis Intervention

Caplan (1986) discussed two interventions for use in crisis situations. The first, *anticipatory guidance and emotional innoculation*, is used when a stressful situation can be anticipated, such as nonemergency surgery. With this technique, what can be expected in the upcoming time of stress is described, as well as the emotions that these circumstances can be expected to elicit. The crisis situation is described in a way that promotes a moderate level of anticipatory distress, and then the individual (and, in some cases, his or her family) is provided with assistance in working out ways to cope with the present distress and the distress of the upcoming crisis situation. Expectations of mastery are raised by focusing on the time-limited nature of the situation and suggesting ways the individual can control the situation or obtain relief. The intervenor also gives assurance that the confusion, distress, and negative emotions experienced by the individual are normal responses to a difficult situation rather than indicators of psychopathology.

Unlike the technique described above, *preventive intervention* is used during a crisis. Its purpose is to help the individual cope more effectively. As Caplan (1986) pointed out, because the goal of this type of intervention is simply to provide immediate, here-and-now assistance in weathering a crisis, it can be done by persons without training in psychological interventions. The activities included in preventive intervention are: (a) short contacts to satisfy dependency needs; (b) help to the individual in finding meaning in their situation; (c) encouragement to seek help without viewing it as a sign of weakness; and (d) actions to counteract feelings of hopelessness, such as reminding the individual of his or her precrisis identity, encouraging action, and emphasizing the normality of reactions.

One of Caplan's (1986) recommendations for intervention at the time of crisis is that the helper support strategic withdrawal when the individual reaches the height of the crisis. Caplan (1989) discussed this recommendation in detail, characterizing this withdrawal as a defense against pain and distress, which the individual in crisis is not yet able to bear. In his book, Caplan (1989) cited his group's findings concerning bereavement outcomes for widows, and Wallerstein and Kelly's (1974) work on adolescent's coping with parental divorce, as the basis for this recommendation. In both cases, it appeared that avoidance did not lead to negative outcomes and, in the case of adolescents, was associated with better outcomes than other coping styles. The notion of strategic withdrawal and concomitant longer periods of adjustment runs counter to earlier characterizations of normal reactions to crises as lasting only 4–6 weeks (Lindemann, 1944).

As mentioned earlier in the chapter, crisis-related roles for mental health professionals include orchestrating preventive intervention activities in times of crisis, examining community hazards to anticipate and lessen crises, consultation to community caregivers regarding clients in crisis, and education for persons in other professions about normal and abnormal coping patterns (Caplan, 1974).

Mental Health Consultation

In part, because consultation has been proclaimed as ". . . a major, if not the major technique and focus of community psychology, community psychiatry, and community mental health" (Mannino & Shore, 1971, p. 1), we regard mental health consultation as one of Caplan's most significant contributions. Due to its importance, we devote greater attention to consultation than to other Caplanian techniques. In this section, we describe the fundamental assumptions and modal process of Caplan's (1970) approach to mental health consultation, and present his four types of consultation, with an emphasis on consultee-centered case consultation.

Basic Description   From the definition that opened this chapter, one can see that specialists such as psychologists provide consultation to other caregiving professionals (i.e., consultees) to assist them in dealing with the psychological aspects of a current work problem involving specific clients or programs. Consultees often are professionals whose backgrounds do not include extensive exposure to mental health issues, and include family doctors, nurses, teachers, lawyers, welfare workers, probation officers, police, and clergy. By providing consultation, a community's mental health can be enhanced by: (a) helping consultees work out ways to conduct their work activities that also promote mental health in their clients, and (b) dealing with personality factors in consultees that interfere with their professional functioning, thus reducing their effectiveness with clients. The primary goals of consultation are to help consultees improve their handling or understanding of the current work problem and to increase their ability to solve future, similar problems (Caplan, 1970, 1974).

Fundamental Assumptions   In their book, Brown, Pryzwansky, and Schulte (1987) explicated five major assumptions that underlie mental health consultation. Because Caplan's consultation model is sometimes misinterpreted as exclusively intrapsychically oriented and these assumptions are not explicit in his work, they are listed here.

1   *Both intrapsychic and environmental factors are important in explaining and changing behavior.* More than any other model of psychological consultation, Caplan's mental health consultation focuses on intrapsychic variables that are important in behavior change. However, perhaps less widely acknowledged is that Caplan (1970) promoted a strong environmental focus with his emphasis on making social institutions (e.g., schools) function more effectively by improving their capacity to deal with the mental health problems of their clients.

2   *More than technical expertise is important in designing effective interventions.* A consultee's adoption of an intervention technique is not solely a function of its effectiveness, but is influenced by many factors, including elements of the consultee's professional role and organizational culture. In Caplan's view, it is unlikely that consultants will be able to design interventions that are wholly appropriate for consultees from other institutions and professions. This is because the consultant does not and cannot understand the consultee's work as well as the consultee himself or herself.

3   *Learning and generalization occur when consultees retain responsibility for action.* Responsibility for problem resolution belongs to the consultee. In fact, the direct involvement of consultants in problem resolution diminishes the consultee's feelings of ownership over problems and solutions generated to resolve them.

4   *Mental health consultation is a supplement to other problem-solving*

mechanisms within an organization. Caplan (1970) assumed that there are several ways of addressing difficulties with clients within an organization and, for many types of problems, procedures other than consultation are more appropriate. As a clear-cut example, skill deficiencies in consultees should be handled through supervision, because consultants are unlikely to understand the skills involved in professions other than their own.

5 *Consultee attitudes and affect are important in consultation, but cannot be dealt with directly.* Instead of focusing on consultee affect, the Caplanian consultant forms hypotheses about the types of personal issues that are interfering with the consultee's functioning and then intervenes *indirectly* by using the work problem as a metaphor for the consultee's problem. Meyers, Brent, Faherty, and Modaferri (Chapter 6) provide an interesting counterpoint to Caplan's indirect methods.

The Process of Mental Health Consultation   Although the process of consultation unfolds somewhat differently within each of Caplan's types of consultation, many concerns and tasks are common to all four types. Because the earlier section on community organization described how the consultant first builds a relationship with a consultee institution, here we summarize Caplan's (1970) description of the consultation process from the next step—the building of relationships with consultees—through follow-up and evaluation.

In establishing relationships with consultees, a Caplanian consultant works to develop a coordinate, nonhierarchical relationship in which professional issues and concerns can be discussed openly. Consultees must learn to view themselves as active participants who can educate the consultant regarding their professional role and its constraints so that the consultant may be most effective. Caplan also emphasized the importance of dealing explicitly with confidentiality issues, assuring consultees that their handling of cases will not be discussed with others, especially their superiors. Consultees also must understand that they retain complete freedom to accept or reject the consultant's advice. Although the consultant has no administrative authority, consultees may feel threatened by the consultant. Thus, the consultant must avoid making judgmental statements regarding consultees' actions because these may reinforce a superior/subordinate, rather than collegial, relationship.

The nature of assessment varies with the specific type of consultation. However, with all types, the consultant privately assesses, to some degree, both the consultee and organizational factors that may have an impact on the consultation problem and its resolution. One important aspect of assessment is the consultant's manner of exploring problems with consultees, which is also an intervention aimed at changing consultees' behavior. Through skillful questioning, consultees' views of their problems may be broadened and later on they may learn to approach new problems in a similar manner.

With respect to intervention, responsibility for action concerning the presenting problem clearly rests with the consultee. However, in consultee-centered consultation, the consultant formulates and carries out interventions to remedy shortcomings within the consultee without the consultee's awareness. These interventions may be relatively simple, such as remaining calm despite a consultee's sense of urgency and anxiety about an issue. Interventions also may be complex, such as in cases of theme-interference reduction. We present theme-interference reduction in greater depth in a later section describing consultee lack of objectivity.

Although not responsible for the outcomes of individual cases or organizational problems discussed, the consultant should indicate an interest in knowing these outcomes. Caplan (1970) also advised the consultant to attempt to evaluate consultation services as a means of increasing professional effectiveness and discussed several evaluation methods.

The Four Types of Mental Health Consultation   Caplan has distinguished four types of consultation based on two major divisions: (a) whether the content focus of consultation is difficulty with a particular client versus an administrative difficulty, and (b) whether the primary goal of consultation is provision of information in the consultant's area of specialty versus improvement of the consultee's problem-solving capacity. We describe the four types of consultation in this section.

Client-Centered Case Consultation   Caplan characterized client-centered case consultation as the most familiar type of consultation performed by mental health professionals. A consultee encounters difficulty with a client for whom he or she has responsibility and seeks in the consultant a specialist who will assess the client, arrive at a diagnosis, and make recommendations concerning how the consultee might modify his or her treatment of the client. Often, the assessment, diagnosis, and recommendations are summarized in a written report submitted to the consultee. The consultee then uses the information provided in the report to develop and implement a plan for dealing with the client with minimal subsequent involvement of the consultant. The primary goal of client-centered case consultation is to develop a plan for dealing with the client's difficulties. Education or skill development for the consultee is a secondary focus.

Consultee-Centered Case Consultation   This type of consultation is most closely identified with Caplan. Consultee-centered case consultation is concerned with difficulties a consultee encounters with a particular client for whom he or she has responsibility in the work setting. The primary goal of consultee-centered case consultation is remediation of the "shortcomings in the consultee's professional functioning that are responsible for difficulties with the present case" (Caplan, 1970, p. 125). Client improvement is viewed as a secondary goal.

Caplan placed the sources of consultee difficulty into four major categories, which necessitate different actions on the part of the consultant. These categories are: (a) lack of knowledge, (b) lack of skill, (c) lack of self confidence, and (d) lack of objectivity. Here we focus on lack of objectivity because of its primary importance within Caplan's approach.

Lack of objectivity   When supervisory and administrative mechanisms are functioning well in a human service organization, the majority of consultee-centered consultation cases will fall in this category. This type of consultee difficulty occurs when consultees lose their usual professional distance or objectivity when working with a client and cannot apply their skills effectively to resolve a current problem involving a client.

Caplan (1970) delineated five categories that reflect most occurrences of consultee lack of objectivity. These categories are: (a) direct personal involvement, (b) simple identification, (c) transference, (d) characterological distortion, and (e) theme interference. Because theme interference assumes a central place in Caplan's writing, we discuss it in detail.

Theme interference   According to Caplan, a theme is a representation of an unsolved problem or defeat that the consultee has experienced, which influences his or her expectations regarding a current work difficulty. The theme takes the form of a syllogism in which the consultee sees an inevitable link between the current situation and an undesirable outcome. In Caplan's (1970) words,

> Statement A denotes a particular situation or condition that was characteristic of the original unsolved problem. Statement B denotes the unpleasant outcome. The syllogism takes the form, "All A inevitably leads to B." The implication is that whenever a person finds himself involved in situation or condition A, he is fated to suffer B, and that this generalization applies universally. (pp. 145–146)

When a consultee experiences theme interference, he or she views the current situation as hopeless and may make several problem-solving attempts that are ill-conceived, hasty, and ineffectual. The unsuccessful outcome of these "constructive" actions confirms the consultee's feelings of hopelessness about the case.

The consultant who encounters a case involving theme interference has two intervention options: (a) *unlinking*, which is only temporarily effective, or (b) *theme-interference reduction*, which brings about a long-term improvement in the consultee. Unlinking occurs when the consultant influences the consultee to perceive the client differently, so that he or she is no longer a member of the initial category. As the consultee begins to see the client more objectively, his or her usual problem-solving skills return.

However, Caplan (1970) considered unlinking a "cardinal error" in consultation technique, because it leaves the consultee's theme intact and theme interference may occur again. The preferred intervention for theme interference is theme-interference reduction, which involves accepting the consultee's unconscious premise that the client's difficulty is a test case for his or her theme and then persuading the consultee that the outcome is not inevitable. This intervention relieves the consultee's anxiety about the case, and he or she is able to resolve his or her problem with the client. This successful experience also serves to invalidate the theme so that the consultee's personal conflict is reduced and his or her future professional functioning is enhanced.

Four principal methods may be used by the consultant to accomplish theme-interference reduction. In each case, the consultant tries to weaken the link between the consultee's initial category and inevitable outcome. The four methods are: (a) verbal focus on the client, (b) the parable, (c) nonverbal focus on the client, and (d) nonverbal focus on the relationship. These techniques can be used alone or in combination to invalidate the theme that causes theme interference, and thus improve the consultee's objectivity and problem-solving capacity with reference to the present case. Iscoe's Chapter 5 offers an intriguing view of theme interference on a system-wide level.

Program-Centered Administrative Consultation   Program-centered administrative consultation is similar to client-centered case consultation. In both types, the consultant is considered a specialist who is called in to carefully study a problem and to provide recommendations for dealing with the problem. However, in client-centered case consultation the consultant's assessment, diagnosis, and recommendations deal with the problems of a particular client; in program-centered administrative consultation, the consultant considers the problems surrounding the development of a new program or some aspect of organizational functioning.

Program-centered administrative consultation typically begins with initial contacts from the organization to explore the possibility of consultation. The consultant then uses these contacts to assess the match between his or her skills and the perceived problem, as well as to identify at what level of the organization sanction will be needed for consultation, and the person or persons who will have the authority to implement consultative recommendations. Unlike case-centered consultation, where a single consultee usually has primary responsibility for a client, the identity of the appropriate consultee who has responsibility for an organizational problem may not be readily known.

Furthermore, unlike consultation concerning a case, organizational factors that are important in administrative consultation may lie outside the mental health specialist's usual area of expertise. Thus, Caplan (1970) cautioned that, in addition to his or her clinical skills, the administrative consultant should have an understanding of organizational theory, planning, financial and personnel management, and administration. The primary goal of program-centered administrative consultation is the development of an action plan that can be implemented by the organization to resolve the administrative problem that prompted consultation.

Consultee-Centered Administrative Consultation   The goal of consultee-centered administrative consultation is to improve the professional functioning of members of an administrative staff. Although consultee-centered administrative consultation may assume different forms, such as consultation with a program director or with a particular group of administrators, much of Caplan's (1970) description of consultee-centered administrative consultation was based on a more broadly conceptualized role for the consultant.

The consultant agrees to work with an organization on a long-term basis; however, the exact focus of consultation and the particular consultees to be involved frequently are not specified. In addition, the consultant is allowed to move freely throughout the levels of the organization. This freedom offers the consultant a view of the entire organization that cannot be obtained by consultees who have a more prescribed role in the organization. Therefore, the consultant does not limit consultation to problems brought to his or her attention by consultees, but instead takes an active role in identifying organizational problems and then approaches potential consultees to discuss these issues.

Because the consultant acts to understand the consultees and their organization, he or she looks for barriers to effective consultee functioning at many different levels. As Caplan (1970) stated,

> [the consultant] must appraise individual personality characteristics and problems among the key administrators, intragroup and intergroup relations in and among the various units of the enterprise, organizational patterns of role assignment and lines of communication and authority, leadership patterns and styles, vertical and horizontal communication, and traditions of participation in decision making. (p. 280)

Interventions in consultee-centered administrative consultation can be directed toward individuals, groups, or the entire organization. At the individual level, the consultant may attempt to expand the list of factors a consultee considers when trying to understand subordinates' actions. At the group level, the consultant may act to improve communication between members of a group, or between a supervisor and his or her staff members. Finally, the consultant may work more globally to improve the overall health of the organization, perhaps by having consultees consider the development of system-wide policies that promote and maintain the mental health of staff members and their clients.

Later in this volume, Backer (Chapter 8) and Levinson (Chapter 11) offer further commentary on program-centered administrative consultation and consultee-centered administrative consultation. Also, Knoff and Batsche (Chapter 7) provide an extended description of a comprehensive school-based organizational consultation effort. Finally, Conoley and Wright (Chapter 10) comment further on mental health consultation in the schools and, more generally, examine the potential future applications of Caplan's ideas in that setting.

Caplan's approach to mental health consultation has inspired many writers in the human services to further develop and expand on his ideas, and Table 5 contains a selective listing of these books. Also, *Mental Health Consultation*

Table 5 A Selective Listing of Books on Consultation

Author(s)	Year published	Title
R. Newman	1967	*Psychological Consultation in the Schools: A Catalyst for Learning*
E. Schein	1969	*Process Consultation: Its Role in Organization Development*
G. Caplan	1970	*The Theory and Practice of Mental Health Consultation*
R. R. Blake & J. S. Mouton	1976	*Consultation*
J. R. Bergan	1977	*Behavioral Consultation*
S. C. Plog & P. I. Ahmed	1977	*Principles and Techniques of Mental Health Consultation*
L. D. Goodstein	1978	*Consulting with Human Service Systems*
J. Meyers, R. D. Parsons, & R. P. Martin	1979	*Mental Health Consultation in the Schools*
J. J. Platt & R. J. Wicks	1979	*The Psychological Consultant*
A. S. Rogawski	1979	*Mental Health Consultations in Community Settings: New Directions for Mental Health Services*
J. C. Conoley	1981	*Consultation in Schools: Theory, Research, Procedures*
J. C. Conoley, & C. W. Conoley	1982, 1992 (2nd ed.)	*School Consultation: Practice and Training*
P. O'Neill & E. J. Trickett	1982	*Community Consultation*
J. L. Alpert	1982	*Psychological Consultation in Educational Settings*
J. Gallessich	1982	*The Profession and Practice of Consultation*
J. L. Alpert & J. Meyers	1983	*Training in Consultation*
S. Cooper & W. F. Hodges	1983	*The Mental Health Consultation Field*
F. V. Mannino, E. J. Trickett, M. F. Shore, M. G. Kidder, & G. Levin	1986	*Handbook of Mental Health Consultation*
L. Idol, P. Paolucci-Whitcomb, & A. Nevin	1986	*Collaborative Consultation*
D. Brown, W. B. Pryzwansky, & A. C. Schulte	1987, 1991 (2nd ed.)	*Psychological Consultation: Introduction to Theory and Practice*
S. A. Rosenfield	1987	*Instructional Consultation*
J. R. Bergan & T. R. Kratochwill	1990	*Behavioral Consultation and Therapy*
G. Caplan & R. B. Caplan	1992	*Mental Health Consultation and Collaboration*
J. E. Zins, T. R. Kratochwill, & S. N. Elliott	in press	*The Handbook of Consultation Services for Children: Applications in Educational and Clinical Settings*

and Collaboration (Caplan & Caplan, 1993) provides an important update on many principles discussed in this chapter.

Collaboration

Consultation is an indirect helping technique that allows the mental health professional to reach a large number of clients. However, this broad reach comes at a cost, and the mental health professional sacrifices direct participation and control over outcomes. There are times when clients' difficulties are sufficiently complex or serious that the mental health professional will not find it feasible or ethical to operate in this indirect role. At these times, a direct service role may be called for, such as assessment, therapy, or counseling. However, an option that combines direct service and indirect service and still retains elements of a preventive approach is *collaboration* (Caplan, 1981; Caplan & Caplan, 1993; Caplan et al., 1981).

Within collaboration, the mental health professional accepts responsibility for the mental health aspects of a case and works directly within a setting to improve conditions that are counter to mental health goals (Caplan et al., 1981). For example, in a school, a psychologist might work directly with a child who has school phobia, but also would work with the child's teacher and principal to assure that the school environment was positive for the child. In a hospital, a psychologist might work with a team of medical personnel treating a chronically ill child to assure that treatment strategies took into account the child and family's psychological needs and coping capacity.

(Caplan & Caplan, 1993) have placed this collaboration at the midpoint of indirect versus direct approaches because there are direct service components, but there also are attempts to educate and influence other staff with regard to the mental health aspects of their role. When these attempts are successful, the mental health professional has functioned in an indirect, preventive role, helping the client and affecting the staff's treatment of other clients in similar circumstances.

Collaboration is often the technique of choice when the mental health professional is internal to an organization. Many of the assumptions on which consultation is based, such as confidentiality, complete consultee freedom to accept or reject advice, and no consultant responsibility for client outcome, are impractical or difficult to achieve when both consultant and consultee belong to the same organization (Caplan & Caplan, 1993). Thus, there is a better fit between the mental health professional's role and the helping technique.

In his writings, Caplan has devoted less attention to collaboration than to the other preventive techniques described in this chapter. Yet the concept is an important one because, as discussed above, there are many situations where the mental health professional may find an opportunity to combine both indirect and direct service roles. Pryzwansky (1974, 1977; Brown, Pryzwansky, & Schulte, 1991; West, 1990) has written extensively about collaboration, particularly in the school setting. In studies of school personnel's service delivery preferences, collaboration is consistently preferred over more indirect service approaches (Babcock & Pryzwansky, 1983; Schulte, Osborne, & Kauffman, in press; West, 1985).

Support Systems Interventions

As noted in the previous section describing the support systems model, an understanding of the importance of social support in promoting adaptive functioning has profound implications for preventive intervention. In Caplan's words, "Professionals interested in promoting mental health on a widespread scale in a population should devote significant effort to fostering the development of support systems" (Caplan, 1974, p. 26).

In designing and providing support systems interventions, the mental health professional monitors the adequacy of social supports for persons under stress and provides or organizes support if the existing social supports are inadequate (Caplan, 1986). More broadly, focused preventive efforts are targeted toward increasing (or improving) professional and nonprofessional supports available in a community.

Support systems interventions that are more narrowly focused on individuals or families under stress include providing and orchestrating professional support, convening a support group for a target individual, and organizing a mutual help couple (Caplan, 1986). In providing support directly to a person or family under stress, the activities of the mental health professional are very similar to the activities of the lay person providing preventive intervention, as described earlier in the "Crisis Intervention" section. The professional has frequent, nurturant contacts with the individual in crisis and his or her family. The professional also supports strategic withdrawal by the individual at peak times of stress, promotes problem solving, and provides encouragement. The professional also complements these with activities requiring more expertise, such as anticipatory guidance, or acts as a mediator between the family and other professionals—interpreting information to the family and interpreting the needs of patients and family to other staff members (Caplan, 1986). The mental health professional also may orchestrate support from other professionals with whom the individual has contact during the crisis period.

Organizing a mutual help couple and convening a support group for a single client are support systems interventions that are targeted at an individual, but do not directly involve the mental health professional. For example, a professional working in a hospital might arrange for an individual about to undergo chemotherapy for cancer to meet a similar individual who has successfully completed chemotherapy. Caplan (1986) termed this dyad a "mutual help couple," because benefits accrue to both the experienced and inexperienced individuals in the pair. The individual about to undergo chemotherapy receives information and a role model for mastering the challenges ahead. The successfully treated individual's own feelings of mastery are reinforced. In other instances, when a mental health professional sees that natural supports are not sufficient to meet a stressed individual's needs, he or she may convene a support group by seeking out family members, community caregivers, or others to provide the needed support.

Support systems interventions may be more broadly focused and, in these cases, serve population-oriented preventive goals. Broadly focused support systems interventions include initiating or organizing new support systems within community institutions or in the community at large, and offering consultation to organizers of existing formal and informal support systems (Caplan, 1974).

Aiding in the development of a mutual help organization is an example of helping to organize a new support system within a community. One of the earliest programs described in community psychiatry is the widow-to-widow program (Silverman, 1976), developed with the Harvard Laboratory of Community Psychiatry. In this program, widows provided support to newly widowed women in the form of friendship, information about coping with common problems, and help finding a job or contacting various agencies (Caplan, 1974). Several chapters of Caplan and Killilea's (1976) book are devoted to describing the formation and functioning of several types of mutual help groups, as well as the mental health professional's role in facilitating their development.

With already existing mutual help organizations, the mental health professional may offer assistance in a variety of forms. For example, he or she may provide consultation to leaders, work to enrich members' understanding of mental health issues, or increase the skills of informal help-givers. Finally, the professional may provide expert guidance in emergency situations where the support provided by a mutual help group is insufficient.

In sum, the notion of providing social support to promote individuals' functioning has spawned a range of interventions. Like other preventive techniques, the strength of these interventions is that they allow many more persons to be reached, and take advantage of existing, but untapped, resources in communities.

Mediation

Mediation is a method whereby a third party promotes communication between hostile individuals or groups freed from distortions linked with dissonances in their perceptions, expectations, interests, values, and attitudes. The aim is to help each side learn enough about the semantic framework and sensitivities of the other and control their own feelings sufficiently to transmit their ideas in an acceptable form to each other. A mediator may personally collect information from each party and transmit selected items to the other party as a way of establishing sufficient common ground to enable the organization of face-to-face discussions. The mediator will then control these discussions to prevent undue interference by the hostile feelings of the participants. (G. Caplan, personal communication, March 23, 1992).

Within population-oriented psychiatry, there is a compelling need for mental health professionals to serve as third-party mediators, because disputes inevitably will arise between community institutions that have resources and consumers who need resources, and between groups sharing disparate views. Because these community disputes often involve sensitive, emotionally-laden issues such as racial prejudice, mental health professionals may be better suited for this activity than recognized community mediators (e.g., judges, attorneys). It is a curious phenomenon that society has legitimized the role of mediator in labor and management negotiations, but not in mental health needs and resources within a community (Caplan, 1970).

To promote the use of mental health mediation, Caplan has defined four possible roles for the mediator (Caplan & Caplan, 1980). First, the professional may align with the institution, helping its staff conduct business more effectively to provide better services to the dissatisfied consumers. Second, the professional may align with the consumers, serving as an advocate and helping them organize their limited resources to obtain greater power and knowledge. Third, the professional may serve on a team that provides an individual consultant to each party, with the expectations that the consultant will help his or her party focus on the objective elements of the dispute and/or will argue the party's position in joint meetings. Fourth, the professional may act as a "true" mediator who safeguards the interests of both sides, but owes primary allegiance to neither. In this case, the mediator helps to clarify each party's priorities and facilitates the negotiation of settlements. In all four roles, the professional must obtain and maintain the sanction of one or both parties, thereby establishing trust is critical to the success of mediation.

Caplan's own work as a mediator in community conflicts was documented extensively in *Arab and Jew in Jerusalem* (Caplan & Caplan, 1980). Using methods derived from community psychiatry (e.g., mental health consultation), ethnography, cultural anthropology, and other fields, from 1969 to 1977 Caplan explored the historically troubled relations between Jerusalem's Arabs and Jews. Caplan's sensitive examination of interpersonal communication (e.g., bargaining, negotiation, social influence) in settings such as government offices and the community marketplace led him to understand fundamental similarities and differences in these two populations. This understanding further led him to serve as an effective mediator in community disputes, and, as mentioned earlier, resulted in his involvement in developing a vocational education program for the Arab population.

Although mediation is a significant role for the population-oriented professional to assume, it is not as prominent in daily practice as consultation, collaboration, or crisis intervention. However, with the recent publication of books such as *Community Mediation: A Handbook for Practitioners and Researchers* (Duffy, Grosch, & Olczak, 1991), mediation may develop a higher profile within psychology and allied fields.

CONCLUSION

Included in Caplan's legacy are contributions both timely and timeless. Although the authors of succeeding chapters provide elaboration, we wish to comment specifically on Caplan's influential contributions relating to prevention, mental health consultation, and support systems before concluding this chapter.

At a time when psychiatry was engaged primarily in the practice of long-term psychoanalysis of individual patients, Caplan (although trained for just such a practice) had the foresight to advocate a population-oriented approach that saw prevention as the ultimate goal. In developing this approach within the mental health field, Caplan adapted public health concepts, including the typology of primary, secondary, and tertiary prevention. This typology continues to serve an organizing function within the field of prevention and, relatedly, one might argue that the *Journal of Primary Prevention* owes its name to Caplan's explorations of public health practice.

A major tool employed to achieve the goal of prevention is mental health consultation, which Caplan initiated in the late-1940s. The community mental health movement saw the widespread use of consultation, and it is certainly a great tribute to Caplan that consultation was included as one of five essential services mandated by P.L. 88-164, the Community Mental Health Centers Act. However, the waning of this movement did not result in the demise of consultation. Rather, specialists such as school psychologists adopted consultation as a primary professional activity, along with assessment and intervention. Other psychologists, as well as counselors and special educators, also came to regard consultation as central to their work. The emergence of three professional journals, *Consultation*, *Consultation: An International Journal*, and the *Journal of Educational and Psychological Consultation*, also may be attributable to Caplan's groundbreaking work in consultation.

We agree with Heller and Monahan's (1977) observation that, because Caplan's model of consultation is embedded within a psychoanalytic perspective, its more general utility is obscured. Regardless of a consultant's theoretical leanings, he or she can learn a great deal from Caplan's writings, especially from his depiction of the consultant–consultee relationship, the consultation process, and the four major types of consultation, as well as his emphasis on both individual and environmental factors in achieving change. These contributions will continue to influence the practice of consultation for decades to come.

The merits of mental health consultation notwithstanding, Caplan also recognized that the population's needs would outstrip available professional resources, and that many people in crisis were not likely to seek out professional help anyway. Thus, in the early 1950s, Caplan first became aware that friends and neighbors could be organized to offer supportive networks to individuals enduring crises, as well as to individuals merely needing an augmentation of existing strengths. The number of mutual help groups and scholarly articles written about them has grown exponentially since the publication of Caplan's two edited books in the mid-1970s, and this trend can be expected to continue well into the next century. In addition, social support has taken new forms not imagined (e.g., electronic bulletin boards offering advice and outreach for persons with disabilities) as computer technology and communication methods have expanded.

Despite of our efforts to isolate three of Caplan's most notable contributions, we conclude by returning to Figure 1, which displays his conceptual models and methods for practice. Ultimately, it is Caplan's entire framework for promoting mental health and preventing mental illness that constitutes his greatest contribution to professional psychology and allied fields. Although Caplan realizes that all professionals do not enthusiastically endorse a population orientation (see Chapter 2), his seminal framework certainly will influence many more generations of professionals who do.

REFERENCES

Aguilera, D. C., & Messick, J. M. (1970). *Crisis intervention: Theory and methodology*. St. Louis: Mosby.

Aguilera, D. C., & Messick, J. M. (1986). *Crisis intervention: Theory and methodology* (5th ed.). St. Louis: Mosby.

Albee, G. W., & Joffe, J. M. (Eds.). (1977). *Primary prevention of psychopathology Volume 1: The issues*. Hanover, NH: University of New England Press.

Alpert, J. L. (Ed.). (1982). *Psychological consultation in educational settings*. San Francisco: Jossey-Bass.

Alpert, J. L., Meyers, J. (Eds.). (1983). *Training in consultation: Perspectives from mental health, behavioral and organizational consultation*. Springfield, IL: C. C. Thomas.

Auerbach, S. M. (1986). Assumptions of crisis theory and a temporal model of crisis intervention. In S. M. Auerbach & A. L. Stolberg (Eds.), *Crisis intervention with children and families* (pp. 3–37). Washington, DC: Hemisphere.

Auerbach, S. M., & Stolberg, A. L. (Eds.). (1986). *Crisis intervention with children and families*. Washington, DC: Hemisphere.

Babcock, N. L., & Pryzwansky, W. B. (1983). Models of consultation: Preferences of educational professionals at five stages of service. *Journal of School Psychology, 21*, 359–366.

Bellak, L., & Small, L. (1965). *Emergency psychotherapy and brief psychotherapy*. New York: Grune & Stratton.

Bellak, L., & Small, L. (1978). *Emergency psychotherapy and brief psychotherapy* (2nd ed.). New York: Grune & Stratton.

Bergan, J. R. (1977). *Behavioral consultation*. Columbus, OH: Merrill.

Bergan, J. R., & Kratochwill, T. R. (1990). *Behavioral consultation and therapy*. New York: Plenum.

Blake, R. R., & Mouton, J. S. (1976). *Consultation*. Reading, MA: Addison-Wesley.

Bloom, M. (1981). *Primary prevention: The possible science*. Englewood Cliffs, NJ: Prentice-Hall.

Brown, D., Pryzwansky, W. B., & Schulte, A. C. (1987). *Psychological consultation: Introduction to theory and practice*. Boston: Allyn & Bacon.

Brown, D., Pryzwansky, W. B., & Schulte, A. C. (1991). *Psychological consultation: Introduction to theory and practice* (2nd ed.). Boston: Allyn & Bacon.

Burgess, A. W., & Baldwin, B. A. (1981). *Crisis intervention theory and practice: A clinical handbook*. Englewood Cliffs, NJ: Prentice-Hall.

Caplan, G. (1960). Patterns of parental response to the crisis of premature birth. *Psychiatry, 23*, 365–374.

Caplan, G. (1961a). *An approach to community mental health*. New York: Grune & Stratton.

Caplan, G. (Ed.) (1961b). *Prevention of mental disorders in children: Initial explorations*. New York: Basic Books.

Caplan, G. (1963). Types of mental health consultation. *American Journal of Orthopsychiatry, 3*, 470–481.

Caplan, G. (1964). *Principles of preventive psychiatry*. New York: Basic Books.

Caplan, G. (1970). *The theory and practice of mental health consultation*. New York: Basic Books.

Caplan, G. (1974). *Support systems and community mental health*. New York: Behavioral Publications.

Caplan, G. (1976). Introduction and overview. In G. Caplan & M. Killilea (Eds.), *Support systems and mutual help: Multidisciplinary explorations* (pp. 1–18). New York: Grune & Stratton.

Caplan, G. (1981). Partnerships for prevention in the human services. *Journal of Primary Prevention, 2*, 3–5.

Caplan, G. (1982). Epilogue: Personal reflections. In H. C. Schulberg & M. Killilea (Eds.), *The modern practice of community mental health: A volume in honor of Gerald Caplan* (pp. 650–666). San Francisco: Jossey-Bass.

Caplan, G. (1986). Recent developments in crisis intervention and in the promotion of support services. In M. Kessler & S. E. Goldston (Eds.), *A decade of progress in primary prevention* (pp. 235–260). Hanover, NH: University Press of New England.

Caplan, G. (1989). *Population-oriented psychiatry*. New York: Human Sciences Press.

Caplan, G., & Bowlby, J. (1948, April). The aims and methods of child guidance. *Health Education Journal*, pp. 1–8.

Caplan, G., & Caplan, R. B. (1980). *Arab and Jew in Jerusalem: Explorations in community mental health*. Cambridge, MA: Harvard University Press.

Caplan, G., & Caplan, R. B. (1993). *Mental health consultation and collaboration*. San Francisco: Jossey-Bass.

Caplan, G., & Killilea, M. (1976). *Support systems and mutual help: Multidisciplinary explorations*. New York: Grune & Stratton.

Caplan, G., LeBow, H., Gavarin, M., & Stelzer, J. (1981). Patterns of cooperation of child psychiatry with other departments in hospitals. *Journal of Primary Prevention, 4,* 96–106.

Caplan-Moskovich, R. B. (1982). Gerald Caplan: The man and his work. In H. C. Schulberg & M. Killilea (Eds.), *The modern practice of community mental health: A volume in honor of Gerald Caplan* (pp. 1–39). San Francisco: Jossey-Bass.

Cassell, J. C. (1974). Psychiatric epidemiology. In G. Caplan (Ed.), *American handbook of psychiatry, Vol. 2* (pp. 402–410). New York: Basic Books.

Clark, E. G., & Leavell, H. R. (1953). Levels of application of preventive medicine. In H. R. Leavell & E. G. Clark (Eds.), *Textbook of preventive medicine* (pp. 7–27). New York: McGraw-Hill.

Clark, E. G., & Leavell, H. R. (1958). Levels of application of preventive medicine. In H. R. Leavell & E. G. Clark (Eds.), *Preventive medicine for the doctor in his community: An epidemiologic approach* (2nd ed.) (pp. 13–39). New York: McGraw-Hill.

Cohen, S., Tyrrell, D. A. J., & Smith, A. P. (1991). Psychological stress and susceptibility to the common cold. *New England Journal of Medicine, 325*(9), 606–612.

Conoley, J. C. (Ed.). (1981). *Consultation in schools: Theory, research, procedures.* New York: Academic Press.

Conoley, J. C., & Conoley, C. W. (1982). *School consultation: Practice and training.* Boston: Allyn and Bacon.

Conoley, J. C., & Conoley, C. W. (1992). *School consultation: A guide to practice and training* (2nd ed.). Elmsford, NY: Macmillan.

Conyne, R. K. (1987). *Primary preventive counseling: Empowering people and systems.* Muncie, IN: Accelerated Development.

Cooper, S., & Hodges, W. F. (Eds.). (1983). *The mental health consultation field.* New York: Human Sciences Press.

Cowen, E. L. (1973). Social and community intervention. *Annual Review of Psychology, 24,* 423–472.

Cowen, E. L., & Hightower, A. D. (1990). The Primary Mental Health Project: Alternative approaches in school-based preventive intervention. In T. B. Gutkin & C. R. Reynolds (Eds.), *The handbook of school psychology* (2nd ed.) (pp. 775–795). New York: Wiley.

Dixon, S. L. (1979). *Working with people in crisis: Theory and practice.* St. Louis: Mosby.

Dohrenwend, B. S., & Dohrenwend, B. P. (Eds.). (1981). *Stressful life events and their contexts.* New York: Prodist.

Duffy, K. G., Grosch, J. W., & Olczak, P. V. (Eds.). (1991). *Community mediation: A handbook for practitioners and researchers.* New York: Guilford.

Duggan, H. A. (1984). *Crisis intervention: Helping individuals at risk.* Lexington, MA: Lexington Books.

Edelstein, B. A., & Michelson, L. (Eds.). (1986). *Handbook of prevention.* New York: Plenum.

Erikson, E. H. (1950). *Childhood and society.* New York: Norton.

Erikson, E. H. (1959). Identity and the life cycle: Selected papers by Erik H. Erickson.

Psychological Issues Monograph, 1(1), 18–166. New York: International Universities Press.

Felner, R. D., Jason, L. A., Moritsugu, J. N., & Farber, S. S. (Eds.). (1983). *Preventive psychology: Theory, research, and practice*. New York: Pergamon.

Forgays, D. G. (Ed.). (1978). *Primary prevention of psychopathology Volume 2: Environmental influences*. Hanover, NH: University Press of New England.

France, K. (1982). *Crisis intervention: A handbook of immediate person-to-person help*. Springfield, IL: C. C. Thomas.

Gallessich, J. (1982). *The profession and practice of consultation*. San Francisco: Jossey-Bass.

Gartner, A., & Riesmann, F. (1977). *Self-help in the human services*. San Francisco: Jossey-Bass.

Golan, N. (1978). *Treatment in crisis situations*. New York: Free Press.

Goodstein, L. D. (1978). *Consulting with human service systems*. Reading, MA: Addison-Wesley.

Gottlieb, B. H. (Ed.). (1981). *Social networks and social support*. Beverly Hills, CA: Sage.

Gottlieb, B. H. (1983). *Social support strategies*. Beverly Hills, CA: Sage.

Hafen, B., Peterson, B., & Frandsen, K. J. (1982). *The crisis intervention handbook*. Englewood Cliffs, NJ: Prentice-Hall.

Heller, K., & Monahan, J. (1977). *Psychology and community change*. Homewood, IL: Dorsey.

Idol, L., Paolucci-Whitcomb, P., & Nevin, A. (1986). *Collaborative consultation*. Rockville, MD: Aspen Systems.

Jacobson, G. F. (Ed.). (1980). *Crisis intervention in the 1980's*. San Francisco: Jossey-Bass.

Janis, I. (1958). *Psychological stress*. New York: Wiley.

Jason, L. A., Hess, R., Felner, R., & Moritsugu, J. (Eds.). (1987). *Prevention: Toward a multidisciplinary approach*. New York: Haworth.

Katz, A. H., & Bender, E. I. (Eds.). (1976). *The strength in us: Self-help groups in the modern world*. New York: New Viewpoints.

Kessler, M., & Goldston, S. E. (Eds.). (1986). *A decade of progress in primary prevention*. Hanover, NH: University Press of New England.

Klein, D. C., & Goldston, S. E. (Eds.). (1977). *Primary prevention: An idea whose time has come* (NIMH, DHHS Publication No. ADM 77-447). Washington, DC: U.S. Government Printing Office.

Lieb, J., Lipsitch, I. I., & Slaby, A. E. (1973). *The crisis team: A handbook for the mental health professional*. Hagerstown, MD: Harper & Row.

Lieberman, M. A., & Borman, L. D. (Eds.). (1979). *Self-help groups for coping with crisis: Origins, members, processes, and impact*. San Francisco: Jossey-Bass.

Lindemann, E. (1944). Symptomatology and the management of acute grief. *American Journal of Psychiatry, 101*, 141–148.

Lindemann, E. (1979). *Beyond grief: Studies in crisis intervention*. New York: Jason Aronson.

Mannino, F. V., & Shore, M. F. (1971). *Consultation research in mental health and related fields*. Public Health Monograph No. 79. Washington, DC: U.S. Government Printing Office.

Mannino, F. V, Trickett, E. J., Shore, M. F., Kidder, M. G., & Levin, G. (Eds.). (1986). *Handbook of mental health consultation* (NIMH, DHHS Publication No. ADM 86-1446). Washington, DC: U.S. Government Printing Office.

McGee, R. K. (1974). *Crisis intervention in the community*. Baltimore: University Park Press.

Meyers, J., Parsons, R. D., & Martin, R. P. (1979). *Mental health consultation in the schools*. San Francisco: Jossey-Bass.

Newman, R. (1967). *Psychological consultation in the schools: A catalyst for learning*. New York: Basic Books.

Oakland, T. (1984). The *Journal of School Psychology*'s first twenty years: Contributions and contributors. *Journal of School Psychology, 22*, 239–250.

O'Neill, P., & Trickett, E. J. (1982). *Community consultation*. San Francisco: Jossey-Bass.

Parad, H. J. (Ed.). (1965). *Crisis intervention: Selected readings*. New York: Family Service Association of America.

Pearson, R. E. (1990). *Counseling and social support: Perspectives and practice*. Beverly Hills, CA: Sage.

Platt, J. J., & Wicks, R. J. (1979). *The psychological consultant*. New York: Grune & Stratton.

Plog, S. C., & Ahmed, P. I. (Eds.). (1977). *Principles and techniques of mental health consultation*. New York: Plenum.

Price, R. H., Ketterer, R. F., Bader, B. C., & Monahan, J. (Eds.). (1980). *Prevention in mental health: Research, policy, and practice* (Vol. 1, Sage Annual Reviews of Community Mental Health). Beverly Hills: Sage.

Pruett, H. L., & Brown, V. B. (Eds.). (1990). *Crisis intervention and prevention*. San Francisco: Jossey-Bass.

Pryzwansky, W. B. (1974). A reconsideration of the consultation model for delivery of school-based psychological services. *American Journal of Orthopsychiatry, 44*, 579–583.

Pryzwansky, W. B. (1977). Collaboration or consultation: Is there a difference? *Journal of Special Education, 11*, 179–182.

Rappoport, R. V. (1963). Normal crisis, family structure and mental health. *Family Process, 2*, 68–80.

Reppucci, N. D., & Haugaard, J. (Eds.). (1991). *Prevention in community mental health practice*. Brookline, MA: Brookline Books.

Roberts, M. C., & Peterson, L. (Eds.). (1984). *Prevention of problems in childhood: Psychological research and applications*. New York: Wiley.

Rogawski, A. S. (1979). *Mental health consultations in community settings: New directions for mental health services*. San Francisco: Jossey-Bass.

Rosenfeld, J. M., & Caplan, G. (1954). Techniques of staff consultation in an immigrant children's organization in Israel. *American Journal of Orthopsychiatry, 24*, 42–62.

Rosenfield, S. A. (1987). *Instructional consultation*. Hillsdale, NJ: Erlbaum.

Sarason, B. R., Sarason, I. G., & Pierce, G. R. (1990). *Social support: An interactional view*. New York: Wiley.

Schein, E. H. (1969). *Process consultation: Its role in organization development*. Reading, MA: Addison-Wesley.

Schulberg, H. C., & Killilea, M. (Eds.). (1982). *The modern practice of community mental health: A volume in honor of Gerald Caplan*. San Francisco: Jossey-Bass.

Schulte, A. C., Osborne, S. S., & Kauffman, J. M. (in press). Teacher responses to two types of consultative special education services. *Journal of Educational and Psychological Consultation*.

Silverman, P. R. (1976). The widow as caregiver in a program of preventive intervention with other widows. In G. Caplan & M. Killilea (Eds.), *Support systems and mutual help: Multidisciplinary explorations* (pp. 233–243). New York: Grune & Stratton.

Silverman, P. R. (1980). *Mutual help groups: Organization and development*. Beverly Hills, CA: Sage.

Simon, A., Lowenthal, M. F., & Epstein, L. J. (1970). *Crisis and intervention*. San Francisco: Jossey-Bass.

Slaikeu, K. A. (1984). *Crisis intervention: A handbook for practice and research*. Boston: Allyn & Bacon.

Slaikeu, K. A. (1990). *Crisis intervention: A handbook for practice and research* (2nd ed.). Boston: Allyn & Bacon.

Smith, L. L. (1976). *Crisis intervention theory and practice*. Washington, DC: University Press of America.

Steinberg, J., & Silverman, M. (Eds.). (1987). *Preventing mental disorders: A research perspective*. (NIMH, DHHS Publication No. ADM 87-1492). Washington, DC: U.S. Government Printing Office.

Trickett, E. J., Dahiyat, C., & Selby, P. (in press). *Primary prevention in mental health 1983–1991: An annotated bibliography*. Washington, DC: U.S. Government Printing Office.

Wallerstein, J. S., & Kelly, J. B. (1974). The effects of parental divorce: The adolescent experience. In E. J. Koupernik & J. C. Koupernik (Eds.), *The child in his family: Children at psychiatric risk* (pp. 479–507). London: Wiley.

West, J. F. (1985). *Regular and special educators' preferences for school-based consultation models: A statewide study* (Tech. Rep. No. 101). Austin, TX: The University of Texas at Austin, Research and Training Institute on School Consultation.

West, J. F. (1990). The nature of consultation vs. collaboration: An interview with Walter B. Pryzwansky. *The Consulting Edge, 2*(1), 1–2.

Williams, R. B., Barefoot, J. C., Califf, R. M., Haney, T. L., Saunders, W. B., Pryor, D. B., Hlatky, M. A., Siegler, I. C., & Mark, D. B. (1992). Prognostic importance of social and economic resources among medically treated patients with angiographically documented coronary artery disease. *Journal of American Medical Association, 267*(4), 520–524.

Zins, J. E., Kratochwill, T. R., & Elliott, S. N. (in press). *The handbook of consultation services for children: Applications in educational and clinical settings*. San Francisco: Jossey-Bass.

Chapter 2

Mental Health Consultation, Community Mental Health, and Population-Oriented Psychiatry

Gerald Caplan

Jerusalem Center for the Study of Psychological Stress

INTRODUCTION

The basic thesis of my 1970 book on mental health consultation (Caplan, 1970) was that community professionals, who are not mental health specialists, are the primary agents in preventing mental disorders in a population. Specialists can best make their contribution to prevention by working inside their agencies rather than in their own mental health clinics or hospitals.

I proposed mental health consultation as a tool to help other professionals incorporate a preventive mental health element into their daily work.

My book explained the principles that guided our techniques and that might be utilized to develop new techniques in other settings. In this regard, it may be valuable to ask which of the ideas of 1970 seem to have stood the test of time. One way to approach such an assessment is to ask myself which techniques and concepts I personally make use of today, following 20 years of psychiatric

Based on a lecture delivered at the Annual Convention of American Psychological Association, Boston, MA, August 13, 1990.

experience in a variety of practice settings in different countries. The following points emerge:

The Noncoercive Consultation Relationship

In the approach proposed in my book, the consultant has a coordinate, non-hierarchical power relationship with the consultee that is expressed by the consultant's nonacceptance of administrative authority over the consultee's actions, or professional responsibility for the client's welfare. The consultee's professional autonomy is fully maintained throughout the consultation, and he or she is free to accept or reject anything the consultant advises regarding the client, the program, or the organizational structure of the consultee institution.

The noncoercive relationship enables the consultant to quickly exert maximum influence on the consultee. The latter must choose from the consultant's formulations which he or she may use in his or her own work. To allow the consultant to leave the consultee free to reject what he or she says, the consultant must have no responsibility for the client or for the actions of the consultee. The consultant is responsible only for doing his or her best to express a sensible opinion about the case. After 20 years, I remain convinced that this approach is valid.

Consultee-Centered Consultation

The 1970 book divides consultation into client-centered case consultation and consultee-centered case consultation. I have continued to appreciate the value of this division in guiding my efforts. For example, in client-centered case consultation I must investigate the client and then communicate my recommendations to the consultee in line with traditional specialist practice. In consultee-centered case consultation, I need not see the client myself, but must focus my investigation on analyzing the consultee's report about the case, as though it were a projective test protocol that reveals the attitudes and perceptions of the consultee, and I must discover whether his or her difficulties are due to his or her lack of knowledge about the issues involved, lack of skill in dealing with them, or lack of professional objectivity. My book conceptualized lack of professional objectivity as being due to the distortion of judgment because of the subjective implications to the consultee of certain elements in the case, the so-called theme interference. How to help the consultee overcome this theme interference was a cornerstone of our consultation method, and it has remained so until this day.

Avoiding Uncovering-Types of Psychotherapy

I am as committed today as I was 20 years ago to keeping the professional role of the consultee separate in my mind and in my formulations from his or her private life. I am just as opposed now, as I was then, to using techniques of uncovering and insight-giving psychotherapy in consultation. My experience has convinced me that I should avoid drawing attention to the specific personal source of a work difficulty in the mind of the consultee. We must maintain our status as two professional colleagues objectively discussing a case, even when I am working hard to understand the elements that are triggering his or her loss of objectivity and how I can help him or her overcome them without endangering his or her professional confidence and poise.

Use of Displacement Object

This cardinal element in consultation technique has indeed stood the test of time. A consultee may become emotionally involved and may express his or her inner conflicts "once removed," as it were, by identifying personally with certain elements in his or her client's drama.

The consultant can also exploit these elements by discussing them in ways that send potent messages to the consultee that have deep psychological significance, without the consultee having to become aware of what is happening and without the consultant making the process explicit. The consultant thus avoids arousing the resistance that would inevitably appear if he or she were to weaken the consultee's defenses by uncovering the nature of his or her unconscious displacements. It is safe for the consultee to feel and express intense feelings about an issue, as long as it is believed that he or she is talking about the client and not about himself or herself.

Orderly Reflection

Increasing experience has emphasized the value of orderly and unhurried reflection during consultation discussions, which increases the consultee's awareness of the range of options and counteracts premature emotionally based closure. Emotional arousal usually distorts cognitive operations, narrows perceptual focus, and prevents rational problem-solving. Consultation combats stereotyping and "complicates the thinking" of consultees because the consultant, as it were, supplements the consultee's ego strength with his or her own.

Widening Frames of Reference

A consultant using our approach, guides the consultee in collecting information about the case and analyzing his or her work problem within the interpenetrating contexts of intrapsychic, interpersonal, and institutional psychosocial systems of client, consultee, and consultant. The consultee is freed to widen his or her own frame of reference and his or her cognitive focus because the consultant supports him or her in feeling safe while dealing with emotionally sensitive issues.

The Consultation Contract

I have repeatedly confirmed the importance of paying particular attention to making explicit and formalizing the successive agreements between the consultee and the consultant institutions that provide the matrix for the development of the individual consultant–consultee relationships. A consultant is not merely a person of good will who is offering help to a colleague. He or she is the representative of the agency that has worked out a partnership agreement, which seeks to fulfill the professional missions of both institutions. This implies that much of the consultant's work must be devoted to exploring feelings of need in the consultee organization, preparing the ground, and negotiating and maintaining sanction, as well as periodically involving the consultees in assessing results and changing needs so that the contract may be renegotiated. This process was discussed in detail in the 1970 book, and experience over the years has convinced me that it is a crucial element in determining whether interactions between a consultant and his or her consultees remain fruitful, or whether they deteriorate into relatively meaningless talk that sooner or later is discarded.

The Consultation Method Must Be Learned

My book gave a precise description of a body of concepts and techniques that were not then and are not today, with certain exceptions, an accepted part of the discipline of any of the traditional mental health professions. It must be learned as a separate method and as an addition to the usual professional curriculum. A professional may be a competent psychologist, but unless he or she has systematically studied this method or some analogue, he or she will not be an effective consultant. Consultation is not modified counseling, modified psychotherapy, or watered-down psychoanalysis, and its skills do not come naturally on the basis of a specialized knowledge of these other methods or through "understanding human nature." In this connection, we should avoid semantic ambiguity. I do not use the term *mental health consultation* to denote any type of extramural interaction of a specialist with another professional, but as one defined and circumscribed type of intervention that conforms to certain specifications.

My book refers to other extramural methods that use different techniques to achieve different goals, such as collaboration, mediation, and community organization. Twenty years later, the process of defining, refining, and evaluating these and other methods of interprofessional influence is still continuing. But one thing is clear: A practitioner must learn each of these as a separate body of skills consciously guided by its own system of concepts if he or she wishes to achieve consistent results, and not to waste his or her own time and other people's money.

MENTAL HEALTH CONSULTATION
AND COMMUNITY MENTAL HEALTH

In 1950, when I took the first steps in developing my consultation method, I was working in Israel. I was responsible for dealing with the mental health problems of 17,000 children being educated in the residential schools of Youth

Aliyah, an organization for the absorption of immigrant children (Rosenfeld & Caplan, 1954). At that time, I conceptualized our method in terms of improving the operations of the staff in managing, on a daily basis, the psychological problems of a particularly needy group of children. I thought of it as a remedial aid that might reduce the need to remove disturbed children to specialized institutions. But the progress of the method soon became intertwined in our development of a model of primary prevention. After President Kennedy's 1963 message to the U.S. Congress on Mental Health and Mental Retardation, our method became incorporated within the rapidly developing community mental health movement. It became a central element in the organization of community mental health centers. It was the impetus for the move by mental health specialists to extend their operations beyond the walls of their traditional clinics and hospitals into other community organizations and institutions.

At that stage, our prevention model focused mainly on the concept of intervention in a current life crisis as an effective and economical way to improve the adaptation of people involved in stressful life situations. The goal was to prevent maladaptive responses that might lead to mental disorder. This intervention was to be undertaken as part of their daily operations by a whole range of community professionals in the fields of welfare, health, and education, who were likely to be in contact with people at such times. We referred to these professionals as "caregiving agents." Mental health consultation was conceptualized as a method whereby a small group of mental health specialists would guide and support these non-mental-health-specialist caregivers, such as doctors, nurses, teachers, clergymen, and welfare workers, in mastering the cognitive and emotional challenges of this addition to their traditional duties.

My book became a manual for the staffs of community mental health centers; and because the method was an officially required element in centers financed by the federal government, the method was used throughout the country.

The results have been mixed. On the one hand, the method has become fashionable; but on the other hand, what consultants in the field have actually done has often borne little resemblance to what I described in my book. The main reason was that public funds were rarely available for staff retraining. Specialists who were ostensibly fulfilling the federally mandated mission of conducting extramural consultation were using makeshift modifications of their traditional clinical tools of psychotherapy or counseling. When they encountered opposition among the staff of the target institution, who objected to being treated as patients, as often happened, they were either thrown out of that institution or they retreated to nonthreatening social interactions with their purported consultees. The outcome was frustrating to all concerned; but the pattern was continued in that or some other community institution because the federal regulations required so-called "mental health consultation" to be included in the program.

This was part of a general picture of ineffectuality in fulfilling the some-times exaggerated promises of political lobbyists, who had been active in secur-ing the large budgetary allocations for community mental health centers from federal and state governments. The lobbyists were too shortsighted to insist on the need to earmark funds to retrain staff members who had mostly been edu-cated in individual-patient-oriented diagnostic and therapeutic clinical methods.

The technical problems of scientific evaluation of the method turned out to be insurmountable, and so the reputation of mental health consultation became inextricably bound up with the popularity of the community mental health cen-ters. Since I left the United States to move to Israel in 1977, I have not kept up to date on the fate of these centers, but my assessment at that time was that their public reputation was declining. Their fall from favor was similar to what had happened repeatedly in the 19th century to population-oriented programs, as described by Ruth Caplan (1969).

Some criticisms of mental health consultation were more legitimate than those based on the current status of the community mental health centers. The assumption that community caregivers were generally quite competent and ef-fective in dealing with their clients, and that their agency usually had an effi-cient system of supervision by senior professionals who would ensure consis-tent high-quality practice, turned out not always to be valid. Thus, our consultation approach, which was restricted to *enabling* consultees to overcome segmental shortcomings in maintaining high quality by remedying narrow lacu-nae in sensitivity, knowledge, skills, and professional objectivity, was not in-variably useful in assisting the consultee to help his or her client. In the many cases where the caregivers were inadequately trained and supervised, another tool needed to be used by a mental health specialist to improve the lot of the client by working inside the domain of the community caregivers rather than organizing referral of the client to his or her own clinic or hospital for special-ized diagnosis and treatment. Since 1970, this other method, which I have named "mental health collaboration," has been developed in community mental health centers and in other population-oriented programs as well.

The essential difference between *collaboration* and *consultation,* as I use the terms, is this: In *collaboration,* the mental health specialist joins the care-giving team inside the community institution, such as a school system or a general hospital, and accepts responsibility for the mental health outcome of its cases. The specialist may fulfill his or her mission by ensuring that the other team members deal effectively with the clients, in line with his or her assess-ment of their needs, or else he or she may undertake to implement part or all of the diagnostic and remedial plan him- or herself. This involves a "hands-on" approach by the specialist, in contrast to the "hands-off" approach of mental health consultation.

Another criticism of mental health consultation is a serious shortcoming in its rationale. We originally proposed consultation as a means to guarantee help to people while they were involved in a current life crisis, on the assumption that at such a time they would naturally be turning for help to a community caregiving professional. However, increasing experience has questioned this assumption. For instance, our Harvard group spent several years studying the ways in which widows grapple with the succeeding crises of their bereavement. We expected to find that most widows would turn to clergymen for help in their predicaments. But our studies revealed that our basic assumption was not valid.

In fact, widows do not regularly seek help from clergymen, and those who do are often disappointed. Widows do not usually obtain support from other community professionals, either. Most of them get help from other widows or from nonprofessional friends and neighbors. This important finding led our Harvard group to organize our widow-to-widow program (Silverman, 1982).

Experience with this program stimulated the development of probably the most important advance in methodology in our field in recent years—Support Systems Theory and Practice (Caplan, 1974; Caplan & Killilea, 1976).

Empirical research demonstrated that individuals involved in stressful life experiences such as bereavement, family breakup, accidents, and bodily illness, were likely to master their predicament without deterioration in their mental health if they received adequate psychosocial support during their crisis. If such support was not given, their risk of becoming psychologically disturbed would increase markedly (Caplan, 1981).

We began to conceptualize the intervention of caregivers, whether or not buttressed by specialist consultation or collaboration, as one form of support system to people in the throes of life crisis. We began to appreciate that, in very many instances, the human support that might make all the difference in ensuring a mentally healthy adaptation was likely to be support by nonprofessionals—family, friends, neighbors, and the so-called "natural caregivers" of the community, as well as fellow members of religious denominations and mutual help groups. The most potent intervention by mental health specialists might be to augment the efforts of the nonprofessional helpers, either directly or through the mediation of the generalist community professionals, rather than improve the direct help that professionals give to people in crisis.

A major weakness of the community mental health center model was its use of catchment areas. The idea itself was attractive: a geographically circumscribed population that would constitute a "community" (Schulberg & Killilea, 1982). It was supposed that the members of this "community" would have common characteristics and, by virtue of their environment would be exposed to particular stresses and be served by a limited number of caregivers. The community mental health center would relate to those members of the population encountering characteristic predicaments or manifesting particular psychiatric disorders, and would articulate with the organized system of professionals and agencies serving them. Unfortunately, the number of inhabitants included in the federally prescribed catchment areas (75,000–200,000) was very large, and

the geographical boundaries carved out on the maps of large cities or metropoli-
tan areas were rarely coterminous with those of a united community bound by
bonds of common history, culture, or identity. Except in small towns or
semirural areas, the population of a catchment area served by a community
mental health center did not constitute an organized community. Also, because
of the size of the area, the number of professionals serving them was too big for
the staff of the center to relate to personally; usually the caregivers did not even
have meaningful relations with each other because they were not part of an
organized system.

In other words, however attractive the conceptual model, it bore little resemblance to the existential realities of the practice field. Nevertheless, the
huge resources of money and manpower did lead to explorations by many gifted
practitioners, who pioneered the development of new methods and techniques
different from those of individual-patient-oriented diagnosis and treatment clinics.

POPULATION-ORIENTED PSYCHIATRY

Although our Harvard group developed many of the concepts and methods of
community mental health centers such as crisis intervention, mental health consultation, and support-systems, and although the group was influential in molding the planning of community mental health center legislation, we never actually worked in a community mental health center. Since I moved back to Israel
in 1977, I have been further cut off from the community mental health center as
a service modality, and I have continued to develop my concepts and to explore
their practice implementation in other settings.

My latest book, *Population-Oriented Psychiatry* (Caplan, 1989), presents
the results of my recent explorations. I believe that they provide a distillation of
ideas and techniques that actually work in the real world, and those that can be
learned or adapted for use in their own settings by other mental health specialists.

In closing, I will summarize some of the more important principles of
population-oriented psychiatry. These principles are equally applicable for psychologists and other specialists who seek to affect *population* and who do not
restrict their mission to affecting the lives of their own individual patients. I
prefer the term *population* to the term *community* because population refers to a
collectivity of people whether or not they are linked together by the shared
history, identification, culture, and residential boundaries that are the necessary
basis for referring to them as a community. They may be organizationally
linked by being members of the staff or the clients of an institution, such as a
school, an army, or a hospital. Or they may simply share a significant characteristic, such as being children of divorced parents or of a parent suffering from
cancer.

Population-oriented practice demands the acquisition of conceptual models and practice methods and skills in addition to those needed by the individual-patient- or individual-family-oriented clinician. These include accepting responsibility for improving the well-being of an entire population, however it is defined and circumscribed. This implies reaching out to change the lives of members of this population by direct interaction and, more important, by influencing the ways they are dealt with by networks of professional and nonprofessional supporters. Primary, secondary, and tertiary prevention are basic elements in this approach (Caplan, 1964); of these, primary prevention is the most important. It implies intervening in the lives of people who do not currently define themselves as being sick or disordered, but who are located and identified by the specialist as being at risk of becoming so because they are exposed to certain potentially harmful factors in the absence of adequate psychosocial supports.

This focus on a circumscribed subpopulation at risk is the cornerstone of such a primary preventive program. It proceeds to reduce the risk by buffering the impact of the harmful factors and increasing the level of meaningful psychosocial support, which will enable the members of the population to master their life problems in healthy ways. These problems may be acute and may lead to the characteristic upsets of crisis, whether single or repeated. They also may be chronic and may take the form of long-term privations or burdens. The strategy of a population orientation prescribes that the specialist should work within the framework of organized collectivities, actual communities when these exist, or institutions or services in health, education and welfare that are already organized to serve their own missions, but that can be exploited to serve the ends of the mental health specialist in locating and identifying the people at risk and in influencing their lives by "plugging into" the existing organized service.

To illustrate these principles, I end with a short description of a program in which I am currently involved in Jerusalem.

The at-risk population on which we focus are the children of divorced parents. Divorce is not as frequent in Israel as in other developed countries: The ratio of divorces to marriages in the United States is currently 1 : 2; in Israel, it is only 1 : 5. This still means that in Jerusalem 250 Jewish parental couples divorced last year, after being married for a median period of 8 years, thus adding about 450 children to the population of 7,500 children below the age of 18 whose parents had divorced in previous years. The rate of psychopathology or social maladjustment that will eventually appear in this child population is estimated at 30–40%, about three times the expectable rate in children of intact families (Caplan, 1989).

Five years ago, we established the Jerusalem Family Center to lower this rate. It is operated by a charitable organization and financed by philanthropic contributions, as well as by the clients, who pay minimal fees for services in accordance with their means. Until now, we have dealt with 331 parental couples before, during, and after the divorce process and with their 829 children under the age of 18. I have seen all the parents and the children myself, with the assistance of two psychologists. Many of our cases were referred by the divorce courts, which asked for advice about the feasibility of parental reconciliation; or, if divorce was inevitable, about custody and visiting arrangements by the noncustodial parent. Other cases were referred by teachers, welfare workers, doctors, or psychologists; about a quarter of the cases came on their own or on the advice of friends who had been helped by us.

Our program includes: (a) mediation to parents to help them work out divorce agreements that cater to the needs of their children; (b) individual or group counseling of parents and children; (c) diagnosis of disturbed children or parents and referral to appropriate remedial agencies; and (d) responding to the requests of the courts for recommendations on custody and child-care arrangements. Our program has been geared to crisis intervention. We have no waiting list and every new case is seen by me within a few days of the initial request for help and our intervention is concluded within a few weeks. We never close a case file. When we complete our first period of interventions, we tell children and parents to expect their existence to be complicated for years to come, because of the inevitable difficulties of living in a divided family. Although most children master these difficulties, it may be helpful to return to us, as the need arises, for guidance and support as they grapple with their problems.

We think of these 331 families not as former clients, but as a population with which we will maintain links as long as they have children under 18. We accept an on-going service responsibility for them, while continually fostering their own autonomy as they actively adjust to the complications of their family breakup and its consequences. Many of them have turned to us intermittently for one or two sessions of counseling and guidance as they have negotiated crises during the following years.

Because of our crisis approach, and because I do most of the work myself, without the need for time-consuming team conferences, I have had no difficulty in keeping abreast of repeated requests for service so far. But as our population increases, we plan to supplement our professional efforts by organizing a mutual-help association among our clients. This will provide them with person-to-person, nonprofessional support and guidance in times of turmoil, which in turn will be given occasional backing by our professional staff.

I spend a good deal of my time outside the center. I use my experience with our clients to provide the basis for an active education program to the generalist professionals in Jerusalem. I have taught systematic courses to family doctors, welfare officers, and educational counselors. I have also given lectures to the staffs of other community agencies in the area who provide family therapy, marriage counseling, and family life education, as well as to judges of the rabbinic courts, which deal with divorce. More significant than this educational effort have been the partnerships I have built up with the four main professional networks that cater to the needs of divorcing parents and their children.

1 I have offered consultation and collaboration to the welfare officers of the Jerusalem Municipality and the Ministry of Welfare, who have the legally mandated responsibility to investigate and report to the courts on the family situation of children whose parents seek divorce. I have helped them investigate their most complicated cases, and, wherever indicated, I have sent supplementary reports to the courts. I have helped train most of their workers, and this has provided an effective basis for collaboration.

2 I have been working collaboratively with 15 educational counselors who serve the Jerusalem school system. Under my direction and supervision, the counselors have organized a series of seminars within their schools for groups of children of divorced parents. In addition, I have offered consultation to these and other counselors on individual cases under their care. In especially difficult cases, I have personally investigated the children and their parents at our center, and then have worked out with the counselor a joint plan of supportive intervention inside the school.

3 I have begun a partnership with the Public Health Department of the Jerusalem Municipality, which provides preventive health care to children under 3 in a network of well-baby clinics, and to adolescents in a special outreach health program in the school system. In the well-baby clinic collaborative program, we intend to visit each of the 20 clinics and carry out a screening interview, together with the public health nurses, with all mothers who have been divorced. On the basis of our joint assessment of the family situation, we will work out a plan for preventive intervention and support to be implemented by the nursing or medical staff with our specialist assistance. This part of our program has already begun and is being well received by the staff and the patients.

4 Jews in Israel may only obtain a divorce at a rabbinic court. Parents who live in Jerusalem obtain their divorce and have their plans for child custody and visitation ratified in the Jerusalem Rabbinic Court. Since the establishment of our program, it has been my ambition to use that site as a major pivot for exerting preventive leverage. Over the past 5 years, I have built up a store of personal good will, mutual respect, and sympathy for our mission among the judges of the Rabbinic Court. But it is not easy for a group of rabbis, with their traditional backgrounds, to articulate their philosophy with a population-oriented psychiatrist, although they, as much as I, are eager to safeguard the interests of the children.

It is not merely a matter of building good personal relationships of trust and respect between us, although this is clearly necessary. The courts are enmeshed in a complicated web of constraints based on religious law and custom, which is designed to protect judges from being prejudiced by litigants who use outsiders to influence their judgment. Jerusalem is made up of small communities bound together by intense neighborhood, family, and ethnic ties; people often utilize personal influence by intermediaries to achieve their goals. Moreover, neighbors are very interested in each other's affairs, and confidentiality in family disputes must be zealously guarded in the courts to prevent gossip and interference by prying neighbors. Divorce cases are tried behind closed doors, and outsiders, even experts, are excluded except when giving evidence. Because of this, the judges have been reluctant to let me into their courtrooms, although they have welcomed me as an expert witness and have been remarkably appreciative of ideas I have presented in lectures and seminars.

Nevertheless, I have made progress in working out a joint plan with the rabbis, by which my staff and I will be allowed to sit in the court building and systematically interview all parents who reach the final stages of the divorce process. Because these couples number only about 250 a year, this is logistically feasible for us. It also will not be difficult to plan a standard half-hour interview to convey crucial messages about how separating spouses may collaborate as co-parents after their divorce to promote the mental health of their children. I have already prepared a two-page summary list of the principles involved, which I have named "Guide for Perplexed Parents Who Are Considering Divorce," borrowed from the title of the religious classic by Maimonides, *Guide For the Perplexed*. I hope to obtain the court's formal approval to give this as an official court document to each couple I interview.

I also plan to use the interview as an opportunity to screen the entire divorcing population to identify the minority whose children are at greatest risk. I then will try to motivate them to seek specialist guidance in another setting. In this connection, the 5-year experience at our center has given us a promising lead. We have been impressed by the finding that if one or both parents suffer from a personality disorder, particularly of the narcissistic, paranoid, or antisocial types, there is an increased likelihood that the process and the outcome of a divorce will be influenced in ways that particularly endanger the future mental health of the children.

Such cases are very difficult for judges to handle, because unconscious, intrapsychic forces in the parents, as well as their lack of insight, may make them resistant to rational considerations and to the verbal formulations of the judges.

I have discussed this issue with the minister of Religious Affairs, whose ministry controls the Rabbinic Courts, and also with the chief rabbis, who are the supreme authority figures in the courts. The chief rabbis, on the basis of years of experience in presiding over divorce suits, agree that these cases possibly represent the 10–15% segment of the parental population in which the psychological dangers to the children after divorce are highest. At the request of the minister, I have drafted a proposed amendment to our divorce laws. The changes would mandate rabbinic court judges to order an investigation of parents and their children by a court-appointed psychiatrist or clinical psychologist whenever the judges suspect that a parent involved in a divorce suit is suffering from a personality disorder. The results of an expert diagnostic investigation, supplemented by the routine report on the family constellation by a welfare officer, should provide important information to enable the court to arrive at a wise judgment, which may reduce the harm to the children.

Rabbinic tradition holds that prevention of divorce is the best way to safeguard the interests of the children. Judges sometimes delay a divorce decision in contested cases for years in the hope that the passage of time and increasing awareness of their socioeconomic interdependence will heal the rifts between feuding parents. My proposal will cause judges to investigate whether particular children are likely to be more harmed by their victimization in a family that is being held together at the demand of a disordered parent, who insists on maintaining it to satisfy his or her irrational drives, rather than by the privations likely to be caused by enforced family break up. They also may realize that termination of such a marriage is a matter of urgency, because its continuation may interfere with the psychological development of the children.

My proposed amendment is currently being studied by the legal advisor of the Rabbinic Courts. After being redrafted, it may be submitted by the minister to parliament for enactment. If this plan is implemented, it should improve the lot of the subpopulation that may be at greatest risk among the high-risk population of children of divorce. If it does not succeed, at least my proposal illustrates how a population-oriented psychiatrist tries to use his clinical findings with a series of individual cases to energize an existing caregiving system to improve the mental health conditions of a large population; and how he attempts to accomplish this by setting in motion social forces that do not depend on his own future input for their continuation.

CONCLUSION

This Jerusalem project introduced me to an unfamiliar world. I was not operating within the auspices of an established institution, such as a mental health clinic, a community mental health center, a school, or a general hospital, which structured and legitimized my activities. I was intervening, often uninvited, in the private lives of mainly healthy parents and children, who did not share an affiliation with a particular organization, and who had come to Jerusalem from many different countries and communities, each with its own values, family customs, and ways of life, which were quite alien to me. I became involved as an untutored outsider in the intricate procedures of rabbinic courts. Yet I discovered that the basic principles of population-oriented psychiatry that have evolved from ideas discussed in my 1970 book helped me to establish a viable program of primary prevention.

When we moved out of our clinics we gained the opportunity for more than a mere extension or change of venue for our operations. We became immersed in the mainstream of ordinary life, where healthy people behaved very differently from the patients and their families in our clinics, who were quite unrepresentative of the general population. We were faced with the challenge of modifying our clinical ideas to conform with our new perceptions of real life. Our professionalized view of human relations appeared to oversimplify the ways ordinary people actually behave. Like emigrants from their native land, when we left our clinics we often left behind the privileges and prerogatives of our former professional status, including the right to involve ourselves in the private life of other people. With each encounter with a new individual or group, we had to begin afresh to negotiate an acceptance of our role and status, not infrequently in the face of derogatory stereotypes and prejudices.

Nevertheless, many of us believe that we have managed, as I have done in Jerusalem, to work productively in many different types of normal populations in pursuit of our professional goals. This has demanded that we be continuously alert and active in questioning and modifying our assumptions, theories, and techniques in the light of our new perceptions of different realities. This is cognitively difficult and emotionally burdensome. We are constantly exposed to the seduction of defending against these difficulties by retiring into professional orthodoxy and the canonization and petrification of theory and practice, followed by selective inattention to those ideas and people who do not fit. Another defense might be laissez faire eclecticism, like drifting in a rudderless boat, which we should reject as being the antithesis of our professional approach, as well as being an ineffectual way to achieve our goals.

Population-oriented psychiatry or psychology will not be to everybody's taste. But to those of us who are exhilarated by the challenge of constantly exploring and mastering novel predicaments, this field is very exciting. For me, it has been supremely satisfying. Over the years, I have come to realize that my accumulating store of basic principles provides a useful guide to deal effectively with continually changing and unpredictable realities. I am happy when I can add to this store on the basis of my new experiences. I have seen evidence that I have improved the lives of many people with whom I have been involved, although they did not initially ask for my help. Above all, I have seen signs that I have contributed to setting in motion social forces that are likely to benefit the lives of countless people with whom I have had no personal contact.

REFERENCES

Caplan, G. (1964). *Principles of preventive psychiatry*. New York: Basic Books.

Caplan, G. (1970). *The theory and practice of mental health consultation*. New York: Basic Books.

Caplan, G. (1974). *Support systems and community mental health: Lectures in concept development*. New York: Behavioral Publications.

Caplan, G. (1981). Mastery of stress. *American Journal of Psychiatry, 138*(4), 413–420.

Caplan, G. (1989). *Population-oriented psychiatry*. New York: Plenum.

Caplan, R. B. (1969). *Psychiatry and the community in nineteenth-century America: The recurring concern with environment in the prevention and treatment of mental disorder.* New York: Basic Books.

Caplan, G., & Killilea, M. (Eds.). (1976). *Support systems and mutual help: Multidisciplinary explorations.* New York: Grune and Stratton.

Rosenfeld, J. M., & Caplan, G. (1954). Techniques of staff consultation in an immigrant children's organization in Israel. *American Journal of Orthopsychiatry, 24,* 45–62.

Schulberg, H. C., & Killilea, M. (Eds.), (1982). *The modern practice of community mental health.* San Francisco: Jossey-Bass.

Silverman, P. R. (1982). People helping people: Beyond the professional model. In H. C. Schulberg & M. Killilea (Eds.), *The modern practice of community mental health* (pp. 611–632). San Francisco: Jossey-Bass.

Chapter 3

Reflections
on Mental Health Consultation:
An Interview
with Gerald Caplan

William P. Erchul
North Carolina State University

INTRODUCTION

Gerald Caplan's thoughts regarding the delivery of psychological services through a consultation approach have had a profound effect on the practice of professional psychology. As one example, Caplan's (1970) *The Theory and Practice of Mental Health Consultation* is the most widely cited book in articles published in the *Journal of School Psychology* from 1963 to 1982 (Oakland, 1984). Oakland's review showed that the only reference cited more frequently was the Wechsler Intelligence Scale for Children-Revised (Wechsler, 1974), a mainstay of school and clinical practice. Furthermore, many community, school, organizational, and clinical psychologists regard the general term "mental health consultation" to be synonymous with the specific model of consultation advanced by Caplan.

As described earlier in this volume, Caplan was honored at the 1990 convention of the American Psychological Association for his multifaceted career achievements related to furthering our understanding of mental health issues. In addition to the public convention events detailing his professional contributions, a private interview was conducted with him on August 13, 1990. This chapter was assembled from excerpts of that interview and from a second interview held May 10, 1991. Several annotations and references have been added to the transcribed material.[1]

Erchul: Dr. Caplan, you have been away from this country for some time, and I think many are familiar with your work through the mid-1970s, but are less familiar with it beyond that point. Could you give us an update of what you've been doing since leaving the Harvard Medical School?

Caplan: I was at Harvard Medical School for 26 years. When I took retirement in 1977, I went to Israel, where I set up a department of child and adolescent psychiatry at the University Hospitals. I worked there for 7 years, and since then I've been the director of the Jerusalem Institute for the Study of Psychological Stress for 6 years. Our main project at the Jerusalem Family Center attempts to prevent psychological and social disturbance in children of divorced parents. During the period, we published two books. One was in 1980, which was *Arab and Jew in Jerusalem* (G. Caplan & R. B. Caplan, 1980). This book is mainly about mediation techniques in a very difficult set of circumstances. The living together, side-by-side, of Arabs and Jews is not always tension-free, but with adequate scope for mediation. My latest book is *Population-Oriented Psychiatry* (Caplan, 1989), which deals with the issues of crisis intervention, support systems methods, and the whole conceptual framework of community and preventive psychiatry.

Erchul: Now that's an interesting term, "population-oriented psychiatry." How would you compare that with an earlier term, "community mental health"?

Caplan: Well, first of all, "population" is a better term to use, because it refers to a collectivity of persons who may or may not form a community. They may be designated by living in a certain area or they may be designated by sharing certain characteristics, like being children of parents with cancer or children of divorced parents. I prefer "psychiatry" because it's addressed to psychiatrists, but it could have easily been psychology. What I say in the book refers to the conceptual models and the techniques that are to be used by either a psychiatrist or psychologist who wants to extend his or her domain beyond dealing with his or her individual patients to taking responsibility for a whole population—a whole collectivity of persons.

Erchul: Let me take you from the present day back to a much earlier point in your career. How did your early experiences in mental "ill" health and mental health care facilities in the early 1940s shape your outlook regarding the treatment and prevention of mental illness?

---

[1]Portions of this interview with Gerald Caplan are copyrighted by the Division of School Psychology of the American Psychological Association and are reprinted here with the permission of the Division's Executive Council.

Caplan: From about 1941 to 1945 I was working in two mental hospitals, which, according to the standards in those days, were both very good hospitals. One was the city hospital in Birmingham (England) and the other a city hospital in Swansea (South Wales). In both of those hospitals, I was dealing with a large population of mainly chronic psychotic patients. I was in charge of them and very little was demanded from me. My feeling at that time was that I wanted to do something about getting a more active treatment program developed, rather than just writing notes describing their symptoms and development otherwise of their symptoms, which was all my superiors wanted me to do.

It was at that stage that I began to think of how I could develop more active methods of treatment. In those days, convulsion therapy was the vogue in treating depression and schizophrenia. With this treatment, we injected a camphor drug and the patient had convulsions, which struck me as being very inhumane. At that time I read an article by Cerlitti and Bini (Bini, 1938; Cerlitti & Bini, 1938) in Italy about reducing convulsions by pressing electric current. Being of a somewhat inventive frame of mind, I invented a little machine called the Caplan Electroconvulsive Apparatus, which was portable and relatively simple. I then began to treat the depressed patients with electrically induced convulsions. I continued that when I left Swansea and moved to London to take psychoanalytic training and to train in child psychiatry. While I trained in child psychiatry and did my psychoanalytic training, I made a living by giving electroconvulsive therapy to patients in my Holly Street office.

My development at that time was that I was constantly looking for more active ways of heading off the population of chronic patients that I was dealing with in the mental hospital. So I tried, first of all, active treatment, and that worked to some extent. Then I tried treating people younger and younger, so I moved into child psychiatry. From there I moved into family psychiatry. From there I came to the realization that however far back you went you couldn't get back far enough. This realization eventually led to my interest in public health, crisis intervention, and different models of prevention.

Erchul: Let's look at the origins of your approach to mental health consultation. We know from your writings that this began with your work in post-war Israel. What were some of the conditions, some of the events occurring in that country or in your professional position that led to your approach to prevention?

Caplan: Well, my approach to prevention antedated that. It comes from my period in the Tavistock Clinic in London, just after the second World War when we had idealistic notions about social intervention called "sociatry," which has since dropped out of common usage. At the Tavistock Clinic, I worked with John Bowlby, and began intervening in child welfare centers, which I continued in Israel from 1948 to 1952. But the main source of the move to consultation was work that we did when we accepted responsibility for the mental health care of 17,000 children who were immigrants to Israel, in residential schools of an immigrant organization. We quickly discovered that, at any time, about 1,000 of the 17,000 were denoted by their teachers and child-care workers as being disturbed. We realized we could not deal with them on a one-to-one basis.

Erchul: How large was your staff at that time?

Caplan: Oh, I think that we had about 9 or 10 people.

Erchul: Nine or 10 people to care for 1,000 referrals in 1 year.

Caplan: And the way we did it was to go around to the different institutions and do what we called "counseling the counselors." And that term, we soon discovered, wasn't a good term, so we called it "consultation." That was where we developed consultation to the child-care workers and the idea originally was to help them cope with their children in their own institutions without having to send them to specialized institutions, which didn't exist anyway.

Erchul: I think, too, from your writings it sounds like an issue was the "disturbing" child rather than the "disturbed" child, and the focus was therefore on those who had direct care responsibilities for children.

Caplan: That's true. We discovered that the type of problem referred from different institutions was characteristic of that institution and differed from institution to institution and, because the children were randomly assigned, we came to the conclusion they were disturbing rather than disturbed. They could have been disturbed, too, but they were disturbing, and what we attempted to do was to deal with the "disturbing" aspect of the children to their caregiver.

Erchul: After that period, you met and formed an association with Erich Lindemann.

Caplan: I came to this country in 1951, as part of a tour of people who were going around on their way to Mexico City to an international congress. We gave lectures up and down the country and I met Erich Lindemann in Boston, and discovered that for the previous 3 or 4 years he'd been doing very similar work to mine using very similar language. So I decided to come for a year to be with him. I came for a year and I stayed for 26.

Erchul: How would you characterize Erich Lindemann's contributions to preventive psychiatry generally and crisis theory specifically?

Caplan: Erich Lindemann came into this field after the Coconut Grove Fire, which was in November 1942. That was a nightclub fire in which nearly 500 young people were killed. Those who were injured and the relatives of those who were killed were treated at Massachusetts General Hospital, where Erich Lindemann was one of the senior psychiatrists. As a result of his experience, he wrote a paper, published in 1944, that was called "Symptomatology and the Management of Acute Grief" (Lindemann, 1944).

In this paper, he characterized the grief reactions of the survivors as being something akin to a clinical syndrome. These reactions were what he began to call the "crisis reaction"—the adjustment reactions of a normal population to an abnormal situation. That led him to investigate the symptomatology of acute grief, which appeared to lead to mental disorder—differentiated from the positive reactions and adaptations, which led to increased mental health. It also led him to believe that it would be possible to intervene during this period (which he thought was about 3 or 4 weeks in duration) to help people grieve in a healthy way. It also led him to believe (which turned out to be incorrect) that the community caregivers, namely clergymen, who took care of people who were grieving could very much influence people to grieve in a healthy way. This led him to establish the Wellesley Human Relations Service, the prototype of the community mental health program in the upper-middle-class suburb of Wellesley, Massachusetts. Here he established a population-oriented mental health program with the collaboration of psychiatrists, psychologists, social scientists, and physicians. These developments led him to the idea that it would be possible to intervene in the community to mobilize forces that would help people do their grief work adequately, and that led him more generally to the ideas of crisis. It was at about that stage that he and I joined forces. Thus, the development of the crisis model and crisis theory involved a collaborative endeavor between Erich Lindemann and myself.

Consultation emerged out of these ideas. The first consultation programs in this country, at least in Massachusetts, involved consultation to the school system in Wellesley and also to the Unitarian church with which Lindemann was working. We discovered, not during his day but later on, that clergymen play very little part in helping people with bereavement for a variety of reasons. This led us, in later years, to develop our widow-to-widow project (Silverman, 1976) with mutual help groups of widows rather than expecting that clergymen would help.

Erchul: One of your notable contributions is your taking of elements from public health theory and practice and adapting them for use in the mental health field. One of these adaptations is the typology of primary, secondary, and tertiary prevention. How would you characterize these terms? What do they mean to you, and how did you arrive at this adaptation of concepts from public health to mental health care systems?

Caplan: When I joined Erich Lindemann in 1952, he was in charge of the community mental health division in the Harvard School of Public Health. Over the next 2 or 3 years, I attended lectures there as a member of the faculty. These lectures were given by my public health colleagues, particularly Dr. Hugh R. Leavell, who was one of the major theoreticians of those days in regard to public health concepts and models. I think it was Leavell who, among others, developed a typology of primary, secondary, and tertiary prevention, and I adapted this public health model to our mental health field.[2]

The term *primary prevention* denotes programs that log the incidence of a

[2]An early presentation of the levels of prevention within public health and epidemiological practice can be found in Clark and Leavell (1953). Clark and Leavell (1958) later revised and expanded this presentation to include the now familiar typology of primary, secondary, and tertiary prevention.

disorder or an illness, incidence being the rate in a population of the occurrence of new cases over a period of time. That means that you, as a professional, have to deal with populations of currently well people and with the factors that influence the population to increase the number of people who would be sick.

Secondary prevention refers to programs that reduce prevalence, prevalence being the rate of new and old cases at the particular point in time. And that was the kind of prevention that was traditionally understood to be "prevention" in psychiatry. The idea is implemented by reducing the duration of existing cases of illness. This means early diagnosis and prompt, effective treatment so that it reduces the duration of cases. If you can make a cut, subsequently, in the population (a statistical cut), you pick up less cases because previously you've helped a number of people get better and therefore they don't appear in your sample.

Tertiary prevention refers to programs that reduce the rate of residual defect and disability consequent upon an illness. In our field, this would involve programs of rehabilitation of people who have been mentally ill to reduce the residual defect in role functioning. It turns out that for schizophrenia, for instance, you can have a traditional medical approach to deal with the symptoms of the illness, but you have to realize that parallel with that is the issue of role functioning. Unfortunately, there isn't a one-to-one correlation in the effectiveness of role functioning and symptomatology. In other words, you can have someone who still has hallucinations and delusions but you're able to help him or her learn to work effectively. Conversely, there may be someone whose symptoms you have combatted so he or she is no longer deluded and hallucinating, but he or she may not be effective as a worker. And that's the aspect of tertiary prevention.

Erchul: Let's talk about the 10 or 11 years you spent at the School of Public Health at Harvard (1953–1964). What was going on in terms of your development of mental health consultation during that period of time?

Caplan: That was the really important work, which was mirrored in my book, *The Theory and Practice of Mental Health Consultation* (Caplan, 1970). I probably did more work preparing for that book than any of the other books that I've written. Mainly we were working as consultants with the Visiting Nurses Association of Boston—a very special group of nurses who did bedside nursing in the home, who were a very competent, highly trained, well-supervised group of public health nurses. We also worked with the public health nurses of the Boston City Health Department, who were not as competent, but who were pretty well organized. In addition to that, we extended into various school systems in the Boston area. We eventually became consultants in the Boston school system, which at that time was an innovation.

Erchul: There are some landmark ideas that are contained in your *Theory and Practice of Mental Health Consultation,* and what I'd like to do is have you elaborate on some of those concepts. You claim the cornerstone

of a successful consulting relationship or consulting experience is the coordinate nonhierarchical relationship that the consultant forms with the consultee. How would you characterize that relationship, and how would you achieve it as a consultant?

Caplan: It is the cornerstone, and it depends on the finding that the more coercive power you have over someone who is asking for help, the quicker maybe they take what you say to them, but they discard it pretty quickly because it's an alien idea that's come into their orbit. Whereas if you have no power over them and you say whatever you say hoping that it will be meaningful to them, then they have to be actively involved in taking ideas that make sense to them and tailoring it to their situation. You achieve that by having an agreement with the consultee institution (and it's usually the one that hires the consultant and within which the consultees work) that you are not responsible for the outcome for the client, nor have you any administrative responsibility for the consultee. Everything you say to the consultee and that they say is absolutely confidential. Under those circumstances, you can allow a situation where you're primarily interested in changing the attitudes and influencing the consultee to change attitudes and sensitivities, but you're not bound by the feeling that they're not doing the right thing by this particular client. You can only do that if you don't have responsibility for the client or for the consultee.

You achieve it, first of all, by working it through with the consultee institution. The consultee institution has to be fairly sophisticated to realize that when they hire a specialist to come in from the outside the most productive use of their money is not by using the specialist to do his or her specialized work on a few cases, but to modify the attitudes and behavior of the staff. If they also see consultation as part of a support system for their staff, which includes education of their staff, inservice training, supervision so that in addition they'll also have consultation, then they can afford to do this. If they do it, then you've got the stage set to develop your coordinate relationship. The essence of the coordinate relationship is that you respect continually—it sounds a bit idealistic, but in practical terms you do it—the autonomy and the specialized competence of your consultee who is usually of a different profession from you, so that's relatively easy. If I, as a psychiatrist, consult with a public health nurse, I know that I don't know much about public health nursing; therefore I say what I say as a psychiatrist, and he or she, as a public health nurse, is able to take from it what may make sense to him or her.

Erchul: Is that relationship able to be achieved if the consultant is internal to the organization? What are some special issues that might arise? It sounds from your description that it's facilitated if the consultant is external to the consultee organization.

Caplan: If he or she is external and just comes in for two or three sessions with a particular consultee, then the consultee is impeded in developing an overly dependent relationship on him or her and, also, if he or she is of a different profession. In the case of a school psychologist consulting with school teachers, hopefully he or she will be regarded as of a different profession from the teachers, although maybe he or she has done some teaching in the past. That's the first thing. Second, if it's a big organization, a big school system, then he or she can leave his or her base in the office and move into the domain of the teachers, in which case you could achieve the same thing. But in a small organization, its very difficult.

Erchul: There's one technique you describe in *The Theory and Practice of Mental Health Consultation* **that isn't described extensively. You don't explain much about the principle, but I would like you to elaborate on the term "onedownsmanship" (Caplan, 1970, pp. 96–97) as a way to facilitate the coordinate nonhierarchical relationship.**

Caplan: Well, when consultees are involved in the total work problem, they feel in a state of disequilibrium or crisis and they're turning for help. It's only human for them to want to give up their autonomy and be dependent on this specialist who has come in and, even though it's been set up not to be that way, they try and twist it along these lines. If you're alert to that, then you notice some of the signs of their self-effacement. They sort of lie themselves down and say, "Please walk over me," for instance, or "You're a very busy man and I'm not busy, so you can fix the appointments to suit yourself." Every time they do that, you should go down to their level or you should bring them up to your level. Instead of the oneupmanship, where you try to achieve a higher status than the people you're dealing with, you try to achieve a lower status than what they are trying to get you into. Eventually you come to the same level.

Erchul: Could you look at mental health consultation and, particularly, your model of mental health consultation, as a type of interpersonal influence process?

Caplan: It's very much so. The less power, the more influence—the issue here is influence. But another way of looking at it is that it's part of a support system. My daughter, Ruth Caplan, wrote a book entitled *Helping the Helpers to Help* (R. B. Caplan, 1972). This relates to some work we did in the Episcopal Church, where we were offering group consultation to parish priests. She developed this title and it places consultation very clearly where it should be. It is an enabling supportive technique that helps to help other people who are helping their clients.

Erchul: Another major point in your *Theory and Practice of Mental Health Consultation* **is your emphasis on consultees' lack of objectivity as a reason for which they may seek assistance from a consultant. What are your current thoughts on lack of objectivity?**

Caplan: Well, as I said before, the consultation method was worked out with a group of very highly trained, very competent, well-supervised professionals. Under those circumstances, if they had problems in a case that were based upon lack of knowledge, lack of skill, or lack of confidence, they would turn to their supervisors who would help them over it. They didn't need to have a specialist—psychologist or psychiatrist—come in from the outside. So what was left for us were the cases where it wasn't due to these particular shortcomings. Since then, I've dealt with many consultee populations, and I must say that many of them do not share the characteristics of the Visiting Nurses Association of Boston. They're professionals who are somewhat inadequately trained, poorly supervised, and their administrative system does not provide them with adequate support and guidance. Most of the cases that come for consultation are cases where the consultee has difficulties because of lack of knowledge or lack of skill. Under those circumstances, you don't see so much of the lack of objectivity, but if you were dealing with a competent group of consultees, I'm sure that lack of objectivity would be, even today, a primary reason for people coming to us.

Erchul: I think that's a major point—that you can entertain a lack of objectivity as a primary reason for consultee difficulty only after lack of skills and knowledge have been ruled out. It sounds like you need to deal with a skilled, knowledgeable consultee and, having such a person, it's only then that you can look toward lack of objectivity to explain his or her difficulty.

Caplan: Yes, but you don't have to do it only on an individual assessment basis. You do it on a system basis, because you know that, in this particular system, the majority of cases that come to you will be cases where the professionals lack skills and knowledge. They are the ones who are obtrusive so you have to deal with those. The lack of objectivity is part of your assessment. You come to that conclusion if that's what you find. Of course, you may have both.

Erchul: Let's look at lack of objectivity in a little more detail. A primary mechanism for lack of objectivity, as you put forth in the 1970 book, is theme interference. You also proposed some indirect ways to look at combating or reducing theme interference. How do you view those ideas today?

Caplan: I think they are as valid today as they ever were. Theme interference, of course, is only one of the reasons for lack of objectivity. There could be personal involvement, transference, or characterological problems that emerge in the work setting, but theme interference relates to normal people and normal professionals who may have some precariously solved problem in the past and it's triggered by the current work situation. They displaced their personal problem onto the work situation. The indirect way to deal with it is to accept their displacement and not to uncover it, not to interpret it. I think the reason you, the consultee, are sensitive to this situation is that something happened to you in the past; but if I were to draw your attention to it, I would be lowering your autonomy. I would be raising my own and I would be moving away from this coordinate relationship. You might be very happy to have me deal with your personal problem, but after I've gone, either you or the people you talk to would feel that they don't want a psychiatrist or psychologist coming in and brainwashing them or reading their minds.

Erchul: Let me step aside a bit from the notion of lack of objectivity and theme interference. Your model describes consultees as other professionals whose backgrounds don't include mental health, or they are paraprofessionals or caregivers. But you don't describe your method as having applicability to parents as consultees, because of a number of reasons that you spell out in your book, their lack of objectivity being one. Can your model be seen as useful or adapted for use by parents as consultees, or do the basic assumptions of your approach preclude that adaptation?

Caplan: I think in the main they preclude it. But certain techniques, certain parts of the model, are applicable. For instance, the idea that when you're dealing with a person, it should be safe for the person. The main difference between a parent and a teacher dealing with the same child is that the parent is and should be personally involved, whereas the teacher should not be personally involved. The teacher is professionally involved—there's distance between the teacher and the student and the consultation method is designed to emphasize, support, and strengthen the professional role of the professional. For parents, that would be quite inappropriate.

Erchul: Do you have any special issues that emerge for the consultant who practices in the public schools? Is it something about that setting or the nature of the work that would lead to an adaptation of your model? Are there special issues that might be considered?

Caplan: I don't know. I think the main issue would be preparing the ground for the consultation program—negotiating and obtaining sanctions for the kind of role that is occupied by the consultant—and that depends on the school policies and the way the school system is run and so on. There are certain schools that would be quite inimical to this approach, so that has to be taken into account. The other issue is the main issue of the content—the content in the schools. Many consultations are likely to be focused on the current life problems of the children—children under stress whose stress gets brought into the school operation—and the question is how the teachers can handle this. These are usually hot topics because everyone is likely to be in the same boat—illness or death in the family or divorce in the family. In this country, about one in two children are now or very soon will be children of divorced parents and broken homes. It's very likely that these situations will trigger sensitivities in the teachers. Under those circumstances, consultation is likely, from a content point of view, to be focusing on these core issues.

Erchul: What is the relationship between mental health consultation and support systems intervention? Is it accurate to state, given its major development in the 1970s (Caplan, 1974; Caplan & Killilea, 1976), that support systems intervention "evolved" from the principles of consultation, or do you regard them as rather separate?

Caplan: No, but they're both related to the basic theories as they evolved over time. The basic theoretical model was the model of crisis, and what I said before about Erich Lindemann lays the foundation for that. As we studied normal people undergoing crisis episodes, we realized that there were significant people in their milieu, professional caregivers, who could influence them. We also discovered that nonprofessional members of their families and neighborhoods could also influence them. Consultation was then developed as an attempt to ameliorate and improve the operations of the professional caregivers. It wasn't until later that we realized that these people operating during crises— natural caregivers and professional caregivers—were one example of a more general situation that we began to call the "support system," which impinged upon individuals. This related to many research findings from the stress research literature that began to show that people's reaction to stress could not be just pathological, as we originally thought, but could be positive, and that high stress in the presence of high support would not increase the danger to mental health. But high stress in the absence of high support would increase the danger to mental health. People who faced life change circumstances on their own were more likely to become sick afterward, whereas those who had a good relationship with a supportive individual were not in danger by having gone through a high stress situation. That, plus our findings in crisis, led us to reformulate the intervention of caregivers—professional or nonprofessional—as one example of support systems. And that led us to support systems matters.

Erchul: Let me change direction again. Many of us base our understanding of you philosophy on your *Theory and Practice of Mental Health Consultation*, which came out 20 years ago. But you changed your thoughts somewhat, or modified them, or moved on from those ideas. I have some quotes from some writings that were published in the early 1980s. For example, in 1981, you wrote in an article, ". . . a purely enabling role has not proved optimally effective. We have found that in order to achieve our preventive goals we must also take part in dealing directly with clients in the community facility" (Caplan, 1981, p. 4). And in a similar way, in a 1982 epilogue chapter, you stated that you had moved ". . . beyond the consultation method to methods of collaboration and mediation" (Caplan, 1982, p. 651). Could you describe this evolution of thought?

Caplan: One thing I want to make clear is that I didn't negate the consultation approach—I added to it. In adding to it, I took into account the fact that many of the cases that we dealt with were professionals who were not optimally trained and supervised. And if you move into that organization, that institution—incidentally, all consultation implies moving out of your own domain into the domain of the consultee—if you move into the other domain with the goal, with the ultimate mission of reducing mental disorder or psychological disorder, then consultation is good, but not enough. Therefore, you've got to develop other techniques that are already mentioned in the 1970 book. In the

1970 book, I even talked about collaboration, although it's a sort of "dirty" word if you use it in the lay sense. But mental health collaboration refers to another kind of interprofessional activity, which I've come to use more and more as time has gone on, as I've moved into other domains than say a school system or nursing agency, which is a rather tight-run organization—in the pediatric or surgical wards, out in the open community, in courts, and so on. There one deals with people, other professionals, who may not be "sophisticated" enough—they don't mirror our ideas and don't realize the importance of consultee-centered consultation. Under those circumstances, we did develop this collaboration method and if I had to rewrite the consultation book, which at the moment I'm considering because it's gone out of print, I will add to it a very significant section on mental health collaboration.[3]

Erchul: Could you elaborate more on situations in which a mental health professional may choose collaboration over a consultation type of approach? Is there a road map that could be provided in terms of what one might choose?

Caplan: Well, in both cases you're moving into the domain and into the institutional setting of the other person, the other professional. If your belief or if your contract calls for you to have responsibility for the client, you can't use consultation by definition; therefore, that's one of the reasons. The other thing is that you may decide when you move in there that you see glaring examples of clients whose mental health development is being infringed upon or is not being supported. Under those circumstances, you will feel that I can't wait for consultation techniques to work—I've got to move in as a collaborator. As a collaborator, the main difference is that you are accepting responsibility for the outcome of the client, and therefore you must leave your coordinate status with your consultee. You must be able to argue, persuade, and, if necessary, coerce him or her to do certain things with his or her patients. Let's say you're collaborating with a doctor on a ward—a pediatrician—and his or her patients. If he or she won't do it, then you've got to move in and do it yourself, because if the kid you are dealing with dies, you will be blamed and correctly so. You allowed certain things to happen. I said "die" because I'm referring to certain cases that were quoted in my recent book (Caplan, 1989), where, in fact, I wasn't active enough and I was still hung up with the idea that the pediatricians were ruling the roost, had the ultimate say, and I allowed them to do things that I felt were wrong.

Erchul: Could you elaborate on that case? That's a very interesting case that's in Chapter 8 of the 1989 book (pp. 169–173). I think there is some interest in seeing how you would go about acting in a case such as this. Many would know how you would act as a consultant, but clearly how

[3]*Mental Health Consultation and Collaboration,* by Gerald Caplan and Ruth B. Caplan, was published by Jossey-Bass Inc., in November 1992.

you acted in this case study you provide in *Population-Oriented Psychiatry* **involved a variety of roles: working with parents, working with staff, etc. Could you give us a rundown of your approach in that particular case?**

Caplan: Well, I think the work that comes out in my recent book is that the consultant has a variety of techniques available and uses them as appropriate. One of the methods is to become a member of the team, my staff and I were members of the team in the pediatric surgery ward, the oncology ward, the pediatrics ward, and so on. Or a school psychologist may be a member of the task force or team in the school. Once you become a member of the team, you have lower authority than the head of the team unless you are the captain of the team. But usually you're not. In pediatric surgery, obviously the surgeon is the captain of the team so he or she has the overall responsibility and you're dependent on him or her for the final decision. But within that, if you feel as a member of the team, that you are involved in collecting data and you come to a diagnostic assessment like we did in that case, you must act. I think the case you've referred to was a mother who didn't bond to her infant.[4] She was an unbonded mother and therefore didn't relate to the infant and didn't protect him. The infant had a problem with stopping breathing in the middle of the night (nocturnal apnea), for which they hooked the infant up to an instrument that sounded an alarm if he stopped breathing. It was my feeling that the child was discharged from the hospital against my wishes before the mother had yet bonded to the child, and this was a dangerous situation. The pediatrician in charge of the case said, "Well, I see no reason to keep the infant in the hospital where he would be exposed to infections. He'll be much safer at home." And he went home. Then the machine broke down. The social worker who had gone out to visit the case saw that the machine had broken down and said, "You come in tomorrow with the machine." Well, that night the kid died. Now that was my fault and I felt quite guilty about the case, because I had allowed my good relations with the head of the team, with whom I wished to maintain good relations, to override my responsibilities as the psychiatrist in charge of my side of the case. What I should have done, and what I did subsequently in similar cases, was go to the head of the department, go up above, and say to him, "If you don't want to accept my advice on this, I will resign and you'll be left with the responsibility." Whenever you do that, they say, "Oh no, no, no! We want you to continue." So they talk to their subordinate, who is the head of the team, and they say, "Look here, you've got to humor this fellow. He may be right, he may be wrong, but if he's going to resign on this basis, he would only do that if it was a matter really of life and death." When you're working on a pediatric

---

[4]Caplan's professional interest in mother–infant bonding may be traced, in part, to his association with John Bowlby at the Tavistock Clinic in London during the mid-1940s. In addition to Caplan's (1989, Ch. 8) treatment of the topic, Klaus and Kennell (1976) and Birns and Ben-Ner (1988) have provided interesting views of mother–infant bonding within a psychoanalytic perspective.

ward, they're all problems of life and death. You don't see it so much in schools, but maybe even there, too, with suicide and such issues.

Erchul: In 1991, you were living in Jerusalem for the duration of the Persian Gulf War. This situation obviously brought a great deal of stress and trauma to citizens of Jerusalem. What was your personal experience during that time, and what did you do to help?

Caplan: The war, as far as Jerusalem was concerned, was mainly a war of nerves. It was psychological warfare when in fact no missiles landed in Jerusalem. But the population was significantly burdened, including me, by the continual threats of Saddam Hussein, who said that he was going to send over missiles with poisoned gas warheads. We had to prepare for this. My operations were part of what I think was a very positive contribution that some of my colleagues made at that time. We're talking only about a month or two ago (March 1991), in which we operated to strengthen the population so that they could continue to function despite the feelings of anxiety and fear related to the impending danger of poison gas.

At the time, I was operating as the advisor on morale to the mayor of Jerusalem. This was a job that I had also had in the previous war, when I had come over from Boston especially to take part in helping the population withstand the real dangers of the Yom Kippur War. That was when I built up my relationships with the mayor and his staff and so on. So in the Gulf War, I reopened those relationships, reactivated them, and organized a committee of psychologists and psychiatrists who were advising the major and his staff, as well as the media (insofar as we had access to them), on how to support the population at this time.

What we were trying to do and, what in fact we did manage to do, was to deliver the message that when you're in that dangerous a situation, it is an adaptive response to be scared, to be frightened, to be uneasy, to be extra alert, not to be able to sleep at night, and so on. Because if you don't sleep at night, then you're alert. If something happens in the middle of the night, then you're prepared for it. It was important for the population to see these reactions as healthy, adaptive reactions (even though to many people they were unpleasant and unusual) and not to regard them as signs of weakness or impending illness. That was mainly what we were doing.

It so happened that the most important job was not done by me, but was done by some psychologists in the Tel Aviv area who formed a team of consultants and collaborated with the army spokesman and the chief radio announcing team. My psychologist colleagues helped them develop a program of support for the population during the periods of the air raids. This was the time when all the population had to go into rooms that were hermetically sealed against incoming gas, and they had to put on their gas masks. Some felt that this made the people completely isolated in their own homes. In point of fact, it was part of the system that every hermetically sealed room should have a radio in it. During the alert, the announcer and the army spokesman on the radio (who were part of the team that was being advised by psychologists) promoted the idea that the whole nation was one large supportive group. This was facilitated by the announcers telling the people step by step what to do, how to seal the doors, where the missiles had landed if they had landed, when to put on the gas masks, when to take them off, and so on. All of this led to supporting the population in a very real way by (a) encouraging them to be active in a purposive way, to do something to save themselves in case there should be a gas attack; (b) encouraging them to help each other—mutual help; and (c) continually informing them about what was happening. There was a constant flow of authentic communication. These three elements of information, purposive activity, and mutual help were the strengthening elements that allowed people to withstand the burden of the anxiety and fear.

Erchul: As we draw this interview to a close, I was wondering, of all your ideas relative to our further understanding of mental health issues, which do you see as your most enduring?

Caplan: That's a hard question. First of all, I think the conceptual models that I developed of prevention and their meaning in the mental health field—the ideas of population-at-risk, the guidance that this gives to us to move in, to leave our ordinary clinics and offices, and move out into the domain of others. Then the series of methods and techniques that we've evolved—crisis intervention, support systems methods, mental health consultation looms large, mental health collaboration, mediation, and so on. All of these are the armamentarium of a specialist who leaves his or her place and moves out there. The reason he or she moves out into the domain of others, into other people's institutions, is that that's where the action is. That's where the decisions are taken in regard to the factors that may be reducing or exacerbating tension and stress and that may also raise the support for the other individuals exposed to these situations so they come out in a healthy way and not with an increased likelihood of mental disorder.

Erchul: Certainly your contributions are many, and certainly we in the mental health and educational arena appreciate them all. Thank you very much, Dr. Caplan.

Caplan: It has been my pleasure.

REFERENCES

Bini, L. (1938). Experimental researches on epileptic attacks induced by the electric current. *American Journal of Psychiatry, 94*(Suppl.), 172–183.

Birns, B., & Ben-Ner, P. (1988). Psychoanalytic constructs of mother. In B. Birns & D. Hay (Eds.), *The different faces of motherhood* (pp. 47–72). New York: Plenum.

Caplan, G. (1970). *The theory and practice of mental health consultation.* New York: Basic Books.

Caplan, G. (1974). *Support systems and community mental health*. New York: Behavioral Publications.

Caplan, G. (1981). Partnerships for prevention in the human services. *Journal of Primary Prevention, 2,* 3–5.

Caplan, G. (1982). Epilogue: Personal reflections. In H. C. Schulberg & M. Killilea (Eds.), *The modern practice of community mental health: A volume in honor of Gerald Caplan* (pp. 650–666). San Francisco: Jossey–Bass.

Caplan, G. (1989). *Population-oriented psychiatry.* New York: Human Sciences Press.

Caplan, G., & Caplan, R. B. (1980). *Arab and Jew in Jerusalem: Explorations in community mental health.* Cambridge, MA: Harvard University Press.

Caplan, G., & Killilea, M. (1976). *Support systems and mutual help: Multidisciplinary explorations.* New York: Grune & Stratton.

Caplan, R. B. (1972). *Helping the helpers to help: Mental health consultation to aid clergymen in pastoral work.* New York: Seabury Press.

Cerlitti, V., & Bini, L. (1938). L'elettroshock. *Achiva Generale Neurologia Psychiatria Psicoanalysia, 19,* 266.

Clark, E. G., & Leavell, H. R. (1953). Levels of application of preventive medicine. In H. R. Leavell & E. G. Clark (Eds.), *Textbook of preventive medicine* (pp. 7–27). New York: McGraw-Hill.

Clark, E. G., & Leavell, H. R. (1958). Levels of application of preventive medicine. In H. R. Leavell & E. G. Clark (Eds.), *Preventive medicine for the doctor in his community: An epidemiologic approach* (2nd ed.) (pp. 13–39). New York: McGraw-Hill.

Klaus, M., & Kennell, J. (1976). *Maternal-infant bonding: The impact of early separation or loss on family development.* St. Louis, MO: Mosby.

Lindemann, E. (1944). Symptomatology and the management of acute grief. *American Journal of Psychiatry, 101,* 141–148.

Oakland, T. (1984). The *Journal of School Psychology's* first twenty years: Contributions and contributors. *Journal of School Psychology, 22,* 239–250.

Silverman, P. R. (1976). The widow as caregiver in a program of preventive intervention with other widows. In G. Caplan & M. Killilea (Eds.), *Support systems and mutual help: Multidisciplinary explorations* (pp. 233–243). New York: Grune & Stratton.

Wechsler, D. (1974). *Wechsler Intelligence Scale for Children-Revised.* New York: The Psychological Corporation.

Part Two

Caplan's Contributions to the Practice of Psychology

Chapter 4

Gerald Caplan's Paradigm: Bridging Psychotherapy and Public Health Practice

James G. Kelly
University of Illinois at Chicago

INTRODUCTION

In 1958, as a brand-new PhD in clinical psychology, I was accepted as a post-doctoral research fellow in community mental health at Massachusetts General Hospital and the Wellesley Human Relations Service (HRS). I had the privilege of working with Erich Lindemann and Don Klein during the first year (Kelly, 1984, 1988). My work at HRS was so satisfying that I enrolled as a degree student in the Harvard School of Public Health for further training with Gerald Caplan. Those two years (1958–1960) have been a major source of conceptual inspiration for my subsequent work. I was captivated by the potential of preventive interventions. I was particularly inspired by the commitment that Erich

These comments were prepared for a symposium, "Gerald Caplan's Contributions to American Psychology: Views from the Discipline," at the 98th annual meeting of the American Psychological Association, Boston, MA, August 13, 1990.

I benefited from comments and suggestions given to me by Eileen Altman, Seeley Chandler Kelly, Jack Glidewell, Chris Keys, Don Klein, and Phil Mann. I thank them for their interest in the ideas expressed on this occasion.

Lindemann, Don Klein, and Gerald Caplan gave to the status of community process in developing prevention programs (Klein, 1968).

The concept of mental health consultation, as developed by Caplan and his colleagues, emerged for me as the major point of view for the practice of a public health approach to mental health work. (Caplan, 1964, 1967, 1970). Mental health consultation was the explicit operational technique that gave concrete meaning to how a mental health professional could become transformed and become a public health practitioner.

What I had learned in my clinical training was that a clinical psychologist focused on internal psychological processes. This focus was accompanied by very explicit role expectations for both the psychologist and the person who was being helped. This role contract required a privileged relationship that was confidential and inaccessible to others.

Public health work, on the other hand, involved community factors, organizational variables, cultural topics, and political issues. These issues became equally salient and as essential as internal psychological states. What mental health consultation represented was a way to take into account how external processes and events affect the internal psychological states of key community resources such as school teachers, clergy, and public health nurses. The role relationship of the consultant to the consultee, although confidential, was defined solely by the workplace of the consultee. The workplace became the context for the integration and clarification of internal psychological and external social processes.

During those two years when I was consulting with elementary school teachers in Wellesley, Massachusetts, and with public health nurses in the Codman Square Health Unit in Dorchester, Massachusetts, I experienced the excitement of being able to help without conceiving of either the teachers or the nurses as "patients." The efficacy of Caplan's ideas was being borne out—I could see classroom teachers and nurses using our consulting relationship as one resource to increase the efficacy of their own working relationship with *their* clients (e.g., their students and mothers with small infants). I learned firsthand that clinical knowledge could be adapted for broader use. I began to appreciate this broader role for mental health concepts. I could begin to appreciate the context of the consultee. As I understood context better, I could process more salient information. My help could become more grounded and more specific to person–environment role relationships. If I was, in fact, helpful, the teacher or nurse could more easily become a mental health resource within his or her own *role*.

I discovered that mental health concepts—particularly knowledge of informal psychological processes—could be accessible to key persons in the community. The intriguing facet of mental health consultation was that I could draw on my clinical knowledge of individuals, yet use and express that knowledge so that it was available for more systemic effects. I discovered that I was learning a skill that gave authentic meaning to what was unique, distinct, and valid about community mental health. I was able to realize my preferred role—to be a clinician and to work in the community. Caplan's methods provided a practical, concrete, and plausible operational definition for how community mental health could be practiced as a public health enterprise.

The development of mental health consultation was a commanding illustration that a bridge could be created between the practice of individually-oriented psychotherapy and public health practice. For me, this was a major paradigm shift.

CAPLAN'S FOUR "LAWS"

I will mention four topics that Caplan and his colleagues were among the first to articulate. I have experienced these four topics as fundamental insights regarding the consultation process. I refer to them as "Caplan's Laws." I have continued to experience the validity of these insights time and time again during the past 30 years. These four insights may not be Caplan's fundamental or most elegant ideas, but they are ideas that I personally have found to be most stimulating. They have pragmatic validity. I mention them to illustrate the potency of Caplan's work.

Law No. 1—Effective and Sustained Innovations Require Sanction and Access from the Top Administrator of the Host Organization

> Sanction must be continually maintained. It is important that the consultant keep the upper echelons of the authority system informed of his activities and solicit their suggestions for modification. (Caplan, 1964, p. 233)

It is both strategic and educational for the top executive of an organization to be informed about the proposed work of an outside consultant and to interpret and facilitate the work of the consultant. Most importantly, when other members of the organization realize that their chief executive is informed and implicitly "O.K.s" the work of the consultant, the members of the organization feel protected. If and when they expend energy to work with a consultant, they can do so without penalty. The staff also is reassured that when the chief executive sanctions the work of the consultant and the staff finds that the consultant is inadequate or not behaving appropriately, or not working according to agreed upon expectations, the staff then has sanctions to complain. In this sense, the staff is not completely vulnerable to be controlled or demeaned by an outside consultant.

What also is compelling about this "law" is that once initial sanction has been given by the chief executive, the consultant can have access to him or her for feedback, clarification, and negotiating new agreements. Sanction is a rare trust. It is nourished and given special status in the consultation relationship.

As someone trained in individual therapy, I rarely had to consider this issue. When I became a consultant, I assimilated from Caplan and colleagues the importance of Law No. 1. This law focused my attention on the context where mental health work was to be done, not only on the various individuals. Thus, I was introduced to the presence of organizational issues when I was a sojourner in the consultee's workplace.

The implicit idea vested in the presentation of mental health consultation was that the consultant attended to the significance of organizational dynamics and the change process. I learned that being a consultant in an organization contrasts with the role relationships defined in psychotherapeutic relationships. In this new context, I was more vulnerable to the power dynamics of the consultees' organization. I was in a more ambiguous situation, as I began to educate myself about the specific site in which I was working.

Power relationships are generic to organizations. Sanctions provide the consultant with access to the formally designated officials of the organization and the various informal power relationships. I discovered ways to assess power, and then to cultivate power to create a framework for the consulting work that followed (Kelly, 1983). Most of all, I learned that if I follow Law No. 1, I could more easily develop access to the many different formal and informal levels of the organization. As time went on, applying this law helped me appreciate that consultation embodies not only a technique, but also a political process.

Law No. 2—Managing the Consultant's Entry Involves Dissipating Stereotypes

> The essential goal in building relationships and obtaining sanction is common perception of mental health problems and role expectations. The consultant and consultee must be mutually understood and recognize certain rules for interaction—ground rules of procedure and cues for expected behavior. . . . The development of free communication is impeded by preconceived stereotypes, and these must be identified and dissipated. This is a two-way process. (Caplan, 1964, p. 233)

I truly learned this law when I was stereotyped. The experience of being stereotyped and the experience of moving beyond my own stereotypes about the consultee organization helped me appreciate the barriers that impede entry. The mental health consultant will be perceived by consultees not only in terms of their actual experiences with mental health professionals, but according to their *fantasies* of what the consultant will learn or know about them. It is expected that all participants in consultation bring to the consultation process undifferentiated, invalidated perceptions and anxieties about each other. This second law addresses this observation. The consultant must realize that to be able to consult, he or she first must be prepared to understand and confront his or her own anxieties about consultees and their anxieties about the consultant. The consultant and consultee then can become more free from mutual anxieties to commit time and energy to develop their new working relationship. Dissipating stereotypes makes it possible for the consultant and consultee to disengage from their anxieties and to attend to their shared perceptions of the consultees' work role experiences.

The usual concerns that a consultee might have about a mental health consultant relate to such factors as the following: (a) how much and how well the consultee believes the consultant can actually read their minds, whether the consultant will be a therapist for them; (b) whether the consultant will require the consultee to express innermost thoughts and feelings; (c) how much confidence the consultee has that the consultant will keep confidences; and (d) how demeaning it could be to be perceived by work colleagues to be meeting with a consultant who is a "shrink." Organizational values can be expressed by the norm that if you ask for help from an outside consultant, you are "weak," "helpless," or "incompetent."

The initial stages of beginning the consultation relationship mean that the consultant is aware and committed to address these stereotypes. The consultant realizes that when an outsider comes into an organization to help, the very presence of that outsider activates anxieties about the intrigues and power struggles, the hidden secrets, and the unresolved issues that are characteristic of any organization. The consultant realizes and accepts the reality that members of the organization may ascribe to the consultant ongoing issues within the organization.

The significance of this issue is that, in beginning any relationship, each partner is likely to perceive and construe the other with expectations and explanations for why the relationship cannot begin, should not begin, or, if begun, may fail.

This anxiety over beginnings is a fundamental phenomenon that needs to be understood as a generic process of creating relationships, not as marks of individual frailty, or idiosyncrasy, or limitation. This issue offers the opportunity to assess consultation in terms of how well the consultant can deal with his or her anxiety in developing a working relationship as a guest in someone else's house (Glidewell, 1959).

The consultant's anxieties about building a relationship can affect how soon and how well the consulting relationship will begin. If the consultant is primarily concerned with being "potent," "intelligent," "witty," or "likeable," in contrast to being helpful, the consultant may activate in the consultee unintended affective responses. Whether the feelings will be positive or negative will depend on the consultee's previous experiences and attitudes about asking for help. This is particularly true when the consultant is a stranger who is presented as an "outside expert."

An important implication of this law is that the diagnostic process of the organization shifts from assessing not only the consultee but also assessing the quality of the relationship between consultant and consultee. Focusing on the quality of working relationships and requiring that the mental health consultant be effective in developing ongoing working relationships is pivotal. Such an understanding makes it possible for the consultant to work in a variety of settings, such as courts, churches, schools, civic groups, voluntary organizations, and citizen task groups. The consultant's ability to develop working relationships enhances the possibility that the consultant can become a resource to a variety of sectors and groups in the community. Until Law No. 2 was articulated, there was little expectation that a mental health practitioner could work outside a psychotherapeutic role. Law No. 2 opened up the practice of mental health work as a public health enterprise.

The first two laws focus on getting ready to do consultation (e.g., what steps the consultant takes to ensure that the consultation can begin on a sound foundation). The next two laws refer to the process when the actual formal helping begins. In my experience, when the consultant understands the workings of these first two laws, the efficacy of consultation is experienced more quickly. Paying attention to all four laws greatly enhances the longevity and impact of the consultation.

Law No. 3—The First Consultee Who Agrees to Meet with the Consultant Is a Deviant Member of the Organization

> In the initial stages of interaction, the first members contacted are often peripheral to the core group of the institution or are deviant. . . . An eager consultant may welcome the outstretched hands, but if he builds too close a relationship with these people, he may find himself categorized by the central group as peripheral or deviant. (Caplan, 1964, p. 234).

This law pays particular attention to organizational dynamics. This law asserts that there is something about organizational and group dynamics—independent of the qualities of individuals—that affects which persons assume specific roles in an organization. This law proclaims the power of the concept of "role" and alerts the mental health practitioner to attend to the nature of the organization as well as to the nature of individuals. This law is apt for consulting situations where the executive of the organization is not requesting consultation for him- or herself. The top executive instead requests the consultant to work with other members of the organization, particularly line personnel.

This law is a strategic insight. I have found that the first person who *does* meet with a consultant does not share or represent modal values within the organization. In fact, the first consultee is often perceived by others within the organization as outside the normal channels of influence and is not likely to be a creditable member of the organization. When this law was being developed, the caution to all new consultants was not to become trapped by the initial excitement of having a "first" consultee. I learned to bind my anxiety to have a "first" case. I found that if I could manage the anxiety over not expecting to connect to consultees too quickly, I could devote my time and energy to learn more about the consultee's organization.

If a consultant gives too much help to the first consultee, and concentrates on this consultee to the exclusion of other possible consultees, the consultant can be perceived by other members of the organization as not understanding the "real" issues and "real" power alliances in the organization. Concentrating the consultant's total energies on the first consultee can reduce opportunities for the consultant to meet and work with other members of the organization. By over-emphasizing the first consultee, the consultant can inadvertently wall him- or herself off from the potential of working with other members of the organiza-tion. This third law tests the consultant's self-confidence in tempering the ex-citement about making an initial connection. Instead, the consultant's task is to cope with the uncertainty of not expecting consultees to respond too quickly to the consultant's presence.

In implementing this law, the consultant needs to devote ample time and energy so that other members of the organization can begin to test out and feel secure when relating to the consultant. A process that I personally have found useful is to arrange to be a part of gatherings or informal social settings in the organization. In this way, the consultant can interact more casually and appreci-ate the nature of informal interactions among the participants. Teachers' lounges, secretaries' offices, and lunchtime and breakfast meetings can create opportunities for all participants, including the consultant, to be oneself, unen-cumbered completely by the "role" of consultant or consultee. By being a participant in such settings, the consultant is communicating that he or she realizes the nature of power relationships in organizations. It is important that members of the organization feel comfortable and, at the same time, be skepti-cal before developing the initial trust for starting the consultative relationship.

This third law communicates again the ecological wisdom of understanding context. The consultant learns to understand how power is defined in various organizations and how alliances are formed in particular organizations. Work-ing from this law confirms that when the mental health consultant moves from psychotherapeutic work to community work, the anxieties over beginnings must be understood in terms of the unique qualities of the individual members *and* the unique dilemmas of the organization.

The challenge for the consultant is to perceive that the first consultee is not deviant in terms of mental status, but is simply not functioning within the cultural norms of the organization. It is often the case that the first consultee will be *more* caring, or *more* concerned with solving organizational problems, in contrast to other members of the organization. In fact, the first consultee's expression of care and investment in the organization may help to define the person to be "deviant." Other members of the organization may have become socialized to become "adjusted," "conforming," "resigned," or "comfortable" with the current ways of working with the organization.

The consultant can learn much from a first consultee in terms of how norms for social support are defined, and how the norms for self-validation, autonomy, and trust become operational within the organization. There are several ways to attend to the consultee, while also attending to the other potential consultees. One is to invite the top executive to arrange conversations with other consultees who may have similar concerns. Another is for the consultant to invite persons in similar roles or who are experiencing similar work demands to meet with the consultant and first consultee. A third is to watch for an expression of interest from other potential consultees as a result of the informal conversations that have occurred between the first consultee and other members of the organization. A fourth is to request a meeting from the top executive in which the consultee uses the material provided by the first consultee to inform others about the potential scope of consultation. In each of these examples, the consultant is attempting to establish connections and linkages between the consultant and representative members of the organization. The consultant is not being held captive by the first consultee.

The pivotal challenge for the consultant is to provide support to the "deviant" person without the consultant reducing access to other members of the organization. This process in itself requires skill in being responsive and being committed to individual consultees while being realistic and savvy when beginning to work with the entire organization.

Law No. 4—The Success of Consultation Is Measured by the Consultant's Ability to Translate Mental Health Concepts to Meet the On-Going Role Requirements of the Consultee

> The consultant is invited to the consultee institution to improve the work performance of the consultees. He is not assigned the role of treating their personal psychological ailments. (Caplan, 1964, p. 243)

The consultant gives time and energy to understand the role requirements of the consultee, and is committed to translate, adapt, and redefine insights gained from the consultee. The pivotal task is for the consultant to communicate these insights in terms of the consultee's work role. If this is done, the consultant can expect to observe changes in *clients'* behavior. The efficacy of this translation from consultant to consultee to client is communicated indirectly in the consultee's relationship to the client. When this law is implemented, the consultee's clients will change their behavior. Actualizing this law distinguishes the average consultant from the premier consultant.

Implementing this fourth law for me is a very demanding activity. It requires me to be sufficiently informed and educated about the intricacies of the organization and the role requirements, expectations, constraints, and culture of the consultee. Given the historical and even elite status of mental health professionals and our socialization, we mental health professionals do not often take time to assess the complexity and resources of the organization in which we are working.

This law affirms that for the consultant to really *do* consultation, he or she must know the territory. It requires that the consultant be informed about the role requirements of the consultee *and* be empathetic about these demands to present insights and needed advice and problem solving. The requirement is for the consultant to suggest actions that can be carried out not as the consultant would do them as a mental health expert, but as consultees can carry them out in their own work roles. The consultant knows the constraints on the consultee, understands the reward structures for the consultee, and understands what the consultee needs to do to create personal and organizational resources to carry out the work role. The consultant knows that the formal and informal roles that are defined and expressed also reflect the values and norms of the organization (Katz & Kahn, 1978).

Many persons aspiring to be consultants can provide apt and valid insights about what the problem is and how it can be solved. This fourth law affirms that the art of consultation is realized when the consultant can conceptualize and express these ideas so that they are consonant within the role demands of the consultee. In this way, the consultant is being a resource in communicating and working with the consultee so that the created solutions are organic and natural within the day-to-day activities of the consultee.

Implementing this law requires being active and being a part of the consultee's settings. It is these settings, these "natural" resources of other staff and participants, that provide the competence and support structures to define and realize help for consultees. In the same way, it is essential for the consultant to appreciate from these settings the constraints and hassles that consultees experience. Effective consultation requires the consultant to adapt psychological insights so that the available competences and natural supports within the consultee organization can be made available and connected to the consultee (Glidewell, 1972).

Activating this law is dependent on the consultant implementing the three previous laws. The consultant's prior efforts provide a personal history and ongoing assessment of the organization in appreciating the daily role demands of the consultee. Implementing this law requires the consultant to perceive the task of consultation not only as a dyadic relationship between consultant and consultee, but as a multifaceted, multilevel activity within a larger social system. This law further confirms the nature of the paradigm shift when the mental health professional moves from the therapist's office to social settings, such as elementary classrooms, principal's offices, rectories of the clergy, and executive offices of corporate organizations. This law affirms that the promise of a public health approach to mental health is most fully realized to the extent that the consultant can appreciate the role demands, role strains, and role stresses of the consultee.

CONCLUSION

On this occasion, I have noted four of the many contributions that Caplan and his colleagues developed that have supported my own work (Kelly & Hess, 1987). They also have stimulated others in a continued effort to conceive mental health consultation as a public health practice rather than as solely an entrepreneurial act (Altrocchi, Spielberger, & Eisdorfer, 1965; Gallessich, 1982; Grady, Gibson, & Trickett, 1981; Hansen, Himes, & Meier, 1990; Heller, 1984; Lippitt & Lippitt, 1978; Mann, 1971, 1973; Mannino, MacLennan, & Shore, 1975; Mannino, Trickett, Shore, Kidder, & Levin, 1986; Singh, Tarnower, & Chen, 1971; Spielberger, 1967; Zusman & Davidson, 1972).

These four laws embody and express the paradigm shift that occurs when the clinician absorbs and owns a public health philosophy—truly becoming a community resource. Caplan's work has made it possible for many clinicians to carry out community work in the spirit of the public's health. Thank you, Gerald Caplan, for the opportunity to help me make my paradigm shift so early in my career.

REFERENCES

Altrocchi, J., Spielberger, C. D., & Eisdorfer, C. (1965). Mental health consultation with groups. *Community Mental Health Journal, 1*, 127–134.

Caplan, G. (1964). *Principles of preventive psychiatry*. New York: Basic Books.

Caplan, G. (Personal Communication, November 19, 1967)

Caplan, G. (1970). *The theory and practice of mental health consultation*. New York: Basic Books.

Gallessich, J. (1982). *The profession and practice of consultation*. San Francisco: Jossey-Bass.

Glidewell, J. C. (1959). The entry problem in consultation. *The Journal of Social Issues, 15*, 51–59.

Glidewell, J. C. (1972). A social psychology of mental health. In S. E. Golann & C. Eisdorfer (Eds.), *Handbook of community mental health*, (pp. 211–246). New York: Appleton-Century-Crofts.

Grady, M. A., Gibson, M., & Trickett, E. J. (Eds.). (1981). *Mental health consultation theory, practice, and research 1973–1978: An annotated reference guide*. Washington, DC: U.S. Government Printing Office.

Hansen, J. C., Himes, B. S., & Meier, S. (1990). *Consultation: Concepts and practices*. Englewood Cliffs, NJ: Prentice-Hall.

Heller, K. (1984). Consultation: Psychodynamic, behavioral, and organization development perspectives. In K. Heller, R. H. Price, S. Reinharz, S. Riger, &

A. Wandersman (Eds.), *Psychology and community change* (pp. 229–285). Homewood, IL: The Dorsey Press.

Katz, D., & Kahn, R. (1978). *The social psychology of organizations* (2nd ed.). New York: Wiley.

Kelly, J. G. (1983). Consultation as a process of creating power: An ecological view. In S. Cooper & W. H. Hodges (Eds.), *The mental health consultation field* (pp. 153–171). New York: Human Sciences Press.

Kelly, J. G. (Ed.). (1984). In honor of Erich Lindemann. *American Journal of Community Psychology, 12*, 511–536.

Kelly, J. G. (1988). 1987 Division 27 Award for Distinguished Practice in Community Psychology: Donald C. Klein. *American Journal of Community Psychology, 16*, 295–303.

Kelly, J. G., & Hess, R. E. (Eds.). (1987). *The ecology of prevention: Illustrating mental health consultation*. New York: The Haworth Press.

Klein, D. C. (1968). *Community dynamics and mental health*. New York: Wiley.

Lippitt, G., & Lippitt, R. (1978). *The consulting process in action*. La Jolla, CA: University Associates, Inc.

Mann, P. A. (1971). Establishing a mental health consultation program with a police department. *Community Mental Health Journal, 7*, 118–126.

Mann, P. A. (1973). *Psychological consultation with a police department*. Springfield, IL: Charles C. Thomas.

Mannino, F. V., MacLennan, B. W., & Shore, M. F. (1975). *The practice of mental health consultation*. New York: Gardner.

Mannino, F. V., Trickett, E. J., Shore, M. F., Kidder, M. G., & Levin, G. (Eds.). (1986). *Handbook of mental health consultation* (DHHS Publication No. ADM 86-1446). Washington, DC: U.S. Government Printing Office.

Singh, R. K. J., Tarnower, W., & Chen, R. (1971). *Community mental health consultation and crisis intervention*. Berkeley, CA: Book People.

Spielberger, C. D. (1967). A mental health consultation program in a small community with limited professional mental health resources. In E. L. Cowen, E. A. Gardner, & M. Zax (Eds.), *Emergent approaches to mental health problems* (pp. 214–236). New York: Appleton-Century-Crofts.

Zusman, J., & Davidson, D. L. (Eds.). (1972). *Practical aspects of mental health consultation*. Springfield, IL: Charles C. Thomas.

Chapter 5

Gerald Caplan's Conceptual and Qualitative Contributions to Community Psychology: Views from an Old Timer

Ira Iscoe
University of Texas at Austin

INTRODUCTION AND BACKGROUND

In casting about how best to make a contribution to the present volume, I recognized that there were already many fine chapters I had the privilege of reading in manuscript form. There is no doubt that Caplan's contributions to community psychology are of lasting significance and of much relevance in today's troubled world. I came to the conclusion that the best contribution I could make was from a historical point of view, taking advantage of my age and early association with Caplan to "look down from the mountain," so to speak. My major purpose is to bring to the reader's attention some of the lesser known but extremely important ideas and concepts that Caplan formulated informally, which still have great importance today in the field of community psychology. Also, I attempt to emphasize how some Caplanian notions about the commu-

Based on a paper presented in the symposium, "Gerald Caplan's Contributions to American Psychology: Views from the Discipline," presented at the 98th annual meeting of the American Psychological Association, Boston, MA, August 13, 1990.

nity, if applied, could be of distinct advantage to certain U. S. institutions, such as public education. I begin with a little of my own background.

I graduated from UCLA in 1951 with a PhD in child clinical psychology. These were the post-war years when clinical psychology was just developing, and the independent practice of clinical psychology had not yet been "legalized." At best, psychologists could "do" psychotherapy under the supervision of a physician. Note that I use the word "physician" rather than "psychiatrist." Psychotherapy was, for all intents and purposes, a medical procedure. The role of the clinical psychologist had been shaped during World War II, dealing with soldiers' suitability for service and resulting mental illness from combat stress. Clinical psychology training programs were set up immediately after the war, first by the Veterans Administration, and later via stipends and training from the newly created National Institute of Mental Health (NIMH). The Scientist-Practitioner Model was agreed on at the Boulder Conference (Raimy, 1950), and many training programs quickly embraced it. (Within community psychology, I feel that the Scientist-Practitioner Model still is extremely important and relevant.) Although scientist-practitioner training may continue to predominate, the Vail Conference (Korman, 1974) introduced the Professional Model of training, which is gaining in strength and visibility. Certainly by the mid-1970s, psychologists were free to practice independently of other disciplines, and clinical psychology had expanded enormously both in number of practitioners and scope of activities.

The theoretical orientation at the time of my graduate study was, for the most part, psychoanalytic. I was convinced that as soon as more psychologists and other mental health professionals were created in my image, mental health would flourish, and that many of the problems of the world would be alleviated. Neuroses would be avoided, and creativity and originality would take their place. Frustrations among young and old would be reduced, and insight would be gained into our many conflicting motivations. Children and youth would be free to grow unencumbered by many developmental traumas, conflicts, and the like.

Despite having rather good clinical skills, I elected to go the academic route following graduation. Teaching undergraduate and graduate classes in child development and clinical and abnormal psychology brought me great satisfaction, but a malaise began to build up in terms of asking myself what I was really accomplishing in training clinical psychologists. As professionals, we clearly were dealing with casualties of social systems, and the more we looked, the more we found.

In the mid-1950s, psychoactive drugs were just beginning to be used, but their effects were already evident. In 1955, Congress set up the Joint Commission on Mental Health and Mental Illness. Fillmore Sanford, a distinguished psychologist and former executive secretary of the American Psychological Association (APA), was the director of the project. Committees were set up and various aspects of mental health were carried out. Soon to emerge were some significant volumes such as *Americans View Their Mental Health* (Gurin, Veroff, & Field, 1960) and *Mental Health Manpower Trends* (Albee, 1959). The book by Gurin et al. (1960) represented the first time a random population was surveyed about their mental health, who they went to for help, and how decisions were made concerning seeking help. Albee, as was to be his role for years to come, amassed data to show the need for changing our conceptions of mental illness, the continuing shortage of traditional mental health manpower, and, in general, the need for innovative approaches and preventive interventions. The entire work of the Joint Commission was summed up in a volume entitled *Action for Mental Health* (Ewalt, 1961).

While these national developments were taking place (and I read about them avidly), I carried on my usual teaching and research activities. Because of my clinical skill and interest in children (plus a very willing school system in Austin, Texas), my graduate students tested children with various problems, and we carried on weekly case conferences.

In our Thursday afternoon case conferences, the usual procedure was for a group of teachers to gather in the cafeteria. The student would present the test results and the teacher would give his or her views and academic status report on the child. Sometimes I even conducted an interview with the child and possibly the parents, and relayed this information during the conference. It took me some time to recognize that some parents have difficulties attending case conferences when they are on hourly wages. This was a community psychology reality that I fear still has not percolated down to some psychologists. In our case conferences, we usually reached some sort of diagnosis and advanced suggestions for helping both the child and the family. The school system was grateful (i.e., they were getting the service for free), my ego was gratified, and most of my students were complimentary about my insightful knowledge and the experiences that they were gaining.

A standard practice then was to place a great deal of blame on the parents, and the usual recommendation was to have the child and family apply to some social service agency or the local child guidance clinic. Of course, all the agencies had a waiting list of at least 3 to 4 months. Like many others, I began to recognize that inappropriate child-rearing practices could not be blamed for all the illnesses, problems, and difficulties that we saw in these school children or that existed in this world. True, the word "prevention" occasionally surfaced, and there also was talk about community action, volunteer services, family involvement, and other activities that now are quite common. But at that time, and in my part of the world (Texas), these activities were of a somewhat primitive nature and of low priority.

How then could I tap into the building ferment and excitement that was taking place in the mental health field? I read and heard about the activities being carried out at the Massachusetts General Hospital under psychiatrist

Erich Lindemann, and about a psychiatrist named Gerald Caplan who had established a Community Mental Health Research Project under the auspices of the Harvard School of Public Health. I knew little about Caplan's background or, for that matter, the details of the program. James G. Kelly (see Chapter 4) was a University of Texas graduate who had gone on to work with Lindemann and earned a master's degree in Public Health at Harvard. I talked to Kelly, and he was enthusiastic about both Lindemann and Caplan.

I applied for and obtained what then was called a senior stipend from NIMH, which allowed my family and me to spend the 1960–1961 academic year with Caplan, who was working on his research and training projects. The project was in an old building that I believe belonged to the Boston Department of Public Health. It was located across from a public housing project in Roxbury, Massachusetts. While at Harvard, I also had the privilege of attending some of the classes at the School of Public Health and became more familiar with public health principles, some of which, of course, are fundamental to effective community psychology practice.

The reader should bear in mind that these activities occurred in the early 1960s, a time during which money was flowing freely into many social programs. There was confidence that the United States could deal with the myriad social, psychological, and educational problems presented by an increasingly heterogeneous population. All it needed was training, personnel, and money. Head Start had not yet begun, and the war on poverty was just getting started. With fewer children from impoverished homes, the education process would be easier and life for every American would be improved. Mental hospitals, due to the drug therapies, would be reduced in size and gradually eliminated. Communities would assume more responsibility for the mentally ill. The practice base of psychology would be expanded, and research findings from universities and institutes would be utilized in our treatment of the mentally ill and emotionally disturbed. Even with the subsequent disappointments, it was wonderful to have these dreams back then.

Looking back, I see that I was a privileged person indeed. Caplan had assembled an excellent team—perhaps not the most skilled in research, but one certainly overflowing with ideas. The Master of Public Health Program and the Community Mental Health Research Project were truly interdisciplinary. Psychiatrists, psychologists, anthropologists, sociologists, social workers, and even some lawyers were involved. NIMH was generous in its support, and public health notions of primary, secondary, and tertiary prevention began to seep into our concepts of mental health.

One of the personal surprises was that, although Caplan had been psychoanalytically trained and was a practicing analyst, he accommodated many views. Although his approach to individuals in terms of intervention was psychoanalytic, his approach to community mental health problems did not follow a psychoanalytic doctrine. Upon reflection, I recognize that even today, psychoanalytically-oriented psychiatrists usually are more likely to accept innovative practices from other disciplines than are their other mental health colleagues.

The Caplan group was engaged in a pioneering study of consultation to public health nurses in the Roxbury area. Louisa Howe, a graduate of the Harvard School of Human Relations, was deeply involved in this research, as were several others. The entire project marked a departure in dealing with mental health problems. The aim was to broaden the skills of public health nurses ("caregivers," in Caplan's terms) so that they could deal more effectively with the many mental health problems of their clients. The Caplan philosophy did not accept the excuse of "I know nothing about mental health," and thus consultation was seen as a form of continuing education that would raise the level of sophistication of the nurses and allow them to handle many of the mental health problems they encountered. I picked up on the notions that the nurses could rely more on community resources than they were currently relying, and that these resources came in strange packages, such as relatives, ministers, police officers, and so on. The reader will recognize some of the parallels in the development of community psychology.

I was not really a part of Caplan's consultation research program, although I sat in on many of the meetings connected with it. These meetings often took place at lunch, almost always at a big table in the public health building. Caplan observed strict kosher dietary laws, and perhaps this explained why he never went out to lunch. He always was generous, however, sharing apples that he cut with surgical precision. Lunchtime also provided an opportunity to catch up with local gossip, to hear about various developments, and to listen to visiting speakers. There was a variety of other activities taking place. For example, David Kaplan, a social worker, was conducting research on the effects of allowing mothers to enter the nursery and thus participate actively in the care of their premature babies. The established procedure then was for the mother to return home and wait until the infant had reached a certain weight. This, however, resulted in unhealthy isolation between mother and child (as it prevented proper bonding) and brought on all types of psychological problems for the entire family. A particularly outrageous notion was advanced that maybe mothers—appropriately gowned and sterile—could be with their premature infants while they were in an incubator in the nursery. This is certainly a common practice today, but in 1960 it marked a revolution in infant care. It also threatened hospital procedure, violated turfs, and so on. I soon learned that a Caplanian technique was to respect the turf of others, but also to proceed with plans that would be beneficial to all concerned.

CONSULTATION TO PUBLIC SCHOOLS

One of my main purposes while at Harvard was to learn consultation, and I soon recognized that, for me at least, consultation was more difficult to master than psychotherapy. I had been accustomed to a type of consultation in which the consultant was superordinate and omniscient, which was quite different from Caplan's emphasis on a coordinate and nonhierarchical consulting relationship. It was also difficult for me to step down from the exalted level of professor to become a student once again. Thankfully, there were many opportunities to learn.

In gaining skill with the Caplan approach to consultation, I was very fortunate to have been supervised by Charlotte Owens, a psychiatric nurse who, in my opinion, is one of the finest teachers and genuine human beings whom I have ever come across. The fact that I was a PhD psychologist and was being supervised by a psychiatric nurse was, I must admit, somewhat of a threatening experience. Later I realized that utilizing appropriate resources, regardless of their professional affiliation, was one of the most important aspects of Caplan's approach, whether he was aware of it or not. As a trainer, Caplan was interested in a professional's competence, not his or her academic discipline.

It was arranged for me to consult with the Lawrence, Massachusetts public school system, as well as a private Catholic school in Lawrence and a school in Arlington, Massachusetts. In beginning my work as a school consultant, one of the things Charlotte stressed was to "know the territory." This meant not only knowing the school, but also its surrounding area. As I walked around the streets of Lawrence, I discovered that many parents sent their children to the public schools only because the parochial school was overcrowded. Likewise, en route to my first consultation, both Gerald and Charlotte warned me that the first teacher with whom I would consult was most likely the "goat," and that despite my orientation meeting with the principal the week before, some teacher who was having a great deal of trouble and who was disliked would be presented to the "psychologist." Sure enough, that is exactly what happened. This forewarning helped me avoid administrative traps and, throughout the years, I have always been very conscious of this principle (see Kelly's Law No. 3, Chapter 4). How to get around such situations was, in essence, part and parcel of the training I received, and may have arisen originally from Caplan's psychoanalytic training (i.e., "know the background"). In later years, while teaching consultation, I made my students aware of these sorts of considerations by requiring them to submit a one-page setting analysis that described the local neighborhood and organizational atmosphere of their respective school placements.

One parochial school said that it "did not need" me, despite a previous agreement. I returned to Boston chagrined and fuming. During an informal meeting, Caplan pointed out that this was common and, if we believed in the concept of crisis, I should wait and we would get a call. Sure enough, in 2 weeks, it happened. I received an anguished phone call from the principal, saying that they had an "insane child," who was probably a "sex fiend," in the form of an 8-year-old girl who had expounded on the sex differences between boys and girls.

The nun asked if I could come out to see the child immediately. I was ready to go, but Charlotte told me to make her wait a day and not to rush into this crisis or else the anxiety generated would be dissipated too rapidly. I made the long drive out to Lawrence the next day, and was greeted by the Sister-in-charge and a trembling little girl. Unfortunately, ethics and the possibility of a breach in confidentiality preclude full elaboration (even after 30 years). Suffice it to say that my consultation was effective. Subsequently, I was much more readily accepted by the school staff, and we all looked forward to our consultation sessions.

I also learned that acceptance of a consultant who deals with consultees rather than clients is sometimes a lengthy process. I frequently had lunch in one of the schools and grew to appreciate the adage that one learns more over the lunch table and in the faculty lounge than exists in the formal records and/or test reports. In addition, I learned a lesson that has stood me in good stead over the years: Within a school, it is not necessarily the principal who really "runs the school." In many cases, it is the executive secretary, a vice-principal, a counselor, or the non-teaching staff who set the tone for the school. In one particular school, while consulting with the custodian I learned more about vandalism and its prevention than from any textbook I have read. The custodian was well-liked and told the kids that if any more commodes were broken or walls defaced, he would get fired. These vandalistic activities stopped.

THE CONCEPT OF THEME INTERFERENCE

At first I did not pay much attention to the concept of theme interference, but later I came to believe in it. Those who are familiar with the Caplanian consultation model know that he makes a point of emphasizing that, when a professional does not perform his or her work effectively, there may be some sort of blockage or difficulty that precludes the optimum exercise of the person's competence and innovation. Caplan admitted the need for training and education to deal with skill and knowledge deficiencies, but also felt that the professional may not be using his or her resources or creativity most effectively. Often this situation would arise due to a lapse in the professional's objectivity.

Caplan's perspective on theme interference perhaps developed when handling a huge number of mental health casualties in Israel following World War II. Vast resources were needed to deal with the children who were the refugees from Europe and the concentration camps; however, these needed resources did not materialize. Notwithstanding, somehow the existing limited resources were stretched and personnel were educated quickly. It was a time of genuine crisis for Caplan and his staff, and consultation emerged as a pragmatic response to the situation. The usual interventions such as psychotherapy were not working, were not going to work, and, therefore, new approaches had to be tried. Caplan was undaunted by this lack of resources, although others in his position might have had this theme cloud their professional objectivity: "The provision of quality services requires a larger staff and greater resources, which we don't have. Thus, we will never be able to meet the existing demands for mental health care here."

The situation Caplan faced more than 40 years ago is relevant as one examines the state of U.S. public education. What are some of the interfering themes that concern America's schools? Below are four that I see as applicable. I am not saying that these themes reside in the individual so much as they reside within the school as an institution, and are shared beliefs among persons who have the power to bring about changes.

1 "Much more money is needed to bring about changes in public education, and yet it seems time after time insufficient funds are earmarked for education. Therefore, meaningful and lasting improvement is impossible to achieve." Included in this theme is that smaller classes are always more effective and better than larger classes. It is true that we need more money for teacher salaries. However, the teacher's role also can be made much more rewarding by changing work conditions and by giving the teacher a more central role in the educational process.

2 "Today's children are simply unmotivated to learn in school because of the many competing interests in their lives. There is little we can do." In some ways, this is another example of "stonewalling." True, hungry children cannot learn, but there are existing school breakfast programs and more should be made available. The schools *can* serve a much more community-oriented function than they presently do. This view certainly is not new with this writer. Zigler (1990) has talked for many years about different utilizations of schools so that they become more community oriented.

3 "Handicapped children must be served in special classes because we simply are unable to meet their needs in the regular classroom. There is no other way." Those of us who work with schools sometimes call this the "Great Shunting Movement." There has been a dramatic increase in the frequency and use of labels to categorize children (e.g., "learning disabled," "attention deficit-hyperactive disorder"). It seems that, when possible, children are placed in special classes where their reentry into the normal educational scheme is very much in doubt. A different approach would be to spend more time finding out ways in which the resources of the school and the community can be organized to deal with whatever problems are presented to the school. This includes not only persons going to the school, but also local merchants, police, health care providers, and others.

4 "Children who come from disadvantaged homes have parents who, by and large, do not care about education. How can we possibly teach these children effectively?" As I mentioned earlier, blaming parents is a time-honored, ineffective strategy. It also does no good to start off with beliefs indicating that there are no incentives for learning, and that all these kids are interested in is fooling around.

Of course, all these themes may contain some truth, but each needs to be examined and, ultimately, reduced. The persons and organizations who hold them have to be disabused and not let the excuses stand as barriers. Here is where well-trained, sophisticated community psychologists acting as participant conceptualizers and policy developers can make an important contribution. This is related to community mental health and, for Caplan, community mental health is grass roots and local in its orientation.

CAPLAN AND THE IMPORTANCE OF LOCAL ACTION

On many fronts, Caplan was way ahead of his time. In my many contacts with him in his office or over lunch, he expounded again and again on the philosophy of local action—the idea that change should be based at the level of the school rather than higher up in the administration. Although not a particularly liberal or democratic person, he always stressed respect for students and teachers and the importance of increasing the dialogue between teachers and parents, even if in the beginning it brought on accusations, hostilities, and so forth. His viewpoint, I suspect, was again related to psychoanalytic principles.

When he and I spoke about resources, I learned something that I now refer to as the "Boston Analogy." Caplan pointed out that, in Boston in the early 1960s, there were more child psychiatrists, child analysts, clinical social workers, clinical psychologists, and, in general, more mental health professionals than in any other U.S. city. Yet, there was no evidence then (and there is not now) that the mental health of Boston's children and adults was any better than that of residents of Boise, Idaho, or Oshkosh, Wisconsin.

I would interpret the emphasis on local action as the power of communities and the imparting of a feeling of worthwhileness to individuals and groups. In my humble opinion, one of the worst plagues in America is the proliferation of graduate degrees in Educational Administration and the great number of school administrators generally. It will come as no surprise to the knowledgeable reader that the New York City public school system contains more assistant school superintendents than there are school superintendents in the entire country of France. (I might add that French children are reportedly well ahead in basic reading and mathematics skills.) The marshalling of families and resources; the agreement on priorities by the school and the community (rather than the central administration); the assumption of greater responsibilities by principals, teachers, and students; and the fostering of a continuing dialogue with parents to deal with problems such as theft, vandalism, and violence all are essential for a well-functioning school system. The hiring of professional school monitors, police guards, and so on only sets one group up against the other in various power struggles, and thus dilutes educational efforts.

What then have been the barriers to schools in performing their mission?

Perhaps in place is the theme, "Community-run schools will offer substandard education in a chaotic, disorganized fashion." There certainly is a variety of political, financial, and other reasons to keep the schools under "tight supervision" within the guild of education.

The philosophy of Caplan then and now calls for a reversal of this trend. His philosophy suggests, as much as possible, to do it at the local level. Tap into resources that you never thought could be used. Emphasize the "holding power" of the schools, and let schools play a more central role in the community. There are some encouraging signs that this philosophy has taken hold. It is in this area that Caplan has perhaps inadvertently made an enormous contribution to community psychology, even prior to 1965, before the discipline as such existed. After all, one of the main tenets of community psychology is empowerment (Rappaport, 1981). What better way to empower schools than to let them have the responsibility for making decisions, and to have local school administrators (i.e., principals) use funds in innovative ways?

MY EXPERIENCE IN THE ROXBURY HOUSING DISTRICT

There is one more implication for training that I feel compelled to mention before concluding this chapter.

The building in which the Community Mental Health Research Project was housed was opposite one of the Roxbury housing units. I was informed that the worse off the family, the higher the priority of receiving an apartment within the huge housing complex. There were hundreds of children playing in the yard and parking lot after school and, sometimes when I came to work, left the subway, and walked to the building, I also saw children and mothers going off to school. I saw very few fathers because the project was under Aid to Dependent Children and, as a matter of policy at that time, an adult male could not live in the apartment. I also noticed that on Monday mornings the parking lot was littered with glass and other debris. I was relatively innocent in those days, but soon gained a better understanding of some of the dynamics of the Roxbury housing community.

The opportunity arose to accompany a public health nurse on one of her visits to the occupants of one of the housing units. I soon realized the great respect the residents had for the public health nurses. We had gone there to see about the condition of a very elderly grandmother. Upon knocking on the door, it was opened and then shut quickly. The nurse knocked again and assured the occupant that I was "not from the welfare agency," but rather that I was a young professor who had come to study with the Harvard project. The door was opened, the woman apologized, and soon the daughter and two babies appeared, later to be followed by her son and another person whom I presumed was the daughter's boyfriend or husband. The girl complained about the "long time" that it took waiting in the clinic. The boy wondered whether he was coming down with a sexually transmitted disease. The grandmother sat in the corner smiling and occasionally mumbling to herself.

As we left the housing unit, I expressed the opinion that we should try to get the grandmother out of the house and possibly into the Boston State Hospital. Innocent me—I learned a lesson. The wise nurse informed me that the grandmother's social security check kept the family going and if we were to remove her to the hospital, the payments would cease and the family would be in much worse circumstances than they were now. The complexities of human service delivery comes as a shock to most middle-class persons, including university professors. It remains a problem, even today.

CONCLUSION

I've looked back some 30 years and tried to bring to the reader a flavor of what it was like to work with Caplan, and how much of his work is directly relevant to the field of community psychology we know today and that we are striving to improve. In some ways, I do not think that Caplan meant to be a community psychologist, so much as he was interested in improving community mental health and expanding the nature of interventions designed to reduce the incidence and prevalence of mental illness. When the antecedents of community psychology are systematically explored in a historical nature, Caplan's many contributions (both formal and informal), his teachings, and his writings will receive the prominence they so richly deserve.

I close this chapter with a final personal observation. Beginning in the early 1980s, and now definitely in the early 1990s, I note a retreat from the idealism and hope that were epitomized by Caplan's work. Prestigious departments of psychiatry and psychology in major U. S. universities have abandoned somewhat the community psychology approach in favor of neurobiological and neurochemical approaches to dealing with problems of human beings. The failure of deinstitutionalization may in one sense be characterized as the failure of "knowing the territory" and understanding the needs of persons with various degrees of mental illness. The method of consultation, that at one time was to be the great hope of prevention, has failed to materialize—not because of a weakness of the method as much as a change in the attitudes of those charged with the design and delivery of mental health care services. Learning consultation and developing an understanding of the dynamic forces in a community are no easy matters, especially for psychologists born and raised in middle-class circumstances. Clearly, the lessons I learned in the Roxbury Housing Project could not be duplicated experientially in a dozen books or lectures.

It is to be hoped that circumstances will again dictate a more compassionate and effective approach to the social pathology of institutions and communities. Certainly the violent aftermath of the recent (May 1992) Rodney King verdict in Los Angeles argues for a stronger behavioral science base, leading to a more effective community psychology.

REFERENCES

Albee, G. W. (1959). *Mental health manpower trends.* New York: Basic Books.

Ewalt, J. (1961). *Action for mental health.* New York: Basic Books.

Gurin, G., Veroff, J., & Field, S. (1960). *Americans view their mental health.* New York: Basic Books.

Korman, M. (1974). National conference on levels and patterns of professional training: The major themes. *American Psychologist, 29,* 441–449.

Raimy, V. C. (Ed.). (1950). *Training in clinical psychology.* Englewood Cliffs, NJ: Prentice-Hall.

Rappaport, J. (1981). In praise of paradox: A social policy of empowerment over prevention. *American Journal of Community Psychology, 9,* 1–25.

Zigler, E. (1990). Shaping child care policies and programs in America. *American Journal of Community Psychology, 18,* 183–193.

Chapter 6

Caplan's Contributions to the Practice of Psychology in Schools

**Joel Meyers, Donna Brent,
Ellen Faherty, and Christine Modafferi**

University at Albany
State University of New York

INTRODUCTION

One of Caplan's most important ideas is presented in the introduction to his classic book, *The Theory and Practice of Mental Health Consultation* (Caplan, 1970), which describes his experience as a psychiatrist in Israel in 1949. The small number of professionals working at a clinic that was responsible for the mental health of 17,000 immigrant children from over 100 residential institutions realized that it was impractical to provide services using a direct service model. Instead, the clinic staff reasoned that if they could help one caregiver provide services more effectively, or if they could facilitate the functioning of a relevant institution, then effective services could be provided to larger numbers of children with the potential of reducing waiting lists.

These overwhelming numbers and long waiting lists have always been and will continue to be a problem for those concerned with the provision of mental health services in schools. That is why Caplan's experience in Israel over 40 years ago still has profound implications for the practice of psychology in schools. School psychologists should be guided by the principle that for each teacher or school that a psychologist helps there will be a positive impact on hundreds of children in the present and in the future. If this view is correct, then those of us who have been influenced by Caplan's work on mental health consultation have helped thousands of students. The publication of this book presents a unique opportunity for psychologists to thank Caplan for his marked contributions to the delivery of psychological services in schools.

Caplan's work can be conceptualized as falling into two major areas: mental health consultation and the prevention of psychopathology. The purpose of this chapter is to examine Caplan's work in these two major areas and to consider the impact of this work on the practice of psychology in the schools. This task will be approached by discussing his impact on the school psychology literature, reviewing his ideas about mental health consultation and the prevention of psychopathology, and presenting suggestions for future research designed to extend Caplan's work. Particular attention will be paid to those of his books and articles that have been written prior to 1980, because sufficient time has passed for these works to influence the field of school psychology.

CAPLAN'S INFLUENCE ON THE SCHOOL PSYCHOLOGY LITERATURE

A review of the school psychology literature helps to underscore Caplan's contributions. Consider, for example, textbooks in the field of school psychology. Many early texts in the field refer to consultation or prevention as part of the psychologist's role (Cutts, 1955; Gottsegen & Gottsegen, 1963; Gray, 1963; Magary, 1967; Valett, 1963; White & Harris, 1961), and some of these texts recognize the preventive potential of consultation as an approach to indirect service (Gottsegen & Gottsegen, 1963; Gray, 1963). Others ignore the preventive potential of school psychology and refer to consultation more as a necessary part of the psychologist's direct service role. This perspective suggests that consultation with those who have regular contact with the child should be used to augment the effectiveness of psychodiagnosticians (Valett, 1963). Although these early school psychology texts mention consultation, and some recognize the potential of preventive approaches, there is minimal space (i.e., one or two pages at most) devoted to the discussion of this part of the role, and there are almost no details about the procedures needed to consult effectively in schools.

In contrast, more recent texts about the practice of school psychology consistently discuss consultation and prevention, and these texts discuss procedural aspects of consultation in some detail (Bardon & Bennett, 1974; Bergan, 1985; Elliott & Witt, 1986; Graden, Zins, & Curtis, 1988; Gutkin & Reynolds, 1990; Kratochwill, 1981; Phillips, 1990; Phye & Reschly, 1979; Reynolds, Gutkin, Elliott, & Witt, 1984). Moreover, these recent texts consistently discuss Caplan's work. For example, Gutkin & Curtis (1990) include a detailed subsection on Caplan's approach to mental health consultation in their comprehensive chapter on school-based consultation.

In addition to being referenced in texts on school psychology, Caplan's work is frequently cited in school psychology journals such as the *Journal of School Psychology, Psychology in the Schools, School Psychology Quarterly,* and *School Psychology Review.* Oakland (1984) found that Caplan's (1970) book, *The Theory and Practice of Mental Health Consultation,* was the most frequently cited book in the *Journal of School Psychology* during the 20-year period from 1963 to 1982, and was the second most frequently cited reference overall (24 citations). Only the Wechsler Intelligence Scale for Children (WISC) and the Wechsler Intelligence Scale for Children-Revised (WISC-R) were cited more frequently (51 citations).

Further evidence of his impact on the field of school psychology is revealed from a review of the Social Science Citation Index for the 20-year period since the publication of *The Theory and Practice of Mental Health Consultation* (Caplan, 1970). During that period, this book has been referenced in 38 articles from the *Journal of School Psychology,* in 22 articles from *Psychology in the Schools,* and in 10 articles from the *School Psychology Review.*[1] Also, his seminal article on consultation, "Types of Mental Health Consultation" (Caplan, 1963), was cited in seven articles in these journals. Caplan's books on the prevention of psychopathology also have been cited in the school psychology literature, although less often than his work on consultation. A review of the same three school psychology journals during the past 20 years reveals that *Principles of Preventive Psychiatry* (Caplan, 1964) has been cited in 12 articles during that 20-year period, *Prevention of Mental Disorders in Children* (Caplan, 1961b) has been cited in 3 articles, and *Support Systems in Community Mental Health* (Caplan, 1974) has been cited in 2 articles.

Additional evidence for his impact is the growing emphasis on consultation as an approach to the role of the school psychologist. Not only have there been many books in the school psychology literature focused specifically on consultation (Alpert et al., 1982; Alpert & Meyers, 1983; Bergan, 1977; Brown, Pryzwansky, & Schulte, 1987; Conoley, 1981; Conoley & Conoley, 1982; Curtis & Zins, 1981; Meyers, Martin, & Hyman, 1977; Meyers, Parsons, & Martin, 1979; Parsons & Meyers, 1984; Rosenfield, 1988), but there also have been numerous surveys reporting support by educators and/or psychologists for a consultation role (Fisher, Jenkins, & Crumbly, 1986; Gutkin, Singer, & Brown, 1980; Lambert, Sandoval, & Corder, 1978; Martin & Meyers, 1980; Meacham & Peckham, 1978; Smith & Lyon, 1985). Although not directly attributable to Caplan, the increased focus on consultation in schools has resulted in a new journal devoted specifically to this topic *(Journal of Educational and Psychological Consultation).*

---

[1]*School Psychology Quarterly,* formerly titled *Professional School Psychology,* is not included in these citation counts because it was not published until 1986.

This interest in consultation also has resulted in numerous recent publications focused on consultation, with about one-fourth of these being based on empirical research (Pryzwansky, 1986). Although there is clearly a need for more research in this area, prior research consistently has suggested that consultation can be an effective intervention (Alpert & Yammer, 1983; Duncan & Pryzwansky, 1988; Mannino & Shore, 1975, 1983; Medway, 1979, 1982; Medway & Updyke, 1985; Meyers, Pitt, Gaughan, & Freidman, 1978).

One of the most important recent contributions to the school-based consultation literature has been the description and evaluation of programmatic efforts to implement various school-based consultation models (Alpert et al., 1982; Curtis & Metz, 1986; Graden, Casey, & Bonstrom, 1985; Graden, Casey, & Christenson, 1985; Gutkin, Henning-Stout, & Piersel, 1988; Lennox, Hyman, & Hughes, 1988; Ponti, Zins, & Graden, 1988). These descriptions inform both practitioners and researchers about methods that seem to work and serve as a stimulus for future research and practice in this field.

MENTAL HEALTH CONSULTATION

Definition

Caplan (1970) defined consultation as

> [A] process of interaction between two professional persons—the consultant, who is a specialist, and the consultee, who invokes the consultant's help in regard to a current work problem with which he is having some difficulty and which he has decided is within the other's area of specialized competence. The work problem involves the management or treatment of one or more clients of the consultee, or the planning or implementation of a program to cater to such clients. (p. 19)

In school-based consultation, the consultant is generally a psychologist or other mental health specialist, the consultee is a teacher or other educator, and the client is a student. Throughout most of this chapter, the terms "teacher" and "consultee" will be used interchangeably, as will the terms "student" and "client." This definition, or some variant, has been the basis for most definitions of school-based consultation, and this basic definition has been used by a range of professionals, even those relying on dramatically different theoretical perspectives, such as behavioral (Bergan, 1977) and psychodynamic frameworks (Alpert & Silverstein, 1985).

Process of Consultation

Interpersonal Process A hallmark of Caplan's approach to consultation is its emphasis on a nonhierarchical, coordinate relationship in which the consultee has the freedom to accept or reject the consultant's ideas. This concept includes the notion that consultation takes place between two equal professionals who each have different areas of expertise. In school-based consultation, the mental health consultant may have expertise in psychology or some aspect of mental health, whereas the teacher-consultee would have expertise in education. There is some evidence that consultants who establish a coordinate, nonhierarchical relationship with consultees augment their potential to reduce resistance on the part of the consultee (Meyers, 1981). These ideas are accepted widely by those who practice school-based consultation, and they have had a dramatic impact on the school consultation literature (Conoley & Conoley, 1982; Curtis & Meyers, 1988; Gutkin & Curtis, 1990; Meyers, 1981; Meyers et al., 1979; Osterweil, 1987; Schowengerdt, Fine, & Poggio, 1976). Nevertheless, there continues to be a need for research documenting the efficacy of various collaborative processes.

Although Caplan carefully explains the rationale and techniques for establishing a nonhierarchical relationship, some contradictions appear in his treatment of gender, which could undermine his stated goal for the consultant to interact with the consultee on an equal basis. For example, Caplan (1970) made statements regarding consultee groups such as public health nurses, which could be interpreted as stereotypic when he refers to public health nurses as a group of young, poorly trained, inexperienced professionals ". . . who may leave within a year because of marriage or pregnancy" (p. 84). At times he refers to women as "girls" and uses examples implying that the consultants and other people in power are men, and that the consultees are female. We do not mean to criticize Caplan for being sexist. After all, this aspect of Caplan's writing reflected the views and writing styles of its period, and this description may have been congruent with the realities of the schools and hospitals he consulted with at that time. Still, it is important to point out that this sort of language may influence neophyte consultants who read this work. This may result in consulting behaviors that conflict with a coordinate, nonhierarchical relationship and interfere with the development of a maximally effective consultative relationship. Perhaps most importantly, this early work by Caplan did not consider the role of gender in consultation in a systematic manner, and most of the subsequent scholarship regarding mental health consultation over the past 20 years has ignored gender as well.

Although sexism and the role of gender in consultation generally have not been considered in the consultation literature, there is reason to believe that these may be important factors. Although Caplan (1970) suggested that consultants are male and consultees are female, today this view is not accurate for school-based consultants. It may be true that the majority of teacher-consultees are female. However, the majority of graduate students being trained as school psychologists are also female (Conoley & Welch, 1988), resulting in a steadily growing number of potential consultants who are women. This is compounded by the fact that female school psychologists rate themselves as less competent than males in teacher consultation (Smith & Lyon, 1986).

One investigation of trainees in a school psychology graduate program found that female students were less likely than their male counterparts to exhibit leadership behaviors, to consult with administrators and other consultees high in the power hierarchy, and to engage in relatively risky approaches to consultation, such as advocacy or consultee-centered case consultation (Conoley & Welch, 1988). This may occur because those who train consultants ignore gender issues. It has been suggested that training has the potential to address these issues effectively so that female consultants will have more confidence in their consultation skills and will be more willing to use a range of consultative approaches (Conoley & Welch, 1988). Although the role of gender has received little attention in the consultation literature, it merits further research and should be considered by programs that train consultants.

Stages of Consultation   The literature on school-based consultation is filled with descriptions of the stages of consultation that are consistent with a problem-solving perspective (Bergan, 1977; Gutkin & Curtis, 1990; Meyers et al., 1979). Although these stages can be traced back to Caplan (1970), the current literature defines most of these steps in more detail. However, Caplan (1970) made unique and important contributions to this area through his discussion of two issues related to the entry stage in consultation: (a) building the relationship with the consultee institution (i.e., the school or school system), and (b) building the relationship with the individual consultee (i.e., teacher or other educator). In discussing the development of a relationship with the individual consultee, Caplan (1970) presented many practical suggestions and elaborated on ideas that can facilitate development of a coordinate relationship. Although over 20 years old, that section of his book is still highly relevant to neophyte consultants.

His description of the development of a relationship with the consultee institution is particularly important, because it is still one of the best and most detailed descriptions of how to establish a relationship with the system—a relationship that is essential to the later effectiveness of consultation. In conjunction with his psychodynamic perspective (Gutkin & Curtis, 1990), Caplan maintains a clear awareness of the importance of the environment, the political realities of consultation, and the systemic factors characterizing the institution.

This emphasis on the environment is underscored because that concept helped to revolutionize school psychologists' concepts about the delivery of mental health services. Rather than assuming that all change should be approached intrapersonally based on discussions in the helper's office, this orientation suggested that sometimes the most appropriate approach to intervention is in the client's environment. Here was a psychodynamic theorist stating that: "The best procedure for the consultant is . . . to do his work not in the isolation of his office but by entering the environment of the consultee . . ." (Caplan, 1970, p. 114). This idea was consistent with the viewpoints of other early contributors to the consultation literature (Sarason, Levine, Goldenberg, Cherlin, & Bennett, 1966), and it is still highly relevant today.

Four Categories of Consultation

Caplan (1970) categorized consultation into four different types: (a) client-centered case consultation, (b) program-centered administrative consultation, (c) consultee-centered case consultation, and (d) consultee-centered administrative consultation. This categorization provides the basis for much of the thinking that has been done about the organization of consultation services. Consultee-centered case consultation has been described as the central focus of Caplan's work on mental health consultation (Gutkin & Curtis, 1990), and, therefore, this approach is discussed later in more detail. His work on program-centered administrative consultation and consultee-centered administrative consultation (approaches to organizational consultation) has had less of an impact than his work on client-centered or consultee-centered case consultation. Nevertheless, organizational consultation methods are described in the school-based consultation literature based on their potential to remediate current school problems and to prevent the development of future problems (Schmuck, 1990). Although there have been some beginning efforts to research the efficacy of organizational consultation in schools (Miles, Fullan, & Taylor, 1980; Schmuck & Runkel, 1988), additional research is needed to develop realistic methods for implementation by practitioners, and to expand the research base concerning the efficacy of organizational consultation.

A Model Integrating the Categories of Consultation Caplan made an important contribution by conceptualizing the four categories of consultation described above. This approach has been adapted specifically for application in school settings (Meyers, 1973) and developed into a decision-making model designed to assist the practitioner in determining which category of consultation is most appropriate to a particular problem (Meyers et al., 1979). The most recent version of this model describes three, rather than four, types of school-based consultation, which vary based on how directly services are provided from the consultant to the student (i.e., student-centered consultation, teacher-centered consultation, and system-centered consultation) (Meyers, 1989; Meyers & Kundert, 1988).

The decision-making rule is to choose first the most indirect approach that is appropriate to a case (e.g., system-centered or teacher-centered consultation), even when more direct approaches might also be appropriate (i.e., student-centered consultation). The most indirect approaches are the priority, because they have the greatest potential to reach a maximum number of students, to eliminate the need for current referrals, and to prevent the development of future problems. Case examples have been used to document the utility of this model (Meyers, 1989; Meyers & Kundert, 1988).

Consultee-Centered Case Consultation

Consultee-centered case consultation is certainly one of Caplan's more significant contributions. Despite the widespread focus on consultee-centered case consultation (Alpert & Silverstein, 1985; Caplan, 1970; Curtis & Meyers, 1988; Gutkin & Curtis, 1990; Meyers et al., 1979), there has been almost no empirical research investigating the efficacy of this approach. One exception is a series of studies supporting the effectiveness of consultee-centered case consultation as a technique to facilitate teachers' professional objectivity and to change teacher behavior (Friedman, 1978; Meyers, 1975; Meyers, Freidman, & Gaughan, 1975).

Caplan (1970) discussed four reasons for consultee-centered case consultation: (a) lack of knowledge, (b) lack of skill, (c) lack of self-confidence, and (d) lack of objectivity. It has been suggested that he considered lack of objectivity to be the most important reason for consultee-centered case consultation (Gutkin & Curtis, 1990). Gutkin (1981) investigated these four reasons for consultee-centered case consultation and found that lack of objectivity was discussed infrequently, and lack of knowledge, lack of skill, and lack of self-confidence were more frequently discussed in school-based consultation. Although this does not dismiss the potential importance of lack of objectivity, it does suggest that future work on school-based consultation should focus on the development of consultation techniques designed for lack of knowledge, lack of skill, and lack of self-confidence.

Lack of objectivity occurs when the consultee is unable to maintain professional distance from the client, resulting in impaired judgment and reduced effectiveness on the part of the consultee. Caplan (1970) discussed several sources of lack of objectivity, which are derived from his psychodynamic theoretical perspective and are based on the degree to which the consultee identifies with the client (or some person connected with the client). Caplan (1970) devoted the greatest attention to "theme interference" as a source of lack of objectivity and the related technique of theme-interference reduction.

Our own personal experience with consultation suggests that when lack of objectivity does occur in schools, techniques such as theme-interference reduction are infrequently identified as appropriate interventions. Instead, behavioral descriptions of consultee conflicts may lead to more practical approaches to restore professional objectivity. Examples of such conflicts include teacher conflicts concerning authority, dependency, and hostility, as well as conflicts like those described by Caplan, which relate to consultee identification with the client (see Meyers et al., 1979).

Direct Versus Indirect Confrontation Theme-interference reduction is one of several approaches to indirect confrontation proposed by Caplan (1970) for consultee-centered case consultation. The basic principle is that confrontation should keep the focus off of the consultee. Another example of an indirect confrontation procedure is to discuss the consultee's affective involvement in the case by describing a related problem existing in the child, rather than discussing the consultee's problem directly. For example, instead of saying that the teacher has problems acting as the authority figure, the consultant might suggest that the youngster has difficulty dealing with authority. The consultant might then suggest that, because of this student's particular problem with authority, it may be important for the teacher to take a clear stance as the classroom authority figure.

Although indirect confrontation techniques may have face validity and can be particularly useful when working with resistant consultees, it must be recognized that there is no database to support the use of these techniques. It has been argued that sometimes indirect methods may be too oblique to be clearly understood by the consultee, and, as a result, they may not consistently result in the intended change (Gutkin & Curtis, 1990; Meyers et al., 1979). Moreover, ethical questions have been raised about the use of techniques directed to consultees who are kept unaware of the consultant's goal (Hughes, 1986).

Caplan recommends indirect approaches because ". . . the teacher's internal problems are assumed to be too serious to approach directly without destroying the teacher's defenses. Generally, we think that it is more useful to . . . accept the teacher's emotional strength and trust his or her ability to handle appropriate confrontation" (Meyers et al., 1979, p. 135). Direct confrontation can be used by pointing out and discussing teacher conflicts directly. As a result, the discussion between consultant and consultee ". . . should be more straightforward and more readily understood by both consultant and consultee . . ." (Meyers et al. 1979, p. 135). Case examples have been presented with data based on behavior observation, and with experimental controls indicating the efficacy of direct confrontation in consultee-centered consultation (Meyers, 1975; Meyers et al., 1975).

Preventive Implications of Consultation

One of the most important points made by Caplan (1970) was that mental health consultation has the potential to serve as an approach to the prevention of psychopathology. He viewed consultation as a pragmatic way to eliminate long referral lists. He assumed that if the consultant could increase the effectiveness of the consultee, some emotional problems would be prevented, thus reducing the need to refer the client. In fact, throughout Caplan's writings about prevention, mental health consultation was referred to as an important preventive procedure. This is a powerful concept, yet insufficient work has been done to develop this idea or to reinforce the application of consultation as a primary prevention technique (Meyers, 1989). Instead, school-based consultation is too often considered as a secondary prevention technique that is implemented during a crisis to improve the current functioning of a particular child (i.e., client-centered case consultation).

Perhaps the potential of consultation as a primary prevention method has not been explored fully because of the psychodynamic notions underlying mental health consultation. For example, "themes" and the consultee's identification with the client may imply that there is something internally wrong with the teacher-consultee. Similarly, the four reasons for consultee-centered case consultation imply that there is something wrong with the consultee (i.e., lack of knowledge, lack of skill, lack of self-confidence, and lack of objectivity). This deficit orientation is not consistent with a preventive framework. It has been suggested that consultee-centered case consultation could have a broader, more preventive impact if the four reasons for consultee-centered case consultation were conceptualized positively instead of negatively. Using this framework, the four reasons for consultee-centered case consultation might be conceptualized as *the development of* knowledge, skill, self-confidence, and objectivity, rather than the lack of these characteristics (see Parsons & Meyers, 1984).

There have been some beginning efforts to determine whether consultation does indeed have the kinds of generalized effects it professes in theory. The results of this research can be summarized as finding: improved professional and problem-solving skills for teachers (Cleven & Gutkin, 1988; Curtis & Metz, 1986; Curtis & Watson, 1980; Gutkin, 1980; Revels & Gutkin, 1983; Zins, 1981); modified teacher attitudes regarding the children's problems (Gutkin, Singer, & Brown, 1980); greater understanding of children's problems by teachers (Curtis & Watson, 1980); generalization of consultation effects to other children in the same classroom (Jason & Ferone, 1978; Meyers, 1975); reduced referral rates (Graden et al., 1985; Gutkin et al., 1988; Ponti et al., 1988; Ritter, 1978); and gains in long-term academic performance (Jackson, Cleveland, & Merenda, 1975) (see Curtis & Meyers, 1988; Gutkin & Curtis, 1990).

PREVENTION OF PSYCHOPATHOLOGY

Although Caplan's work on mental health consultation has had dramatic effects on the school psychology literature, his work on prevention has had less impact. This observation is noteworthy, given that his contributions to the prevention of psychopathology in children have had significant and far-reaching effects on the current literature connected with primary and secondary prevention. Moreover, Caplan's decades' old conceptual model of primary, secondary, and tertiary prevention activities (Caplan, 1964) is the foundation for much of the current work on the prevention of learning and adjustment problems in schools. Because his work on primary and secondary prevention has particularly important implications for the practice of psychology in the schools, these two approaches are discussed briefly below.

Primary prevention refers to those methods that are designed to prevent the entire population (or subgroup) from developing mental health problems by implementing those methods before individuals show signs of the problem. In many ways, Caplan's writings about primary prevention (Caplan, 1961b, 1964, 1974) anticipated the theories, models, and approaches discussed in the current literature on primary prevention. It has been suggested that two major approaches to primary prevention include modifying the environment and modifying the individual (Albee, 1982; Alpert, 1985; Cowen, 1985; Meyers & Parsons, 1987), and this conceptualization can be traced back to Caplan's discussion of two approaches to primary prevention referred to as the "nutritional model" and the "crisis model" (Caplan, 1964, 1974).

Primary Prevention Methods Designed to Modify the Environment

The Nutritional Model and Prevention Programs Designed to Modify the Environment   The "nutritional model" (Caplan, 1974) suggested that adequate personality development depends on the availability of appropriate "supplies," those physical, psychosocial, and sociocultural requirements necessary for an individual's current stage of growth and development. Primary prevention programs can be developed systematically by surveying a population to identify those "supplies" unavailable to the population, and by designing a program that provides these supplies and facilitates healthy emotional development by modifying the environment.

Examples of these types of programs are provided, for example, in his edited book, *Prevention of Mental Disorders in Children* (Caplan, 1961b), which includes chapters by several authors who describe prevention activities that attempt to modify the environment. Particular attention is paid to modifying the school environment in a chapter by Barbara Biber, who describes the effects of different educational atmospheres on the development of students' ego strength. Recent research has underscored the potential preventive impact of modifying the school environment (Cowen & Hightower, 1990; Kelly, 1979; Meyers, 1989; Meyers & Parsons, 1987; Moos, 1979).

Community Support Systems   Caplan (1974) has suggested that professionals interested in preventing mental disorders and promoting mental health should devote significant effort to fostering the development of various support systems in the communities they serve. Support systems can be provided through formal institutions, such as church and school, as well as through less formal marital and family groups, groups of friends, neighbors and acquaintances, or organized support groups not directed by caregiving professionals (Caplan, 1974). The development of support systems is an approach to modifying the environment, which can help to provide the individual with needed supplies.

Caplan (1974) provided several illustrations of support systems. For example, he described a program of peer counseling developed by Hamburg and Varenhorst (1972; cited in Caplan, 1974) where junior high students were trained as volunteer counselors. These students visited elementary schools in May and June of the school year to offer counseling to sixth graders preparing for the move to junior high school. The volunteer counselors were then available again to the incoming students in September to help them with transition difficulties. Following Caplan's lead, networks, self-help groups, and support systems have been suggested as powerful primary prevention approaches to modifying the environment (Cauce & Srebnik, 1989; Katz & Hermalin, 1987; Sarason, Carroll, Maton, Cohen, & Lorentz, 1977), and there is a need for more research indicating the efficacy of these procedures in schools.

The Crisis Model and Primary Prevention Methods Designed to Modify the Individual

The "crisis model" (Caplan, 1964, 1974) has a short-term focus on the transitional periods of individual development. Caplan (1974) stated that a person develops through a succession of differentiated phases (e.g., school transitions, divorce, developmental changes such as puberty, etc.), and that between each phase is a period of upset or crisis. Caplan (1964) suggested that the crisis state presents an individual with the opportunity for personal growth as well as an increased risk of mental disturbance. The notion that crises can be growth producing is consistent with Janis' (1958) concept of psychological innoculation and Hollister's (1965) concept of strens, and it has been suggested that these ideas have important implications for prevention in schools (Meyers, 1989; Meyers & Parsons, 1987; Phillips, Martin, & Meyers, 1972). Moreover, there has been recent research on prevention programs designed to modify the impact of life transitions relevant to schooling, such as school transitions, transitions resulting from mobility, and life changes associated with divorce (Felner, Farber, & Primavera, 1983; Felner, Ginter, & Primavera, 1982; Stolberg, 1988).

As early as 1961, Caplan suggested that techniques such as anticipatory guidance, dry runs, dress rehearsals, and preliminary training periods could be useful in lessening the novelty or challenge of crisis situations so that they would become more manageable for the individual (Caplan, 1961b). Although Caplan's early work does not use the term, these techniques are strikingly similar to current discussions of "competence building" in the primary prevention literature (Albee, 1982; Cowen, 1985). For example, a chapter from Caplan's 1961 book, *Prevention of Mental Disorders in Children,* written by Ralph Ojemann (1961), described the effects of a program training students to

develop causal thinking skills. This was the forerunner to many current compe-
tence building programs in the area of social-skills training (Elias et al., 1986;
Shure & Spivack, 1982; Spivack, Platt, & Shure, 1976; Weissberg, Caplan, &
Sivo, 1989).

Secondary Prevention

The goal of secondary prevention programs is to reduce the duration of established cases of mental disorder, thereby reducing their prevalence in the community (Caplan, 1964). This goal can be accomplished through early intervention and the use of prompt, effective approaches to treatment with populations
showing early signs of emotional disorder (Caplan, 1964).

Early Intervention   Caplan (1964) argued that early intervention would
be possible if there were effective approaches to obtaining early referrals. For
example, he suggested public education and dissemination of information about
mental health through mass media, an approach that has been discussed in the
recent literature on prevention (Roppel & Jacobs, 1988). In this same vein, he
suggested offering mental health education courses to key nonpsychiatric professionals (i.e., nurses, teachers, physicians, and clergy) and offering mental
health consultation to caregivers (Caplan, 1964).

Caplan (1964) also advocated the use of screening programs to facilitate the
early identification and intervention strategies that are consistent with secondary prevention. In *Prevention of Mental Disorders in Children* (1961b), a chapter by Eli Bower described an effort to develop screening procedures designed
to identify emotionally disturbed children in school settings. An excellent example of recent work focused on secondary prevention and using early screening
procedures with school children is Cowen's Primary Mental Health Project
(Cowen & Hightower, 1990).

Prompt Effective Approaches to Treatment   Caplan (1961a) advocated
crisis intervention approaches to avoid long waiting lists for treatment. He
suggested a range of interventions consistent with secondary prevention, including mental health consultation and intervention with the mother rather than the
child (Caplan, 1955, 1961a), as well as direct therapeutic intervention provided
to populations identified as having early signs of emotional difficulties (Caplan,
1964). A priority for Caplan was to use the time and skills of mental health
professionals to deliver therapeutic intervention with maximum efficiency. One
effective example from the school psychology literature has been Cowen's pioneering work using paraprofessionals to provide therapeutic intervention to
children showing early signs of adjustment problems in school (Cowen &
Hightower, 1990).

CONCLUSIONS AND FUTURE DIRECTIONS

Toward a Model of Cooperative Professional Development

The definitions, discussions, and examples of mental health consultation presented by Caplan (1970) consistently imply that the consultant is external to the system. However, this aspect of Caplan's work is inconsistent with the experience of most school psychologists, who are typically employees of the systems in which they consult and who serve as internal rather than external consultants. The literature on mental health consultation has not considered this distinction sufficiently, and yet this is likely to have an important impact because there are inherent differences in the expert and referent power of internal and external consultants (see Meyers et al., 1979, for a discussion of expert and referent power).

Psychologists and counselors working in schools represent one obvious group of internal consultants, and special educators make up another group of potential internal consultants. However, the role of teachers as consultants represents a significant departure from Caplan's early work on mental health consultation, because teachers are typically not trained as professionals with expertise in mental health. The notion of using teachers as consultants has emerged as a partial outgrowth of the increased attention to special education and mainstreaming during the past 25 years. Consultant teacher models have been discussed since the late-1960s and early 1970s, particularly through work at the University of Vermont (Knight, Meyers, Paolucci-Whitcomb, Hasazi, & Nevin, 1981). However, there has been a dramatic increase in attention to this role by special educators during the last decade (West & Idol, 1987).

Recently, consulting teacher models have been criticized for their narrow focus on solving problems, which may prevent consulting teachers from interacting with other teachers for broader preventive purposes such as the exchange of ideas, stress reduction, and the development of teacher knowledge (Glatthorn, 1990). This is consistent with recent criticisms of both mental health consultation (Parsons & Meyers, 1984) and client-centered consultation (Witt & Martens, 1988), which suggest that consultation is based on a deficit-oriented model that limits the role to problem solving rather than prevention. Witt and Martens (1988) suggested empowerment (Rappaport, 1981) as a more useful model for consultation than problem-solving approaches, and this is consistent with Glatthorn's (1990) emphasis on "cooperative professional development" among teachers as an alternative to consultation. In both instances, teachers or other educators, including mental health specialists, work together as colleagues to facilitate each other's professional development rather than being limited to the solution of problems.

These ideas imply a definition of the helping relationship that is very different from most definitions of mental health consultation (Caplan, 1970; Meyers et al., 1979), school-based consultation (Curtis & Meyers, 1988; Gutkin &

Curtis, 1990; Rosenfield, 1988), or behavioral consultation (Bergan, 1977). Moreover, a drastically different approach to establishing the helping relationship is implied by these concepts of "empowerment" and "cooperative professional development," because one professional is not set up as *the expert* who receives referrals or requests for help from the needy consultee. Although suggestions can be made for a range of approaches to establish such cooperative professional relationships (Glatthorn, 1990; Witt & Martens, 1988), recent research on mainstreaming special education students suggests one method that has an emerging empirical basis (Gelzheiser & Meyers, 1990; Gelzheiser, Meyers, & Pruzek, 1990; Meyers, Gelzheiser, & Yelich, 1991).

This research investigated a "pull-in" model for mainstreaming, in which the specialist teacher provides instruction in the regular class rather than pulling the special student out of the regular class to receive instruction in the specialist teacher's room (for a description of pull-in models, see Gelzheiser & Meyers, 1990). Because the two teachers work together to provide instruction in the same classroom, this approach requires increased collaborative planning among teachers focused on vital instructional issues (Meyers et al., 1991). The gains in achievement that were observed for pull-in students have been attributed, in part, to the changes in teacher collaboration noted above (Gelzheiser et al., 1990). These results suggest that when educators work together in the classroom, collaborative professional relationships among teachers can evolve with positive effects on instruction.

We do not mean to suggest that participating as a teacher in a pull-in model is the only way to establish cooperative professional relationships. However, these data do suggest that working together on a cooperative educational project provides a strong basis for developing effective professional collaboration. If this notion were taken seriously by school-based consultants, it would require them to spend more time in the classroom to learn to implement and model classroom-based strategies that can facilitate children's mental health.

This represents a dramatic change from the approaches to mental health consultation that are based primarily on two professionals talking together, where only one, the consultee, has professional responsibility for what takes place in the classroom (Caplan, 1970). By working together in the same classroom, both "professional helpers" have direct responsibility for outcome. This notion is alluded to in Caplan's recent discussion of "collaboration" as an alternative to consultation. He suggested collaboration as an appropriate alternative role when it is necessary for the consultant to help implement the intervention (see Caplan, 1989; Caplan, LeBow, Gavarin, & Stelzer, 1981). This represents a shift for Caplan, whose earlier writings about mental health consultation stated that the consultee must have full responsibility for outcome (Caplan, 1970).

Caplan's notion of "collaboration" and the approaches to "cooperative professional development" discussed in this chapter provide a built-in opportunity for each of the professional helpers to model effective procedures for instruction, behavior management, and prevention of learning and adjustment problems. This may be a unique benefit of these approaches, because modeling is a potentially effective technique that has received too little attention in the literature on school-based consultation. It is suggested that future research investigate the potential benefits of modeling techniques when implemented in the context of "consultation," "collaboration," and/or "cooperative professional development."

Despite these similarities between "cooperative professional development" and Caplan's approach to "collaboration," there are some important distinctions. Whereas Caplan's description of "collaboration" implies that the helping relationship is initiated by attempting to solve a problem associated with the client (Caplan, 1989; Caplan et al., 1981), cooperative professional development has broader preventive goals focused on developing the professional competence of the participating professionals. In addition, this approach to cooperative professional development extends Caplan's concept of a coordinate, nonhierarchical relationship between consultant and consultee by suggesting that each party in the relationship is equally likely to help the other.

The collaborative relationship between two co-equal professionals implied by the concept of cooperative professional development raises questions about the expertise of these professionals. It might be assumed that because two equal professionals work together, it is not necessary, or even possible, for one to have special expertise. This view seems shortsighted. Similar to Caplan's (1970) description of mental health consultation, each professional in cooperative professional development must contribute expertise pertinent to the issues being discussed. However, this new approach extends Caplan's notions of expertise by implying that both professionals need to be skilled in the *process* of helping as well.

A final difference is that cooperative professional development may be implemented without the direct involvement of a mental health professional, because those involved in cooperative professional development may all be teachers. This implies that mental health professionals may need to give up power to teachers to facilitate the learning and adjustment of all children in schools, an idea that is consistent with Rappaport's (1981) discussion of empowerment as an alternative framework for prevention.

A Research Agenda Extending Caplan's Contributions

This chapter has reviewed Caplan's work on mental health consultation and the prevention of psychopathology to document the dramatic impact he has had on the practice of psychology in the schools. Several suggestions were made for future directions of the field in an effort to extend Caplan's work, and these can be summarized by considering the research agenda implied by these suggestions.

This research agenda is based, in part, on prior criticisms of research in school-based consultation (Gresham & Kendell, 1987; Meyers et al., 1978). For example, process-outcome research needs to include the use of adequate experimental control. Also, small-N designs should be considered when large-N designs are impractical, given a limited knowledge base or various logistical factors. When possible, consultation research should focus on outcome in both students and teacher-consultees, and outcome criteria should include directly observable behavior, as well as various self-report measures.

The following questions, derived from the discussion in this paper, should be considered in relation to the above guidelines for consultation research. They are presented to serve as a stimulus in developing a research agenda. Each of the questions focused on the outcome of consultation is concerned with outcome for both students and consultees and with criteria that are based on observable behavior as well as various self-report measures.

1 What are the most effective ways to implement "cooperative professional development," and what are its effects?

2 What is the role of gender in consultation, and how does it influence practice? What are the implications of gender for training school-based consultants?

3 How does the role of internal versus external consultant influence the process and outcome of school-based consultation?

4 How can modeling be used as a consultation technique, and what are its effects on the outcome of school-based consultation?

5 What are the effects of various theories and specific techniques for establishing a coordinate, nonhierarchical consultation relationship?

6 What are the effects of a decision-making framework that favors the most indirect approaches to service delivery (i.e., consultee-centered and system-centered consultation)?

7 What are the preventive effects of school-based consultation? How do the effects on students generalize to other settings? How do the effects on teacher-consultees generalize to other students both in the present and the future? How can such generalization be facilitated?

8 What methods can be used to develop the knowledge, skill, and self-confidence of teacher-consultees, and how should these methods be implemented in school? How does consultee-centered consultation affect the development of knowledge, skill, and self-confidence, as well as professional objectivity?

9 What are the effects of direct and indirect confrontation techniques in school-based consultation?

10 What are practical ways for psychologists in schools to implement approaches to primary and secondary prevention? What are the effects of these preventive efforts?

Answers to these questions would do a great deal to extend Caplan's work and to facilitate the practice of psychology in the school, and this would require significantly increased attention to research in consultation. To increase the research base regarding school-based consultation, a substantial increase in research funding is necessary. Researchers and practitioners can help move toward this goal by communicating clearly and forcefully to funding agencies that this must be a priority. The long-term result should be growth in the learning and adjustment of school children.

REFERENCES

Albee, G. W. (1982). Preventing psychopathology and promoting human potential. *American Psychologist, 37,* 1043–1051.

Alpert, J. L. (1985). Change within a profession: Change, future, prevention, and school psychology, *American Psychologist, 40,* 1112–1121.

Alpert, J. L., & Associates. (1982). *Psychological consultation in educational settings.* San Francisco: Jossey-Bass.

Alpert, J. L., & Meyers, J. (Eds.). (1983). *Training in consultation.* Springfield, IL: Charles C. Thomas.

Alpert, J. L., & Silverstein, J. (1985). Mental health consultation: Historical, present, and future perspectives. In J. R. Bergan (Ed.), *School psychology in contemporary society: An introduction* (pp. 281–315). Columbus, OH: Charles E. Merrill.

Alpert, J. L., & Yammer, M. D. (1983). Research in school consultation: A content analysis of selected journals. *Professional Psychology, 14,* 604–612.

Bardon, J. I., & Bennett, V. D. (1974). *School psychology.* Englewood Cliffs, NJ: Prentice-Hall.

Bergan, J. R. (1977). *Behavioral consultation.* Columbus, OH: Charles E. Merrill.

Bergan, J. R. (Ed.). (1985). *School psychology in contemporary society: An introduction.* Columbus, OH: Charles E. Merrill.

Bower, E. (1961). In G. Caplan (Ed.), *Prevention of mental disorders in children* (pp. 353–377). New York: Basic Books.

Brown, D., Pryzwansky, W. B., & Schulte, A. C. (1987). *Psychological consultation: Introduction to theory and practice.* Boston: Allyn and Bacon.

Caplan. G. (Ed.). (1955). *Emotional problems of early childhood.* New York: Basic Books.

Caplan. G. (1961a). *An approach to community mental health.* New York: Grune & Stratton.

Caplan. G. (Ed.). (1961b). *Prevention of mental disorders in children.* New York: Basic Books.

Caplan. G. (1963). Types of mental health consultation. *American Journal of Orthopsychiatry, 33,* 470–481.

Caplan. G. (1964). *Principles of preventive psychiatry.* New York: Basic Books.

Caplan. G. (1970). *The theory and practice of mental health consultation.* New York: Basic Books.

Caplan. G. (Ed.). (1974). *Support systems and community mental health.* New York: Behavioral Publications.

Caplan. G. (1989). *Population oriented psychiatry.* New York: Human Sciences Press.

Caplan. G., LeBow, H., Gavarin, M., & Stelzer, J. (1981). Patterns of cooperation of child psychiatry with other departments in hospitals. *Journal of Primary Prevention, 2,* 40–49.

Cauce, A. M., & Srebnik, D. S. (1989). Peer networks and social support: A focus for preventive efforts with youth. In L. A. Bond & B. E. Compas (Eds.), *Primary prevention and promotion in the schools* (pp. 235–254). Beverly Hills, CA: Sage.

Cleven, C. A., & Gutkin, T, B. (1988). Cognitive modeling to consultation processes: A means for improving consultees' problem definition skills. *Journal of School Psychology, 26,* 379–389.

Conoley, J. C. (Ed.). (1981). *Consultation in schools: Theory, research, procedures.* New York: Academic Press.

Conoley, J. C., & Conoley, C. W. (1982). *School consultation: A guide to practice and training.* Elmsford, NY: Pergamon.

Conoley, J. C., & Welch, K. (1988). The empowerment of women in school psychology: Paradoxes of success and failure. *Professional School Psychology, 3,* 13–19.

Cowen, E. L. (1985). Person-centered approaches to primary prevention in mental health: Situation-focused and competence enhancement. *American Journal of Community Psychology, 13,* 31–48.

Cowen, E. L., & Hightower, A. D. (1990). The primary mental health project: Alternative approaches in school-based preventive intervention. In T. B. Gutkin & C. R. Reynolds (Eds.), *Handbook of school psychology* (pp. 775–795). New York: Wiley.

Curtis, M. J., & Metz, L. W. (1986). System level intervention in a school for handicapped children. *School Psychology Review, 15,* 510–518.

Curtis, M. J., & Meyers, J. (1988). Consultation: A foundation for alternative services in the schools. In J. L. Graden, J. E. Zins, & M. J. Curtis (Eds.), *Alternative educational delivery systems: Enhancing instructional options for all students* (pp. 35–48). Washington, DC: National Association of School Psychologists.

Curtis, M. J., & Watson, K. (1980). Changes in consultee problem clarification skills following consultation. *Journal of School Psychology, 18,* 210–221.

Curtis, M. J., & Zins, J. (Eds.). (1981). *The theory and practice of school consultation.* Springfield, IL: Charles C. Thomas.

Cutts, N. E. (Ed.). (1955). *School psychologists at mid-century.* Washington, DC: American Psychological Association.

Duncan, C. F., & Pryzwansky, W. B. (1988). Consultation research: Trends in doctoral dissertations, 1978–1985. *Journal of School Psychology, 26,* 107–119.

Elias, M. J., Gara, M., Ubriaco, M., Rothbaum, P. A., Clabby, J. F., & Schuyler, T. (1986). Impact of a preventive social problem solving intervention on children's coping with middle-school stressors. *American Journal of Community Psychology, 14,* 259–276.

Elliott, S. N., & Witt, J. C. (Eds.). (1986). *The delivery of psychological services in schools: Concepts, processes, and issues.* Hillsdale, NJ: Lawrence Erlbaum.

Felner, R. D., Farber, S. S., & Primavera, J. (1983). Transitions and stressful life events: A model for primary prevention. In R. D. Felner, L. A. Jason, J. N. Moritsugu, & S. S. Farber (Eds.), *Preventive psychology: Theory, research, and prevention* (pp. 191–215). New York: Pergamon.

Felner, R. D., Ginter, M. A., & Primavera, J. (1982). Primary prevention during school transitions: Social support and environmental structure. *American Journal of Community Psychology, 10,* 277–290.

Fisher, G. L., Jenkins, S. J., & Crumbly, J. D. (1986). A replication of a survey of school psychologists: Congruence between training, practice, preferred role, and competence. *Psychology in the Schools, 23,* 271–279.

Freidman, M. (March, 1978). *Mental health consultation with teachers: An analysis of process variables.* Paper presented at the annual meetings of the National Association of School Psychologists, New York.

Gelzheiser, L. M., & Meyers, J. (1990). Special and remedial education in the classroom: Theme and variations. *Journal of Reading, Writing and Learning Disabilities International, 6,* 419–436.

Gelzheiser, L. M., Meyers, J., & Pruzek, R. M. (April, 1990). *Effects of pull-in and pull-out approaches to reading instruction for special education and remedial reading students.* Paper presented at the annual meetings of the American Educational Research Association, Boston.

Glatthorn, A. A. (1990). Cooperative professional development: Facilitating the growth of the special education teacher and the classroom teacher. *Remedial and Special Education, 11,* 29–34.

Gottsegen, M. G., & Gottsegen, G. B. (Eds.). (1963). *Professional school psychology: Volume II.* New York: Grune & Stratton.

Graden, J. L., Casey, A., & Bonstrom, O. (1985). Implementing a prereferral intervention system: Part II. The data. *Exceptional Children, 51,* 487–496.

Graden, J. L., Casey, A., & Christenson, S. L. (1985). Implementing a prereferral intervention system: Part I. The model. *Exceptional Children, 51,* 377–384.

Graden, J. L., Zins, J. E., & Curtis, M. J. (Eds.). (1988). *Alternative educational delivery systems: Enhancing instructional options for all students.* Washington, DC: National Association of School Psychologists.

Gray, S. (1963). *The psychologist in the schools.* New York: Holt, Rinehart & Winston.

Gresham, F. M., & Kendell, G. K. (1987). School consultation research: Methodological critique and future research directions. *School Psychology Review, 16,* 306–316.

Gutkin, T. B. (1980). Teacher perceptions of consultation services provided by school psychologists. *Professional Psychology, 11,* 637–642.

Gutkin, T. B. (1981). Relative frequency of consultee lack of knowledge, skill, confidence, and objectivity in school settings. *Journal of School Psychology, 19,* 57–61.

Gutkin, T. B., & Curtis, M. J. (1990). School-based consultation: Theory, techniques, and research. In T. B. Gutkin & C. R. Reynolds (Eds.), *Handbook of school psychology* (pp. 577–611). New York: Wiley.

Gutkin, T. B., Henning-Stout, M., & Piersel, W. C. (1988). Impact of a district-wide behavioral consultation prereferral intervention service on patterns of school psychological service delivery. *Professional School Psychology, 3,* 301–308.

Gutkin, T. B., & Reynolds, C. R. (Eds.). (1990). *Handbook of school psychology.* New York: Wiley.

Gutkin, T. B., Singer, J. H., & Brown, R. (1980). Teacher reactions to school-based consultation services: A multivariate analysis. *Journal of School Psychology, 18,* 126–134.

Hollister, W. G. (1965). The concept of strens in preventive interventions and ego-strength building in the schools. In N. Lambert (Ed.), *The protection and promotion of mental health in schools: Mental health monograph no. 5* (pp. 30–35). Washington, DC: U.S. Government Printing Office.

Hughes, J. N. (1986). Ethical issues in school consultation. *School Psychology Review, 15*, 489–499.

Jackson, R. M., Cleveland, J. C., & Merenda, P. F. (1975). The longitudinal effects of early identification and counseling of underachievers. *Journal of School Psychology, 13*, 119–128.

Janis, I. L. (1958). *Psychological stress.* New York: Wiley.

Jason, L. A., & Ferone, L. (1978). Behavioral versus process consultation interventions in school settings. *American Journal of Community Psychology, 6*, 531–543.

Katz, A. H., & Hermalin, J. (1987). Self-help and prevention. In J. Hermalin & J. A. Morell (Eds.), *Prevention planning in mental health* (pp. 151–190). Beverly Hills, CA: Sage.

Kelly, J. G. (Ed.). (1979). *Adolescent boys in high school: A psychological study of coping and adaptation.* Hillsdale, NJ: Lawrence Erlbaum.

Knight, M. F., Meyers, H. W., Paolucci-Whitcomb, P., Hasazi, S. E., & Nevin, A. (1981). A four-year evaluation of consulting teacher service. *Behavioral Disorders, 6*, 92–100.

Kratochwill, T. (Ed.). (1981). *Advances in school psychology.* Hillsdale, NJ: Lawrence Erlbaum.

Lambert, N., Sandoval, J., & Corder, R. (1978). Teacher perceptions of school based consultants. *Professional Psychology, 6*, 204–216.

Lennox, N., Hyman, I. A., & Hughes, C. A. (1988). Institutionalization of a consultation-based service delivery system. In J. L. Graden, J. E. Zins, & M. J. Curtis (Eds.), *Alternative educational delivery systems: Enhancing instructional options for all students* (pp. 71–89). Washington, DC: National Association of School Psychologists.

Magary, J. (Ed). (1967). *School psychological services.* Englewood Cliffs, NJ: Prentice-Hall.

Mannino, F. V., & Shore, M. F. (1975). Effecting change through consultation. In F. V. Mannino, B. W. MacLennan, & M. F. Shore (Eds.), *The practice of mental health consultation* (pp. 25–46). New York: Gardner.

Mannino, F. V., & Shore, M. F. (1983). Trainee research in consultation: A study of doctoral dissertations. In J. L. Alpert and J. Meyers (Eds.), *Training in consultation: Perspectives from mental health, behavioral and organizational consultation* (pp. 123–141). Springfield, IL: Charles C. Thomas.

Martin, R. P., & Meyers, J. (1980). School psychologists and the practice of consultation. *Psychology in the Schools, 17*, 478–484.

Meacham, M. L., & Peckham, P. D. (1978). School psychologists at three-quarters century: Congruence between training, practice, preferred role and competence. *Journal of School Psychology, 16*, 195–206.

Medway, F. J. (1979). How effective is school consultation? A review of recent research. *Journal of School Psychology, 17*, 275–282.

Medway, F. J. (1982). School consultation research: Past trends and future directions. *Professional Psychology, 13*, 422–430.

Medway, F. J., & Updyke, J. F. (1985). Meta-analysis of consultation outcome studies. *American Journal of Community Psychology, 13*, 489–504.

Meyers, J. (1973). A consultation model for school psychological services. *Journal of School Psychology, 11*, 5–15.

Meyers, J. (1975). Consultee-centered consultation with a teacher as a technique in behavior management. *American Journal of Community Psychology, 3*, 111–121.

Meyers, J. (1981). Mental health consultation. In J. C. Conoley (Ed.), *Consultation in schools: Theory, research, procedures* (pp. 35–58). New York: Academic Press.

Meyers, J. (1989). The practice of psychology in the schools for the primary prevention of learning and adjustment problems in children: A perspective from the field of education. In L. A. Bond & B. E. Compas (Eds.), *Primary prevention and promotion in the schools* (pp. 391–422). Beverly Hills, CA: Sage.

Meyers, J., Freidman, M. P. & Gaughan, E. J., Jr. (1975). The effects of consultee-centered consultation on teacher behavior. *Psychology in the Schools, 12*, 288–295.

Meyers, J., Gelzheiser, L. M., & Yelich, G. (1991) Do pull-in programs foster teacher collaboration? *Journal of Remedial and Special Education, 12*, 7–15.

Meyers, J., & Kundert, D. (1988). Implementing process assessment. In J. L. Graden, J. E. Zins, & M. J. Curtis (Eds.), *Alternative educational delivery systems: Enhancing instructional options for all students* (pp. 173–197). Washington, DC: National Association of School Psychologists.

Meyers, J., Martin, R. P., & Hyman, I. A. (Eds.). (1977). *School Consultation*. Springfield, IL: Charles C. Thomas.

Meyers, J., & Parsons, R. D. (1987). Prevention planning in the school system. In J. Hermalin & J. Morell (Eds.), *Prevention planning in mental health* (pp. 111–150). Beverly Hills, CA: Sage.

Meyers, J., Parsons, R. D., & Martin, R. P. (1979). *Mental health consultation in the schools*. San Francisco: Jossey-Bass.

Meyers, J., Pitt, N., Gaughan, E. J., & Freidman, M. P. (1978). A research model for consultation with teachers. *Journal of School Psychology, 16*, 137–145.

Miles, M., Fullan, M., & Taylor, G. (1980). OD in schools: The state of the art. *Review of Educational Research, 50*, 121–183.

Moos, R. (1979). *Evaluating educational environments*. San Francisco: Jossey-Bass.

Oakland, T. (1984). The *Journal of School Psychology*'s first twenty years: Contributions from contributors. *Journal of School Psychology, 22*, 239–250.

Ojemann, R. H. (1961). Investigations on the effects of teaching on understanding and appreciation of behavioral dynamics. In G. Caplan (Ed.), *Prevention of mental disorders in children* (pp. 378–397). New York: Basic Books.

Osterweil, Z. O. (1987). A structured process of problem definition in school consultation. *School Counselor, 34*, 345–352.

Parsons, R. D., & Meyers, J. (1984). *Developing consultation skills*. San Francisco: Jossey-Bass.

Phillips, B. N. *School psychology at a turning point: Ensuring a bright future for the profession*. San Francisco: Jossey-Bass.

Phillips, B. N., Martin, R. P., & Meyers, J. (1972). Interventions in relation to anxiety in school. In C. D. Spielberger (Ed.), *Anxiety: Current trends in theory and research* (pp. 409–464). New York: Academic Press.

Phye, G. D., & Reschly, D. J. (Eds.). (1979). *School psychology: Perspectives and issues.* New York: Academic Press.

Ponti, C. R., Zins, J. E., & Graden, J. L. (1988). Implementing a consultation-based service delivery system to decrease referrals for special education: A case study of organizational considerations. *School Psychology Review, 17,* 89–100.

Pryzwansky, W. B. (1986). Indirect service delivery: Considerations for future research in consultation. *School Psychology Review, 15,* 479–488.

Rappaport, J. (1981). In praise of paradox: A social policy of empowerment over prevention. *American Journal of Community Psychology, 9,* 1–25.

Revels, O. H., & Gutkin, T. B. (1983). Effects of symbolic modeling procedures and model status on brainstorming behavior. *Journal of School Psychology, 21,* 311–318.

Reynolds, C. R., Gutkin, T. B., Elliott, S. N., & Witt, J. C. (1984). *School psychology: Essentials of theory and practice.* New York: Wiley.

Ritter, D. R. (1978). Effects of a school consultation program upon referral patterns of teachers. *Psychology in the Schools, 15,* 239–243.

Roppel, C. E., & Jacobs, M. K. (1988). Multimedia strategies for mental health promotion. In L. A. Bond & B. M. Wagner (Eds.), *Families in transition* (pp. 33–48). Beverly Hills, CA: Sage.

Rosenfield, S. (1988). *Instructional consultation.* New York: Pergamon.

Sarason, S. B., Carroll, C., Maton, K., Cohen, S., & Lorentz, E. (1977). *Human services and resource networks.* San Francisco: Jossey-Bass.

Sarason, S. B., Levine, M., Goldenberg, I. I., Cherlin, D. L., & Bennett, E. (1966). *Psychology in community settings.* New York: Wiley.

Schmuck, R. A. (1990). Organization development in schools: Contemporary concepts and practices. In T. B. Gutkin & C. R. Reynolds (Eds.), *Handbook of school psychology* (2nd ed.) (pp. 899–919). New York: Wiley.

Schmuck, R. A., & Runkel, P. J. (1988). *The handbook of organization development in schools* (3rd ed.). Prospect Heights, IL: Waveland Press.

Schowengerdt, R. V., Fine, M. J., & Poggio, J. P. (1976). An examination of some bases of teacher satisfaction with school psychological services. *Psychology in the Schools, 13,* 269–275.

Shure, M. B., & Spivack, G. (1982). Interpersonal problem-solving in young children: A cognitive approach to prevention. *American Journal of Community Psychology, 10,* 341–356.

Smith, D. K., & Lyon, M. A. (1985). Consultation in school psychology: Changes from 1981 to 1984. *Psychology in the Schools, 22,* 404–409.

Spivack, G., Platt, J. J., & Shure, M. B. (1976). *The problem solving approach to adjustment.* San Francisco: Jossey-Bass.

Stolberg, A. L. (1988). Prevention programs for divorcing families. In L. A. Bond & B. M. Wagner (Eds.), *Families in transition* (pp. 225–251). Beverly Hills, CA: Sage.

Valett, R. E. (1963). *The practice of school psychology: Professional problems.* New York: Wiley.

Weissberg, R. P., Caplan, M. Z., & Sivo, P. J. (1989). A new conceptual framework for establishing school-based social competence programs. In L. A. Bond & B. E. Compas (Eds.), *Primary prevention and promotion in the schools* (pp. 255–296). Beverly Hills, CA: Sage.

West, F., & Idol, L. (1987). School consultation: I. An interdisciplinary perspective on theory, models, and research. *Journal of Learning Disabilities, 20,* 388–408.

White, M. A., & Harris, M. W. (1961). *The school psychologist.* New York: Harper.

Witt, J. C., & Martens, B. K. (1988). Problems with problem-solving consultation: A re-analysis of assumptions, methods, and goals. *School Psychology Review, 17,* 211–226.

Zins, J. E. (1981). Using data-based evaluation in developing school consultation services. In M. J. Curtis & J. E. Zins (Eds.), *The theory and practice of school consultation* (pp. 261–268). Springfield, IL: Charles C. Thomas.

Chapter 7

A School Reform Process for At-Risk Students: Applying Caplan's Organizational Consultation Principles to Guide Prevention, Intervention, and Home-School Collaboration

Howard M. Knoff and George M. Batsche
University of South Florida

Today's families, schools, and communities are confronting a domestic war that threatens to impact the educational and social success of every child in our nation. This war has no single, defined enemy, yet it has many overt and covert symptoms. Although it might be easy to identify the enemy as poverty, racism, illiteracy, or the demise of the nuclear family, the symptoms would not be explained sufficiently. Consider the following startling facts:

1 Every eight seconds of the school day, an American child drops out.
2 Every 26 seconds of each day, an American child runs away from home.
3 Every 47 seconds, an American child is abused or neglected.
4 Every 67 seconds, an American teenager has a baby.
5 Every seven minutes, an American child is arrested for a drug offense.

6 Every 36 minutes, an American child is killed or injured by guns.

7 Every 53 minutes, an American child dies because of poverty.

8 Every day, over 100,000 American children are homeless. (Children's Defense Fund, 1990, p. 3)

According to the Children's Defense Fund (1990), "[t]he mounting crisis of our children and families is a rebuke to everything America professes to be. It also will bring America to its economic knees and increase violence and discord within this country unless we confront it" (p. 3). Clearly, we need to respond to and address these broad-based problems. To do so, we need a comprehensive organizational perspective, methodology, and interactive system.

From an organizational perspective, the decade of the 1990s may turn out to be one of the most important relative to addressing children's educational and social needs (Knoff & Batsche, 1990; Knoff & Batsche, 1991a). Yet, the work of the 1990s has been driven by the evaluations and needs assessments of the 1980s. Indeed, in the 1980s, an astounding number of diverse national evaluations were published addressing many facets of the comprehensive problems described above:

1 The 1982 National Academy of Sciences report (Heller, Holtzman, & Messick, 1982) addressing the fundamental problems that exist in the provision of services to handicapped and at-risk students;

2 The 1983 *Nation at Risk* report of the National Commission on Excellence in Education;

3 The 1988 William T. Grant Foundation's Commission on Work, Family, and Citizenship's report, *The Forgotten Half: Pathways to Success for America's Youth and Young families,* focusing on those 16–24 year olds who do not attend college and do not achieve their economic, social, and vocational potentials;

4 The 1989 National Council on Disability's report on *The Education of Students with Disabilities: Where Do We Stand?;*

5 The 1989 National Governor's Association report summarizing their educational summit and specifying the nation's educational goals for the coming 10 years;

6 The 1989 Institute of Medicine report, *Research on Children & Adolescents with Mental, Behavioral, & Developmental Disorders,* describing the significant mental health problems besetting today's children and adolescents and summarizing known interventions that, if applied, could begin to remediate these problems;

7 The 1990 Bank Street College report, *At the Schoolhouse Door: An Examination of Programs and Policies for Children with Behavioral and Emotional Problems;* and

8 The 1990 National Advisory Mental Health Council's report to the U.S. Congress on a *National Plan for Research on Child and Adolescent Mental Disorders.*

As a result of these reports, the commitment to social and educational reform has been sounded at national, state, and local levels. In addition, numerous facts have been clearly reinforced:

1 Between 20–50% of all students are at risk for educational, psychological, and/or social failure during their school-aged years (birth–age 21).

2 Services often are not available to meet the needs of disadvantaged, minority, rural, and other families whose children are at risk.

3 Comprehensive preventive services are the most effective to address the long-term impacts of poverty, disability, and inequity.

4 Children spend the second greatest amount of time (next to the home) in the schools.

5 Schools must become interdependent partners with family and community systems to address children's significant social and academic needs.

6 Evaluation procedures, intervention development, and intervention implementation vary greatly among schools, and often students' educational problems are never fully identified or addressed.

7 Parents and students report that schools some have low expectations for at-risk students and establish inappropriate learning objectives and goals.

8 America's educational system must be reformed so that it becomes an institution that can prepare all students for productive vocational, social, and familial lives.

9 Most school reform initiatives appear to be a response to declining academic achievement rather than efforts to find ways for schools to meet the diverse needs of all students.

10 School reform efforts have not specifically addressed the diverse needs of at-risk and minority students.

A CAPLANIAN PERSPECTIVE OF THE PROBLEMS AT HAND

Four predominant facets of Caplan's work can be used to help us respond to the educational and social problems currently entering the schoolhouse door, and to devise a process of systems change in the context of comprehensive school and educational reform: (a) his conceptual model of prevention; (b) his call for integrated community support systems; (c) his organization of consultation into four types; and (d) his focus on the interpersonal aspects of consultation within a process of change.

Caplan's Model of Prevention

Caplan's conceptual model of primary, secondary, and tertiary prevention (Caplan, 1964) has significant applicability to the current status of the American community, family, and school. From a primary prevention perspective, we know that early intervention services have the greatest and most long-standing impact of any other form of service delivery. Primary prevention programs and research clearly have shown significant impact in: (a) improving the educational readiness of at-risk students; (b) developing the interpersonal and social problem-solving competence of children with social skills deficits; (c) training parents to respond to their children's physical, emotional, and developmental needs; (d) decreasing child abuse and specific mental disorders; and (e) responding to individual, familial, and community-wide crises (Buckner, Trickett, & Corse, 1985). Yet, national, state, and community policymakers have largely ignored these projects and outcomes. Policymakers have ignored the facts that:

1 The Special Supplemental Food Program for Women, Infants, and Children (WIC) served 59% of those eligible in 1989, and that $1 invested in this program saves as much as $3 in later short-term hospital costs.

2 Less than half of America's poor pregnant women and children were covered by Medicaid and its Early and Periodic Screening, Diagnosis, and Treatment (EPSDT) services in 1987, and that $1 spent on comprehensive prenatal care saves $3.38.

3 Up to 20% of our children are not receiving comprehensive medical immunizations due to the lack of a social and medical services "safety net," and that $1 spent on childhood immunizations saves $10 in later medical costs.

4 Head Start serves fewer than one in six eligible youngsters, and that $1 invested in quality preschool education returns $4.75 in lowered special education, public assistance, and crime prevention programs.

5 Chapter 1 served about one half of the children who needed remedial education in 1987, and that an investment of $600 for one child in compensatory education can save $4,000 in the costs of a single repeated grade (Children's Defense Fund, 1990).

From a secondary prevention perspective, we now understand that we can positively identify and impact the conditions that relate most to children who drop out, run away, abuse drugs and alcohol, who are adversely affected by poverty and stress, who become abused and neglected, and/or who become teenaged parents. In fact, there now are numerous, sophisticated methodologies whereby we can: (a) evaluate identified groups of children and youth with significant emotional, behavioral, or affective problems; (b) isolate the precursor conditions and variables that most predict or relate to their difficulties; (c) determine how these conditions and variables operate for children and youth before they develop these problems; and (d) implement and evaluate preventive programs such that these problems are eliminated in the next generation of students. For example, we know that children's lack of prosocial and peer relationship skills have been linked to social isolation and rejection, psychiatric disorders, delinquency, dropping out of school, developmental delays, and subsequent adult mental health difficulties. We know that systematic social skills and anger control training, even during the preschool years, can eliminate many of these threats and potentials (Knoff, 1988).

From a tertiary prevention perspective, we know that we must and can respond to the immediate outcomes of a family or child's educational or social problem. Yet, even in this context, we are always trying to prevent the problem itself from recurring and from potentially becoming a problem passed down to the next generation (e.g., as in child abuse). Caplan applies a very systemic orientation to both his analysis of specific problems and their remediation, from a tertiary prevention perspective. This is very apparent in his focus on the integration of community support systems.

Caplan and the Integration of Community Support Systems

Caplan (1974) has provided a very specific focus on the need to coordinate community-based support systems as a way to deliver preventive mental health services. Stroul and Friedman (1986) applied this focus when discussing, in the context of services for emotionally disturbed children, the need to develop multiagency "systems of care" that provide 24-hour "wrap-around" services to students and families in need. These systems involve the educational, health, mental health, welfare, respite, and other social services that allow children to be maintained, as much as possible, in the mainstream and that address their primary and emerging problems. Although this approach is clearly important with emotionally disturbed children, it is becoming increasingly critical given the complexity and severity of the "typical" problems that today's children are now presenting. In fact, if one were to substitute "at risk" for "emotionally disturbed" in Stroul and Friedman's (1986) "core values" and "guiding principles" for the system of care, the result would operationalize Caplan's model for integrated community-based prevention services:

1 The system of care should be child centered, with the needs of the child and family dictating the types and mix of services provided.

2 The system of care should be community based, with the locus of services as well as management and decision-making responsibility resting at the community level.

3 At-risk children should have access to a comprehensive array of services that address the children's physical, emotional, social, and educational needs.

4 At-risk children should receive services that are integrated, with linkages between child-care agencies and programs and mechanisms for planning, developing, and coordinating services.

5 At-risk children should be provided with case management or similar mechanisms to ensure that multiple services are delivered in a coordinated and therapeutic manner, and that they can move through the system of services in accordance with their changing needs.

Critically, the interdependent nature of school and community mental health services must be recognized as a significant part of the system of care (Knoff & Batsche, 1990). Indeed, Knitzer, Steinberg, and Fleisch (1990), after examining our nation's programs and policies for children with behavioral and emotional problems, made the following recommendations:

1 (We need to) Conduct reviews, both within school districts and on a statewide basis, of the scope and quality of the current mix of educational and mental health services available for children with identified behavioral and emotional disorders.

2 (We need to) Strengthen the policy commitment to enhance collaboration between schools and mental heath agencies.

3 (We need to) Encourage the formation of parent support and advocacy groups and expand opportunities for parents to collaborate in school-related efforts to help their children.

4 (We need to) Examine current fiscal strategies at all levels of government to ensure that all available dollars for services are being used in the most cost-effective ways, and to develop strategies to increase resources as appropriate.

In essence, Knitzer et al. (1990) said that the schools cannot be solely responsible for today's students. Families, schools, and communities must share the responsibility for every student at the schoolhouse door. At a policy level, barriers that discourage or disallow the coordination and collaboration of services across school and community lines, to the detriment of our children, must be removed. At a practice level, the interdependence and integration of school and community services can only maximize the resources available, so that the challenges of educating and preparing the next generation of children for school and society can be met successfully.

Caplan (1970) said, "A mental health consultant . . . operates in the field as part of a carefully conceived institutional plan to deal with a community problem" (p. 35). Today, every institutional plan must involve home, school, and community resources. Indeed, all mental health consultants must engage in a strategic, systemic process that utilizes a consultation-based problem-solving process such that any plan of action is carefully conceived, accepted, socially validated, implemented with integrity, and evaluated relative to both process and outcome.

Caplan's Organization of Consultation Processes

Caplan's third major contribution, helping us respond to the child at the school-house door, involves his four types of consultation. Given today's at-risk student, *client-centered case consultation* helps the consultee (e.g., teacher) to improve his or her knowledge and skill such that the client (i.e., the student) can make significant progress in a problematic educational-academic, social-emotional, cognitive-metacognitive, and/or adaptive behavior domain. *Consultee-centered case consultation* helps the teacher or parent develop or maintain the attitudes, beliefs, expectations, and/or attributions that help him or her work objectively and effectively with the at-risk student. This type of consultation can eliminate racial or other prejudice when it exists and/or facilitate a teacher or parent's positive expectations for student progress and success. *Program-centered administrative consultation* helps identify long-standing student problems that are a function of system deficiencies or that need to be addressed through new or improved programs. This consultation approach results in the coordination of community-based support systems, as described above, and helps these systems to identify and remediate system flaws that cause or relate to ineffective child and adolescent services. Finally, *consultee-centered administrative consultation* is analogous to consultee-centered case consultation, but addresses those administrator blindspots that interfere with the development of needed or innovative programs for at-risk students.

Although Caplan does not synthesize these consultation types into a hierarchy or sequence, it is clear that administrative consultation has the greatest potential to deal with the strategic planning of services for at-risk students, whereas the case-centered consultation approaches can respond to either teacher or student needs as they relate to direct, student-focused service delivery. Without a sound program or approach to the comprehensive delivery of services, however, case-centered consultations may never be fully successful. This is because the case-centered consultations may be focused more on symptoms of behavior and not the actual, systemic conditions that can truly change behavior. Nonetheless, the use of consultee-centered case consultation is important as an on-going process, so that teachers and parents can "debrief" and "reenergize" themselves in the face of service delivery that is often frustrating given its focus and realization of small steps rather than large strides.

Caplan's Focus on Consultation Skill and the Process of Change

Caplan's discussions of consultation skills in the context of change have focused heavily on relationship building. From an institutional perspective, Caplan (1970) talked about the need to: (a) understand the social makeup, relate to the leaders, and communicate with the entirety of any consultee organization; (b) build channels of communication that foster trust and respect throughout the organization; (c) identify and eliminate conflicts of interest and distortions of perception and expectation; (d) develop the ground rules and stages of prospective change; and (e) negotiate and follow a contract that encourages change while discouraging organizational dependency on the consultant. From an individual consultee perspective, Caplan has emphasized the need to: (a) devote enough time to develop a relationship with the consultee; (b) foster the consultee's self-respect while decreasing his or her anxiety; and (c) negotiate and follow a contract that is based on confidentiality, collegial collaboration, and the avoidance of psychotherapy.

In further specifying consultant skills that facilitate change, Knoff, McKenna, and Riser (1991) completed a factor analysis from a national sample of school psychologists who rated effective consultant skills drawn from the existing literature. Their results suggested four factors of effective consultant skills: interpersonal skills, problem-solving skills, process skills, and ethical and professional practice skills. The interpersonal skills factor focuses on relationship-building skills that an effective consultant demonstrates throughout a consultation contact. The problem-solving skills factor focuses on consultation skills needed to identify and analyze referred problems, develop interventions, and evaluate the entire process. The process skills factor focuses on specific consultation process skills that facilitate success. Finally, the ethical and professional practice skills factor focuses on skills that facilitate professional and collegial trust.

Each of these factors clearly relates to Caplan's (1970) focus on the need, described above, to build solid consultation relationships when working with institutions and individual consultees. Indeed, the top six rated items from the Knoff et al. (1991) study were: ethical, confidential, skillful, respectful, knowledgeable, and approachable. Caplan (1970) has noted that the ideal consultation relationship is one of coordinate interdependence, and that "[w]hatever the type of consultation, the effect of the consultant's intervention is mediated by the relationship between the consultee and him [or her]self" (p. 80). Future research needs to explore both the coordinate interdependence and the interdependence between the consultant/consultee relationship and specific consultant skills. Caplan has provided us with a significant charge in this respect. We must continue to clarify and extend this charge so we can effectively address the needs of all consultees and clients.

PROJECT ACHIEVE: APPLYING CAPLAN'S ORGANIZATIONAL CONSULTATION PRINCIPLES TO A SCHOOL REFORM PROCESS FOR AT-RISK STUDENTS

The four facets of Caplan's work just described are especially important when developing interventions for at-risk students. Such interventions need to be preventively focused; they need to integrate home, school, and community support systems; they must focus both on programmatic or administrative change, as well as child, teacher, school, and family change; and they can only be accomplished through an interpersonal focus on how to build long-lasting relationships within a process of change. Next, a school reform project that addresses the particular needs of at-risk students is described. Afterward, the project is analyzed within the context of Caplan's organizational consultation principles.

Project ACHIEVE is a joint project between the School Psychology Program at the University of South Florida and the Polk County (Florida) School District. The project is currently based at Jesse Keen Elementary School in Lakeland (Polk County), Florida.

The Polk County (Florida) School District serves approximately 65,000 students (72% White, 22% Black, 6% other) in 110 school buildings, with a total instructional staff of over 3,200 professionals. Polk County is located in the center of Florida's peninsula between the counties that include Tampa and Orlando. It covers 1,820 square miles, and includes a population of 389,336 people. Workers earn a median annual income of $21,163 primarily in agricultural, mining, and service-oriented businesses. Forty percent of the students in Polk County schools receive full or partial free lunch, 4.4% receive Chapter 1 services, 14% are in special education, and 5% are retained each year. The school system's financial base greatly depends on property taxes—its 1990–1991 per pupil expenditure was $4,126.

Jesse Keen Elementary School serves 658 students (57% White, 39% Black, 4% other) in pre-kindergarten through fourth grade in one of the poorest sections of Lakeland, Florida, a city of 76,000 people. With 72% and 11% of the students receiving a federally funded free or partial breakfast/lunch, respectively, Jesse Keen has 32 pre-kindergarten through fourth grade teachers; 9 special education teachers for the learning disability, educably mentally retarded, and severely emotionally disturbed classroom programs; and 9 instructional or pupil personnel specialists (e.g., guidance, reading/math specialists, speech pathologist, school psychologist). Jesse Keen has over $136,000 in computer equipment. Every classroom has at least three computers that are networked to a computer center, which houses an interactive, individualized computerized math, reading, and written expression curriculum. The computer curriculum supplements the teachers' classroom instruction by providing practice toward mastery and remediation of specific skills as necessary. Finally, the school has a paid paraprofessional program and an active volunteer program involving senior citizens and parents from the community. However, even with the resources outlined above, only 30% of the students at Jesse Keen are achieving at or above grade level in reading and math achievement.

Project ACHIEVE is completing its second formal year of full-time operations. Supported by a 3-year federal preservice training grant from the U.S. Department of Education (Office of Special Education Programs), Project ACHIEVE is a dynamic blend of training, service, and research. The training comes as the project directors (the authors) teach and supervise second- through fourth-year psychology graduate students in providing preventive behavioral and curricular services to the school's at-risk students two days each week. The service comes as the entire school's service delivery process has been assessed and reformed such that seven critical components now drive the integrated educational and social program. Finally, the research comes as every training and service delivery component of Project ACHIEVE is evaluated, formatively and from a summative perspective, for efficacy and accountability. Project ACHIEVE is now being extended into at least five additional Polk County schools. As such, the district is committed to continuing this project over the next 5–7 years, ultimately expanding it throughout the district from kindergarten through twelfth grade.

The Need and Specific Goals for Project ACHIEVE

Given the community, home, and other demographic characteristics of the students at Jesse Keen Elementary, many of the students are significantly at risk for educational and social difficulties and/or failure. This is already exemplified in the designation of Jesse Keen as a Chapter 1 school, a status only given to schools that have more than 75% of their students in the federal free-lunch program and whose student bodies collectively average below the 40th percentile on their annual group achievement tests, and because more than 15% of Jesse Keen's students were referred for potential special education services during the 1989–1990 academic year. In addition, approximately 25% of Jesse Keen's kindergarten and first grade students were retained during both the 1988–1989 and 1989–1990 school years, with retention being a significant predictor for students' later academic problems and dropping out. Finally, approximately 10% of the students were suspended during 1989–1990, and over 700 behavioral referrals were forwarded to the office for administrative action.

All of these factors significantly impacted the way teachers in Jesse Keen Elementary structured their instructional programs to facilitate students' academic and social progress. Given the lack of student progress, the need for a new approach that used a systematic organizational assessment and planned change process to increase the effectiveness of the academic, social, behavioral, and parent involvement strategies became paramount. To this end, Project ACHIEVE was designed as a multifaceted prevention program to achieve the following goals:

1 To enhance the problem-solving skills of teachers so effective interventions for academic and social difficulties of at-risk students were developed and implemented;

2 To improve the teachers' classroom management skills and at-risk students' classroom behavior to increase the amount of academic-engaged time through the use of a building-based social skills training program, thus increasing their access to educational opportunities;

3 To improve the school's comprehensive services to students with below-average academic performance so they are served, as much as possible, in the regular classroom setting and have equal access to high-quality educational programs;

4 To increase the academic and social progress of students through enhanced involvement of parents in the education of their children, specifically through direct involvement with the schoolwork of their children and the development of improved parenting skills; and

5 To validate the various components of Project ACHIEVE, and to develop a demonstration training site for district personnel in the expansion of this model districtwide.

Implementation: Project ACHIEVE's Service Delivery Components

The overall intent of Project ACHIEVE is to guide a school reform process that will improve teaching and learning at the school level, specifically with at-risk students, their families, and the teachers who work with them. This is accomplished through the use of seven interdependent components, each of which is based on a sound theoretical foundation with established empirical and applied validity. It is the dynamic combination of these seven components that contributes to the uniqueness of this project. We describe each one below.

Strategic Planning and Organizational Analysis and Development This component assesses the organizational climate, administrative style, and staff decision-making and interactive processes at Jesse Keen Elementary School, and has moved into the development of optimal organizational support patterns that facilitate the academic and social progress of our targeted at-risk and underachieving students. Organizational assessment and strategic planning are significant foundations to any school reform/planned change process. Although many schools talk about school reform and site-based management, they often do not utilize an empirically tested process guided by individuals trained in organizational development. Project ACHIEVE applies the principles of sound business and educational management and planning to systemic change. At Jesse Keen, this is accomplished through (a) community, environmental, and organizational needs assessment procedures and techniques; (b) evaluations of the current efficacy of existing student assessment and intervention programs; and (c) the initiation of strategic planning processes through 1-, 3-, and 5-year action plans (Steiner, 1979). These action plans encourage the communication and decision-making processes that facilitate positive school climates and that support the objectives and activities of the remaining components of Project ACHIEVE.

Significantly, recent studies have suggested it may take longer than was first thought to fully and functionally implement site-based management and true educational reform in individual schools. From an organizational psychology perspective, this is not surprising. Every school needs to coordinate its past administrative and service delivery history with the existing skills of its staff, its resources, its unique family and community characteristics, and the potential rewards and outcomes to competently begin to "take care of its own business." Thus, Project ACHIEVE assists its target school to assess its own strengths, weaknesses, threats, and opportunities, and to build an educational reform process that is strategically tailored to its individual goals and capabilities.

Problem-Solving/Referral Question Consultation (RQC)   This component is grounded in the belief that school systems and buildings must utilize a common language and method of problem solving throughout the system to address referred or arising problems. In addition, this problem-solving process must incorporate the many disciplines that exist in the schools, their various theoretical orientations, and their numerous explanations for specific child problems or other occurrences. To accomplish this, Project ACHIEVE uses the Referral Question Consultation (RQC) process. The RQC process is an innovative, systematic, problem-solving process that provides the foundation to every consultation interaction whether child-focused, teacher- or parent-focused, or program- or system-focused (Knoff & Batsche, 1991a). Developed by Batsche (1984) and expanded by Knoff and Batsche (1991b), the process emphasizes the clarification of referred problems using behavioral description and operationalizations: (a) The use of existing data to develop an understanding of the referred problem and referral situation; (b) the development of hypotheses to explain the referral problem; (c) the multisource, multimethod, multisetting assessment of those hypotheses; (d) the development of interventions to address the now-validated explanations for the referred problems; and (e) the evaluation of those interventions to ensure their success and socially valid change.

The RQC process is taught to an entire building's administration, staff, and support staff so they can use a common problem-solving approach to address all academic, social, and organizational concerns. With this "common language," the RQC process supports the organizational assessment and strategic planning component of Project ACHIEVE, and facilitates functional changes that translate into real student progress. Significantly, the RQC process was the consultation procedure used throughout the 1985–1988 State of Iowa's RE-AIM (Relevant Educational Assessment and Intervention Model) Project, which trained the state's educators in the process of developing, implementing, and evaluating school-based interventions. In addition, over 200 school districts across the country also have been trained to use the RQC process. All told, the RQC process has increased staff communication and the development of more functional academic and behavioral interventions for students, while decreasing unnecessary referrals to special education and wasted time due to ineffective and inefficient problem solving.

Effective Classroom Teacher/Staff Development This component ensures that effective teaching behaviors, combined with effective instructional teacher styles, are used with students in combination with appropriate curricular materials. In addition to using the Referral Question Consultation (RQC) process for effective problem solving, this component reinforces educators' use of the effective teaching techniques that maximize students' educational and social progress (i.e., their time on task, academic engagement, academic learning time). This is done using a clinical supervision model. Professional development teams are developed in each school to provide feedback and skill-building opportunities for all teachers and staff. The Instructional Environment Scale (TIES; Ysseldyke & Christenson, 1987) is used as a conceptual assessment and evaluation model, given its derivation from the effective instruction research. In all, the TIES identifies 12 effective instruction clusters of behaviors: instructional presentation, classroom environment, teacher expectations, cognitive emphasis, motivational strategies, relevant practice, academic engaged time, informed feedback, adaptive instruction, progress evaluation, instructional planning, and student understanding. Where knowledge or skills are found lacking, the school plans and implements a staff development program that leads to functional and demonstrated outcomes.

Instructional Consultation and Curriculum-Based Assessment This component assesses student's learning problems by evaluating: (a) their progress in the curriculum, their ability to succeed in the curriculum, and the match between the students and the processes used by the curriculum to facilitate learning; (b) the quality of instruction and the presence/absence of effective school and schooling characteristics as they relate to student learning and achievement; and (c) the curriculum, its development, task demands, encouragement of sound instruction, and impact of successful learning (Rosenfield, 1987). In this context, project teachers learn how to observe systematically for instructional contingencies, assess curricular placement and performance expectations, and complete curricular task analyses such that assessment is functionally linked to intervention in the classroom.

A critical part of this component is the development and implementation of a curriculum-based measurement (CBM) system that creates local norms of achievement in the areas of reading and mathematics (Shinn, 1989). CBM is an assessment system developed from the actual textbooks used by students in the classroom setting. After systematically sampling the reading and mathematics curriculum at each grade level of the targeted schools, CBM norms are developed for Project ACHIEVE for every grade at Jesse Keen Elementary School. These norms are based on 1-minute reading samples of textbook stories and single-word vocabulary lists, 2-minute samples of 12–17 spelling words, and 2-

minute samples of addition, subtraction, multiplication, and division problems. With these norms, students are assessed with 1- and 2-minute reading, spelling, and math probes, and are compared with same-aged peers to track both individual and intervention progress. This measurement system facilitates the identification of at-risk and underachieving students and the isolation of their specific academic problems. In this way, the academic determinants of their difficulties are more functionally identified, as compared with traditional norm-referenced assessment. As a result, more successful instructional programs are developed and implemented.

Behavioral Consultation and Behavioral Interventions This component implements (utilizing the RQC problem-solving process) effective behavioral interventions to address students' curricular and behavioral problems or teachers' instructional and classroom management procedures. Therefore, these interventions focus on specific referred problems exhibited by students in the school or classroom (e.g., not completing homework, not answering teacher questions, swearing, threatening others), or specific behaviors exhibited by teachers as part of the instructional process (e.g., not providing advanced organizers or appropriate instructional feedback, reinforcing inappropriate behavior through attention, using discipline inconsistently). After learning to discriminate whether a referred problem involves a skill deficit, a performance deficit, or a self-management deficit, teachers are taught to strategically choose among the following behavioral approaches within the context of the student's behavioral ecology: stimulus control approaches, behavioral addition approaches, behavioral reduction approaches, behavioral maintenance approaches, and behavioral generalization approaches. At the same time, support staff are taught methods in behavioral observation, data collection, consultation intervention, and intervention evaluation.

One part of the behavioral consultation/intervention component involves social skills training. This training provides both students and staff with an immensely important set of skills that facilitate positive student behavior and motivation, and thus increase time on task and academic engagement. Critically, the absence of social skills often results in interpersonal difficulties that inhibit students' successful academic progress and often contribute to their dropping out of school or their expulsion or suspension from school. Students are faced daily with conflict, confusion, difficult choices, and a wide variety of other problematic situations. Social skills provide them with procedures to confront and resolve these challenges and problem situations. Inadequate problem-solving skills in the interpersonal and personal areas of functioning result in students' reliance on socially unacceptable solutions to real-life difficulties. Goldstein (1988) and his colleagues have demonstrated that skilled interpersonal behaviors can be taught as viable substitutes for aggression, withdrawal, and other deficit behaviors. Already, all of the teachers and support staff at

Jesse Keen Elementary have learned how to teach and use the social skills training in their classrooms. Although this effort needs to continue, we do have a sound foundation to build on in the years to come.

Parent Training, Tutoring, and Support   This component attempts to increase the involvement of all of Jesse Keen's parents, but especially those of at-risk and underachieving students. Parental involvement in the school and educational process is often absent in the homes of at-risk and underachieving students—a variable that directly discriminates achieving from underachieving students. This component involves: (a) direct training of target students' parents in tutoring strategies, in their children's actual academic curricula, and in positive behavior management approaches; (b) direct supervision of the parents-in-training through a "Parents in the Classroom" program, in which the parents work with students (not their own children) with academic difficulties like their own children's; (c) direct supervision of the parents-in-training through a "Parents and Their Children" program, in which the parents work with their own children in the educational setting; (d) direct consultation with the parents-in-training following initiation of the program in the home setting; and (e) the creation of parent drop-in centers in the targeted schools to encourage parents' participation in the school culture and parent access to learning materials. In all, this component works to provide at-risk and underachieving students with the opportunity to increase their academic-engaged time at home and in school, to give parents the opportunity to expand their understanding and support of their children's academic assignments and teachers' expectations, and to provide teachers the opportunity to guide parent-training programs and to build effective home-school partnerships. It is clear that the role of the parent in the education of children is of paramount importance.

Research and Accountability   This final component focuses on the active researching of critical consultation and/or curricular/behavioral intervention variables and techniques. Part of this research involves collecting specific data that validate various aspects of Project ACHIEVE: the RQC process, the in-service training components, the training and implementation of curriculum/ behavioral interventions, and the effectiveness of the practicum for referred students and their teachers and/or systems. Another part of this research involves relevant aspects of an on-going research commitment, which is investigating consultation effectiveness and identifying the organizational, classroom, and interpersonal characteristics that predict and influence consultation effectiveness.

Implementation: Examples of Activities
Within Project ACHIEVE's
Service Delivery Components

As with any prevention program, each Project ACHIEVE component has specific activities that are tied to the broader strategic objectives and the explicit desired outcomes. Below are samples of these activities drawn from strategic planning, RQC, social skills, and parent involvement components of the Project.

The strategic planning component's primary objective is to complete an organizational analysis and strategic planning process that will yield comprehensive 1-, 3-, and 5-year action plans. These plans aim to facilitate a schoolwide reform/restructuring of Jesse Keen Elementary School, resulting in the active involvement of parents and other community resources, increased efficacy of staff instruction, and overall improvement of student academic and social performance. The activities designed and implemented to achieve this objective are listed below.

1 Initially, a Strategic Planning Team (SPT), comprised of a cross section of every administrative, teaching, service, and paraprofessional group in the school, was formed to conceptualize, plan, and implement (a) an environmental analysis of community and conditions surrounding Jesse Keen Elementary School, and (b) an assessment of the administrative and instructional climate of the school. This latter organizational assessment included force-field analyses of building strengths, weaknesses, resources, threats, opportunities, and limitations, including existing programs specifically designed for at-risk students; an assessment of existing decision-making models and staffing patterns used to identify and address these and other students' needs; and an evaluation of the efficacy of the existing student assessment and intervention programs. The SPT supervised the initial facets of the organizational assessment, strategic planning, and school reform/restructuring process, and then submitted its recommendations to the entire staff for their approval.

2 The SPT and the Jesse Keen staff then evaluated the organizational and needs assessment data to identify problems, explanations, and organizational and other interventions that would facilitate the academic and social progress of students, the instructional excellence of staff, and the active involvement of parents and other community resources.

3 The identified organizational interventions then were integrated into 1-, 3-, and 5-year, interdependent administrative, staff, student, parent, and community-based action plans, which identified in-service needs, resource needs, and system changes needed for success. These action plans had built-in evaluative mechanisms that depended on specific objective and periodically collected data.

The RQC component's primary objective is to increase the academic and social performance of at-risk students through improving teacher problem-solving skills and range of academic and social interventions using the RQC problem-solving model. The activities designed and implemented to achieve this objective are listed below.

1 The teaching staff were trained in the RQC problem-solving process. This training occurred separately for each grade-specific teaching team on a weekly basis.

2   The teaching staff were trained in academic and social interventions. This training occurred as needed interventions were determined through the RQC process. This training was conducted, as appropriate, by building-based resource teachers, the school counselor, the school psychologist, and Project staff, and included cooperative learning, heterogeneous grouping, whole-language curricula in reading, group management procedures, academic motivation strategies, and other academic social interventions validated for use with at-risk students.

3   Students who were at risk for academic and social failure were identified.

4   The RQC process was supervised by the Project directors and advanced doctoral students from the University of South Florida under the direction of the Project staff.

The social skills component's primary objective is to improve the behavior management skills of teachers through training in and implementation of a building-based social skills training program, which will significantly reduce removal of at-risk students from mainstream education and significantly increase the academic-engaged time of such students. The activities designed and implemented to achieve this objective are listed below.

1   Classroom teachers and support staff were trained in the use of social skills designed to improve student-teacher relationships, student classroom behavior, student on-task behaviors, and self-control skills. This training was conducted by building-based resource teachers, the school counselor, the school psychologist, and the Project directors.

2   The social skills program was implemented at a building level, including all classrooms, lunch, PE, art, music and special programs, and school buses.

3   A building-based incentive and support program was implemented to reinforce both teachers and students in the use of the social skills program.

The parent involvement component's primary objective is to increase the academic and social progress of at-risk students by increasing the involvement of parents in working with their children on academic schoolwork and expanding the level of parent management skills through the use of a parent training program. Although it is not fully implemented yet, the activities designed and implemented to achieve this objective include the following:

1   A "drop-in" center, located in the school building, will be developed. This center will be the location of parent training in academic support of their children, as well as parent training in child-management skills.

2   A program designed to teach parents how to help their children with academic work at home will be developed. Initially, parents will be taught the skills their children are working on/having difficulty with and will be observed/ supervised by "parent professionals." The parent professionals will be trained

and employed by the school to work with students, in the school setting, on the same types of activities that the parents will be trained to work on in the home. This activity is seen as a unique strength of this project.

3 Parents will be taught basic behavior management and social skills training processes similar to those employed in the school setting. This activity will provide consistency in treatment of students in the home and school setting. Teachers will meet with parents in the "drop-in" center to discuss the children. The school counselor, the school psychologist, and advanced doctoral students from the University of South Florida will provide the parent training.

4 A control group of students, matched for the demographics of those students whose parents participate in the "drop-in" center, will be identified and followed during the course of this project. The academic and behavioral progress of the two groups of students will be evaluated to determine the short- and long-term effects of the parent involvement component.

PRELIMINARY RESULTS

Project ACHIEVE has completed 1½ years of program implementation at the time of this writing. Thus, an evaluation of the Project is best focused on outcomes from the first year of implementation, as contrasted with data from preproject years. Currently, data are being collected on a number of variables, including: (a) teacher satisfaction with the process and outcomes of consultation; (b) acceptability of the consultation process as measured by requests for assistance; (c) teacher attributions as to the permanence of referred students' academic and social difficulties and their own ability to problem solve these difficulties; (d) effects of the consultation process on special education placements, number of case study evaluations, behavioral referrals to the office, suspensions/expulsions, grade retention, and cost of services; and (e) parent involvement.

Preliminary results suggest the following strong trends: (a) teacher satisfaction and acceptability is high, as evidenced by increasing requests for and use of consultation; (b) there has been a significant reduction (approximately 67%) in the special education placement rate and number of case study evaluations; (c) there has been a significant reduction in suspensions, expulsions, and use of grade retention; (d) there has been a significant reduction in the number of reported behavioral problems, both in school and on the bus; and (e) there has been a significant increase in parent participation for students referred for consultation. At the system level, there has been a significant increase in the number of days of staff training and inservice opportunities, as well as the successful implementation of building-based programs such as social skills training and curriculum-based measurement.

In evaluating these preliminary findings, there is strong evidence that the Caplanian principles described earlier can be institutionalized at building, classroom, teacher, and individual student levels. Indeed, organizational change is evident at the training, administrative support, and policy levels of Project ACHIEVE. It is now the desire of the Polk County School Board to institutionalize this process in all elementary school buildings. Initial plans to implement this project systemwide are underway with an initial focus on funding and resource allocation.

INTEGRATING PROJECT ACHIEVE WITH CAPLAN'S ORGANIZATIONAL CONSULTATION PRINCIPLES

Project ACHIEVE was conceptualized as a comprehensive, systemic approach to service delivery that includes primary, secondary, and tertiary prevention components. The complexity of the problems of society, as evidenced in the schools, is too great to suggest a simple, or singular, approach to problem solving and prevention. The seven components of Project ACHIEVE and Caplan's organizational consultation principles are well integrated and address, in a comprehensive manner, the needs of today's schools and students. It is this integration that serves to strengthen the effect of Project ACHIEVE and to realize the Project's outcomes. Next, an integrated analysis of Caplan's work is presented as it specifically relates to the activities of Project ACHIEVE.

Prevention and Project ACHIEVE

Caplan's conceptual model of primary, secondary, and tertiary prevention is evident in a number of Project ACHIEVE's components. Indeed, prevention is the primary focus of Project ACHIEVE. The Caplanian model of prevention clearly provides a fitting structure for the components of the Project as follows:

1   The RQC problem-solving process guides the development of interventions at all three of Caplan's levels of prevention. For instance, problems identified through the strategic planning component are addressed using RQC problem solving, such that prevention programs like social skills training, home-school partnerships, and preschool program development are chosen and implemented. The RQC problem-solving process also is utilized in the development of building- and classroom-based discipline programs, which are designed to teach students appropriate academic and social behavior so that future individual referral problems are prevented.

2   The staff development component is used to train school staff (professional, paraprofessional, and volunteer) in the skills necessary for both prevention and direct intervention services.

3   The instructional and behavioral consultation components support all levels of Caplan's prevention model. Through instructional consultation, new curricular methods are designed, implemented, and monitored as a way to reduce current and future at-risk students' academic failure. These same processes are used to problem solve the academic difficulties of both entire classrooms and individual students. The behavioral consultation and intervention components are used at building, classroom, and individual student levels. So-

cial skills training at the building level, group behavioral procedures at the classroom level, and individualized behavioral interventions at the student level parallel Caplan's primary, secondary and tertiary prevention model, respectively.

4   The parent-training component also addresses all three prevention levels. At the preschool level, parent training is designed to improve parents' skills in areas of child management, nutrition, home structure, and academic tutoring. Parent training, coordinated with the building- and classroom-based social skills training, is designed to prevent serious behavioral problems through the utilization of more effective management strategies in the home. Finally, individual student referrals utilize the parent-training component to address existing problems through a comprehensive service delivery program. The philosophy of Project ACHIEVE includes the encouragement of active parent involvement in the individual intervention plans of all students referred for assistance.

The Integration of Community Support Systems and Project ACHIEVE

The goal of an integrated community support system is the development of a system of schooling that links classroom, community, and home efforts. Project ACHIEVE specifically addresses all three levels. Changes in our society, different expectations of the schooling process, and educational reform strategies all support a need for this integrated schooling process. Jesse Keen Elementary School is one of four elementary schools in the Lakeland, Florida area participating in a "full-service school" program. Community mental health, public health, early education, public assistance, and educational programming are all provided through the public school setting. Significantly, the various components of Project ACHIEVE help maximize the potential of the "full-service school" program. For example, the strategic planning component integrates and develops action plans that coordinate services between the participating agencies and schools. The staff development component is used to train school (teachers and paraprofessionals), district (bus drivers, psychologists, and counselors), home (parent trainers), and community (mental health workers, parent educators) personnel. The behavioral consultation/intervention component emphasizes and operationalizes the integration of these services across home, school, and community settings. Here, community mental health workers and parents participate with school-based teams to link prevention and intervention plans across settings. Future directions for Project ACHIEVE include expanding the parent "drop-in" center, integrating parent education and training through the GED program, and improving the integration of each "full-service school" component. These efforts will further synthesize available community support systems with school and home programs.

The Conceptual Organization of Consultation and Project ACHIEVE

When engaged in organizational change, Caplan has recognized that consultation, as a process, must address the needs of all parties involved. One group or an individual within a system cannot change without affecting all of the others equally involved in that system. In addition, change for any individual in a system is difficult when the system itself is resistant to such change. One solution to these realities is the simultaneous use of "top-down" (e.g., program-centered administrative) and "bottom-up" (consultee- or client-centered) case consultation. This facilitates a more rapid, effective, and long-term change process, especially when contrasted with the separate use of either "top-down" or "bottom-up" consultation.

Project ACHIEVE was designed to use all four of Caplan's types of consultation. Client-centered (i.e., student) case consultation is reflected in Project ACHIEVE's instructional, behavioral, and RQC components. Consultee-centered (i.e., teacher and parent) case consultation is reflected in the parent-training, behavioral, instructional, and RQC components. Program-centered administrative consultation is seen in the strategic planning, staff development, research, and RQC components. Consultee-centered administrative consultation is evident in the staff development, strategic planning, and research components.

Classroom and individual student referrals by Project ACHIEVE teachers most frequently utilize the client- and consultee-centered case consultation approaches. In each case, the RQC process focuses on both client (home, student, and community) characteristics as well as consultee (teacher, curriculum, and classroom) characteristics. Ultimately, the RQC problem-solving and consultation change processes focus on the role that client and consultee variables must play in successfully implementing prevention and intervention programs. Through this process, consultees (parents and teachers) learn new prevention and intervention skills and develop new attitudes about problem behaviors. Students acquire new academic and social skills that improve their ability to adapt successfully to changing expectations and environments.

The strategic planning, staff development, and research components of Project ACHIEVE directly facilitate program- and consultee-centered administrative consultation. From a program-centered perspective, Project ACHIEVE initiatives are developed as a result of an integration of strategic planning and problem-solving processes. From a consultee-centered perspective, the attitudes and values of the administrators and supervisors involved in Project ACHIEVE have been influenced by those parts of the strategic planning process that involved building-wide needs assessments, evaluations of teacher attitudes and perceptions, and the input of the School Climate Committee. Similarly, staff

development involves teachers, paraprofessionals, and administrators, and facilitates both the development of new child-focused skills and the acceptance of
new values and programs.

As a school reform initiative, change and adaptation have been inherent
and ongoing parts of Project ACHIEVE from the beginning. Indeed, as outcomes of the Project have affected different facets of the school environment,
new and expanded programs have been required to respond to and support the
results. Through it all, the ongoing use of both types of administrative consultation have resulted in continued, strong leadership for the educational restruc-
turing process and in positive attitudes and vocal support for our various
student- and classroom-based programs. To be sure, the dynamic evolution of
the change process has been strengthened by the presence of all four types of
consultation. This has assured the success of both our "top-down" and
"bottom-up" processes.

Specific Consultation Skills and Project ACHIEVE

Resistance to consultation, especially in the context of a comprehensive home,
school, and community project, is fueled by differences in the professional
language, training, and philosophies of those multidisciplinary individuals who
are attempting to work together. Further complicating matters are differences in
education (e.g., of parents, teachers, and paraprofessionals), culture, language,
and values across home, school, and community settings. Each of these factors
can significantly inhibit effective interpersonal communication and may potentially hinder the consultation and change process.

Critically, the RQC component of Project ACHIEVE has prevented this
problem from occurring. The RQC process does not use professional jargon,
labels, or discipline-specific language. Rather, all parties involved in this collaborative, problem-solving process bring their own experience, training (if
any), background, and perspective to the consultation table. There, hypotheses
to explain a referred situation are developed based on the individual and multidisciplinary experience of all those who participate, and the contributions of
parents, teachers, school psychologists, and others are treated and approached
at an equal level. The RQC process uses information from a variety of sources
and takes that information without prejudice or prejudgment. This greatly facilitates interpersonal communication and reinforces the collaborative nature of
the consultation process.

The staff development component of Project ACHIEVE has ensured further the potential for nonhierarchical consultation by training the entire Jesse
Keen staff (teachers, administrators, office and cafeteria staff, bus drivers,
counselors, school psychologists, mental health and parent educators) in the
RQC process. This training has emphasized a number of factors. First, the
interpersonal communication of building staff is built on a common method of
communication that uses a shared, "lay" language. Second, the RQC process

uses information from six areas (child, teacher, peer, curriculum, home/community, and classroom) in its attempt to comprehensively understand and resolve any referral situation. This emphasis on a multifactored problem-solving process relieves any anxiety over who is "responsible" for a problem or program, thereby facilitating communication. Third, the RQC process is constant in its focus on outcome-based/intervention strategies that use multiple resources. Fourth, the RQC process involves a collaborative, team effort, where all parties share the problem-solving and intervention responsibilities. The focus on positive outcomes and the shared nature of this process greatly facilitate interpersonal communication, significantly reduce resistance, and result in a comfort level that increases the number of consultation requests. This increase may be the most salient indicator of the consultation process' acceptability and of its ability to enhance interpersonal communication and consultation effectiveness.

SUMMARY

Caplan has made numerous significant contributions to psychology and the community mental health movement, which have provided a foundation to systems and individual change. Today, our communities confront a number of interdependent factors and circumstances, which have created an underclass of at-risk children whose educational and social success is severely threatened. Through it all, however, four predominant Caplanian principles hold a key that can unlock a plethora of impactful solutions: a focus on the need for (a) prevention, (b) integrated service delivery systems, (c) programmatic and individual consultation, and (d) relationship building within the context of change. Although it is frustrating to know that we have held this key for several decades (with limited impact as it relates to at-risk students), it is still a comfort to acknowledge that the key exists. We must rededicate ourselves to the use of this key. In the end, our successes will not be for ourselves, but for the future generations of children who will grow up in the nurturing environments that fully support their physical, social, psychological, educational, and individual progress and success.

REFERENCES

Batsche, G. M. (1984). *Referral-question consultation.* Washington, DC: National Association of School Psychologists.

Buckner, J. C., Trickett, E. J., & Corse, S. J. (1985). *Primary prevention in mental health: An annotated bibliography.* Rockville, MD: National Institute of Mental Health.

Caplan, G. (1964). *Principles of preventive psychiatry.* New York: Basic Books.

Caplan, G. (1970). *The theory and practice of mental health consultation.* New York: Basic Books.

Caplan, G. (Ed.). (1974). *Support systems and community mental health.* New York: Behavioral Publications.

Children's Defense Fund. (1990). *Children 1990: A report card, briefing book, and action primer.* Washington, DC: Author.

Goldstein, A. P. (1988). *The prepare curriculum: Teaching prosocial competencies.* Champaign, IL: Research Press.

Heller, K., Holtzman, W., & Messick, S. (Eds.). (1982). *Placing children in special education: A strategy for equity.* Washington, DC: National Academy Press.

Institute of Medicine. (1989). *Research on children & adolescents with mental, behavioral, & developmental disorders.* Washington, DC: National Academy Press.

Kazdin, A. E. (1989). *Behavioral modification in applied settings* (4th ed.). Pacific Grove, CA: Brooks-Cole.

Knitzer, J., Steinberg, Z., & Fleisch, B. (1990). *At the schoolhouse door: An examination of programs and policies for children with behavioral and emotional problems.* New York: Bank Street College.

Knoff, H. M. (1988). Effective social interventions. In J. L. Graden, J. E. Zins, & M. J. Curtis (Eds.), *Alternative educational delivery systems: Enhancing instructional options for all students* (pp. 431–454). Washington, DC: National Association of School Psychologists.

Knoff, H. M., & Batsche, G. M. (1990). The place of the school in community mental health services for children: A necessary interdependence. *The Journal of Mental Health Administration, 17,* 122–130.

Knoff, H. M., & Batsche, G. M. (1991a). Integrating school and educational psychology to meet the educational and mental health needs of all children. *Educational Psychologist, 26,* 167–184.

Knoff, H. M., & Batsche, G. M. (1991b). *The Referral Question Consultation process workbook: Addressing system, school, and classroom academic and behavioral problems.* Tampa, FL: Authors.

Knoff, H. M., McKenna, A. F., & Riser, K. (1991). Toward a consultant effectiveness scale: Investigating the characteristics of effective consultants. *School Psychology Review, 20,* 81–96.

National Commission on Excellence in Education. (1983). *A nation at risk: The imperative for educational reform.* Washington, DC: Author.

National Council on Disability. (1989). *The education of students with disabilities: Where do we stand? A report to the President and the Congress of the United States.* Washington, DC: Author.

Rosenfield, S. (1987). *Instructional consultation.* Hillsdale, NJ: Erlbaum.

Shinn, M. R. (1989). *Curriculum-based measurement: Assessing special children.* New York: Guilford.

Steiner, G. A. (1979). *Strategic planning: What every manager must know.* New York: The Free Press.

Stroul, B., & Friedman, R. M. (1986). *A system of care for severely emotionally disturbed children & youth.* Washington, DC: CASSP Technical Assistance Center, Georgetown University Child Development Center.

U.S. Department of Health and Human Services. (1990). *National plan for research on child and adolescent mental disorders: A report requested by the U.S. Congress submitted by the National Advisory Mental Health Council.* Washington, DC.

William, T. Grant Foundation Commission on Work, Family and Citizenship. (1988). *The forgotten half: Pathways to success for America's youth and young families.* Washington, DC: Author.

Ysseldyke, J. E., & Christenson, S. L. (1987). *The Instructional Environment Scale.* Austin, TX: Pro-Ed.

Chapter 8

Consulting on Innovation and Change with Public Mental Health Organizations: The Caplan Approach

Thomas E. Backer
Human Interaction Research Institute

INTRODUCTION: THE CHALLENGES TO PUBLIC MENTAL HEALTH

Public mental health agencies in the United States today face many challenges to providing effective services for people with mental illnesses. Continuing fiscal austerity is perhaps the most compelling of these challenges. Forty of the 50 states currently have general budget crises, and federal support for mental health services is dwindling, making it an absolute requirement to "do more with less." For instance, in 1991, Oregon faced a 15% cut in funding for its public mental health program, forcing significant reduction and reorganization of services (R. Lippincott, personal communication, January 1992).

State and county mental health agencies, community mental health centers, state hospitals, and residential facilities have other challenges to confront as well. These include significant changes in the populations needing service (e.g., increases in the number of homeless mentally ill and mentally ill substance abusers), pressures for decentralization (or centralization) to enhance efficiency, increased liability and legal actions, changing technological and labor force requirements (e.g., the management of racial and ethnic diversity in the mental health workforce), and demands for heightened family and consumer involvement in the service delivery process (including employment of consumers by public mental health agencies in various roles, such as case manager).

Larger system changes in mental health and in America's overall health care system also are a significant factor. Public Law 99-660, passed by Congress in 1988, requires state mental health agencies to create and submit for federal approval comprehensive plans for community-based services. Plans found to be out of compliance can trigger cuts in the state's federal funding. Managed care, the increasingly popular approach to health care cost containment, is coming to public mental health programs in many states. Many policymakers are looking with increasing favor on integrated service agency models, which provide "one-stop shopping" for consumers of mental health services.

In his 1985 book, *Innovation and Entrepreneurship*, Drucker asserted that the rapid changes in today's society, technology, and economy are a greater threat to public-sector organizations than to private businesses. Yet, like the Chinese language symbol for crisis, which contains elements of both danger and opportunity, public mental health agencies do still have some creative, potentially advantageous choices for how to deal with the ongoing crisis they face.

In some respects, crisis is no longer the right word to use, because it connotes temporariness. A mental health administrator said to me recently, "Crisis? We've been in crisis mode for 18 months now. We need some help in how to deal with the aftereffects of constant crisis that doesn't let up." When budgets have been cut to the bone (and then still more cuts are required), and when change after change has been thrust on public agencies still reeling from the last round, then some new options forged out of the damage already done can and do emerge.

For example, parties to the mental health service system can be asked to look at dramatic new options for cutback management, and lessons can be learned from other entities that are facing similar fates (e.g., private businesses in a recessionary economy). In fact, there can be a renewed willingness to innovate when the entire system is in an ongoing "survival mode." This chapter discusses consultation on "survival mode innovation" in public mental health, and the contributions to such an approach that have been made by the pioneering work of Caplan.

SURVIVAL MODE INNOVATION
AND GERALD CAPLAN

Although much of Caplan's early work on consultation models and approaches was carried out in mental health settings, the troubled environment of public mental health just described is one that he scarcely would have imagined more than 20 years ago, when his pioneering book, *The Theory and Practice of Mental Health Consultation* (Caplan, 1970), was first published. Yet the concepts set forth in Caplan's work are even more relevant now than in the less "mean and lean" years, which provided him with the framework for those concepts' initial development.

In fact, organizational consultation on innovation and change to public mental health agencies, using a Caplanian model, can be one essential component in the effort to help these agencies survive and remain effective in the current hostile, crisis-strewn environment. Such outside advice and technical assistance provided by competent consultants can help: (a) deal with some of the psychological and organizational "side effects" of change; (b) provide a supportive framework for managing even the least desired changes so that the well-validated principles of participation and ownership of the change effort are respected; and (c) identify innovations from various sources that assist public mental health agencies to "do more with less" in a creative way (i.e., innovations that are low cost, carrying built-in financing, or offer highly visible cost savings). These are the three key ingredients of what is called "survival mode innovation."

Regrettably, during this time of financial austerity and program instability, the tendency may be to clamp down on any type of innovation. An administrator for one state mental health agency said to me in a recent interview: "Don't offer us anything that isn't 'meat and potatoes' . . . we don't want anything new unless it can help us right now, today." A county mental health director in another state said: "Our state has a lot going for it, and a lot going on, but things are fragmented, not systemic."

Both interviewees agreed on the potential value of training and consultation for mental health staff on a systems approach to coping with change, and on how to search out and implement innovations that would provide more effective services in a tight-resources time. Both agreed that staff in their agencies were wrestling with troubling psychological reactions to the negative events of the last several years. The resulting anxiety, depression, and paranoia stand in the way of change at least as much as lack of funding or good planning.

"Survival mode innovation," based, in part, on concepts originated by Caplan, is presented as one adaptive response to the extraordinary environment currently faced by public mental health agencies. It can help public mental health agencies to move beyond a crisis response (which, as mentioned already, connotes temporariness) to function effectively in a "survival mode" over an extended period of recovery from negative change.

Such efforts might be likened to the American Red Cross' strategies for disaster management, which assume that, after a major disaster (e.g., the October 1991 Oakland, California residential fires), several years of recovery time may be needed for the residents of the community in which the disaster took place. During this period, strategic planning is required that (a) shows how to use customary community resources in a very different way, and (b) attends to the ongoing human, psychological needs associated with this prolonged recovery period.

Organizational consultation to public mental health agencies using the concepts of "survival mode innovation" draws heavily on concepts and techniques first developed by Caplan (1970). Three arguments support the relevance of these concepts to the ongoing crisis in public mental health already described:

1 The Caplan model emphasizes such concepts as "ownership" of solutions by those who have to implement them, and attention to the larger environment in which an organization exists, concepts which are fundamental to dealing effectively with the very complicated realities public mental health agencies face today. (Some of Caplan's basic concepts are briefly reviewed in the next section.)

2 Caplan's consultation approach is especially likely to work with mental health systems, because it is expressed in terms familiar to and comfortable for administrators and staff in these systems, many of whom have training as clinicians. Moreover, during his career, Caplan has trained literally thousands of mental health professionals, many of whom have gone on to significant positions of leadership in public mental health.

3 Paradoxically, Caplan's approach has not been widely used in public mental health systems (at least not in an *integrated* way), partly because it addresses themes of consultee feelings and behaviors that mental health professionals may believe do not apply to them, or that they already know about, and thus can deal with without consultation from the outside.

BASIC CONCEPTS IN ORGANIZATIONAL CONSULTATION: THE CAPLAN VIEW

Brown, Pryzwansky, and Schulte (1991) offered a succinct overview of some of the basic principles underlying Caplan's consultation approach:

1 Both intrapsychic and environmental factors are important in explaining and changing behavior, and both need to be explored in preconsultation assessment. Recipients of consultation are human beings with feelings, attitudes, and beliefs that can have an important bearing on the success of consultation. Anxiety, paranoia, defensiveness, and territorial reactions are common and powerful responses to change, and often may reflect deep-seated personality styles and belief systems. Also important are the larger professional, bureaucratic, and community environments in which the agency receiving consultation exists. These set a context in which the change facilitated by consultation will occur.

2 Consultees typically are members of professional disciplines that have their own norms, roles, language, and body of knowledge; and they are also part of a specific culture in their own organization. These factors must be taken into account in designing a consultation, and consultants who are content-familiar with these factors (i.e., those who also come from a mental health background) may be more successful in such custom designing.

3 Learning and generalization are most likely to occur when consultees retain responsibility for taking action (i.e., "felt ownership" of the proposed change).

4 Mental health consultation is just one of the mechanisms by which organizational challenges can be met. Thus, framing consultation within the larger matrix of problem-solving approaches, such as teaching, supervision, and collaboration, is essential for success.

5 Consultee attitudes and affect are important in consultation, but cannot be dealt with directly. The focus needs to remain on the work problem, which is why the consultant is there in the first place. The consultation process becomes "unequal," and thus less effective, if the personal issues of the consultee are raised directly. Confrontation in this manner also may arouse considerable defensiveness on the part of the consultee.

As is well known, Caplan (1970) has posited four types of consultation, three of which focus on individual consultees and/or clients. The fourth type, "program-centered administrative consultation," is concerned with organizations, focusing either on the problems surrounding the development of a new program or on some aspect of ongoing organizational functioning. Because they are dealing with organizational systems, Caplan (1970) has said that consultants working in this arena need to have a significant understanding of organizational theory, planning, financial and personal management, and administration, in addition to clinical skills.

The primary goal of such organizational consultation is the development of an action plan, usually in the form of a written report, that can be implemented by the organization to resolve the identified problem. Caplan (1970) has indicated four major steps in the consultation process that lead to a written report, usually over a period of days or weeks, and with a definite time frame specified:

1 Initial contact—resulting in a preliminary diagnosis and assessment of fit between the problem, organization, and consultant.

2 Assessment—a more thorough evaluation of written documents, interviews with staff, and other data gathering, learning about the organization and the specific challenges it faces.

3 Problem formulation—which has three stages: an initial definition; followed by a period of "confusion," where the consultant considers multiple possibilities; and then by a "gestalt closure," where the consultant views the problem in a more complex way that makes sense of the data gathered.

4 Development of recommendations—with active participation of the organization's staff, problem-solving formulations take shape, involving staff feedback about appropriateness of recommendations while they are still in "draft" form.

APPLICATIONS TO PUBLIC MENTAL HEALTH ORGANIZATIONS

Caplan's (1970) methods and concepts have been applied in mental health consultation for over 30 years, including many American public mental health systems. In biographical writings about Caplan (Caplan-Moskovich, 1982), mention frequently is made of his many management consultations to public mental health agencies.

These included important systems consultations to the federally sponsored community mental health program in the 1960s, when it was first developed, and to a number of state mental health programs where Caplan offered influential training/consultation to top management staff. Many public mental health leaders of today are graduates of Caplan's training programs at Harvard.

The APA Division of Consulting Psychology provided considerable dissemination of Caplanian concepts to mental health consultants from 1979 to 1984, when the Division collaborated with the Human Interaction Research Institute in providing a number of training workshops on consultation for psychologists, sponsored by the National Institute of Mental Health. The principles already mentioned were a fundamental part of these workshops. For instance, these trainings emphasized use of the strategy of "ownership," in which consultees participated actively in designing the change approach that is at the heart of the consultation. This program of activity also included preparing a chapter on organizational practice of consulting psychology for an edited book on professional practice (Backer, 1982). This and other publications helped to "institutionalize" the Division-sponsored work on consultation approaches.

WHY THE CAPLAN CONCEPTS
ARE NOT USED MORE WIDELY

Some Caplanian concepts have been adopted widely in consultation to mental health organizations, particularly as a result of the increasing application of organization development (OD) consultation in public agencies. The work of such pioneers as Robert Golembiewski at the University of Georgia, and Alan Glassman at California State University-Northridge has helped broaden the impact of this technique, well known in the private sector (Beer & Walton, 1987; Porras & Silvers, 1991), to public sector organizations. Environmental analysis, "felt ownership," and other parts of the Caplan scheme are a fundamental part of OD.

However, other aspects of Caplan's approach have not been used widely in consultation on change provided to mental health settings. For instance, as Levinson (Chapter 11) makes clear, understanding and attention to intrapsychic factors in organizational consultation is by no means universal. It is particularly ironic that such factors usually have not been a part of OD approaches in mental health (Backer & Grant, 1981; Glaser & Backer, 1979). By and large, organizational consulting in mental health settings has not looked at the intrapsychic factors of consultees, nor those of the consultant.

Yet here, too, Caplan (1970) has had much to say. For instance, "theme interference" would be familiar to most clinicians with their treatment hats on, yet the application of this concept to the work of an organizational consultant in a mental health setting is uncommon. The consultant's own history of authority relationships or childhood experiences of being a team player at school can affect the outcomes of consulting with the director or management team of a mental health agency. Consultants often are unaware of how their personalities and styles affect the consultation and its success. Yet many consultants working in mental health settings have a clinical background themselves, which should make applying such principles easier. In real life, however, the "cobblers' children have no shoes" in some cases, and these valuable tools for learning and improvement are ignored.

SURVIVAL MODE INNOVATION:
APPLYING CAPLANIAN PRINCIPLES IN THE 1990s

I am currently conducting a 5-year study with my colleagues for the National Institute of Mental Health (NIMH). In this study, Caplan's concepts are being applied in a highly practical way—offering consultation on innovation and change to public mental health agencies in six states. All of these states are grappling with fiscal constraints and fast-changing program and community environments. The Center for Improving Mental Health Systems is intended to help the six states improve service delivery by promoting the adoption of services or program innovations, and by enhancing the knowledge and skills of the mental health workforce. Psychiatric rehabilitation services for clients, and strategies for family involvement in the mental health delivery process, are the two topical areas in which the Center works. Both are key ingredients of the community-based system of care that public mental health agencies currently are attempting to achieve (National Institute of Mental Health, 1991).

The Center identifies worthwhile innovations in selected topical areas, makes information about them available, coordinates staff training related to these innovations, and provides targeted technical assistance to facilitate the process of innovation adoption. The Center works closely with the existing Human Resource Development (HRD) systems of each state (see Salasin & Backer, in press), but is concerned with much more than training alone. Technical assistance on the dynamics of change and strategic planning to guide the change process are the two key resources the Center provides to these challenge-laden public mental health environments, helping them achieve systems change through adopting innovations.

The Center starts from the assumption that empirically-validated, demonstrably cost-effective approaches to psychiatric rehabilitation and family involvement in community-based care are now available from many sources. But there are significant barriers to full implementation of these valuable technologies, even in states moving the most aggressively and creatively to implement P.L. 99-660 and its amendments. These barriers include limited understanding and use of these technologies by mental health professionals, despite recent dissemination through the literature and demonstration programs; and organizational and psychological resistances to change, some of them stemming from the challenging environment in which mental health services are currently provided in most states.

A six-state consortium (California, New Mexico, New York, Oregon, Texas, and Virginia) collaborates with the Center on this project, with each state serving as a field site for training and technical assistance efforts. The Center is operated jointly by the nonprofit Human Interaction Research Institute, which has conducted research and policy studies on knowledge utilization in health care for 30 years; the UCLA Center for Clinical Research on Schizophrenia and Psychiatric Rehabilitation; and the National Alliance for the Mentally Ill.

The Center's main activities are planned to: (a) assess needs in each of the six states related to the above priorities; (b) develop innovative systems for delivering knowledge, training, and technical assistance (including state-to-state technical assistance (TA) within the six-state consortium) related to these needs; (c) develop knowledge packages and identify validated "best practice" innovations or psychiatric rehabilitation and family involvement; and (d) conduct or facilitate HRD management training programs in each state, oriented toward innovation adoption and system change.

Expected outcomes from the Center's activities for the six participating states will include: (a) an annual needs assessment study addressing training and public mental health system priorities in the three topical areas; (b) access to state-of-the-art knowledge and technology in psychiatric rehabilitation and family involvement; (c) access to cost-effective training, with provision of follow-up consultation and technical assistance; and (d) participation in a communications and resource sharing network with the six states, selected academic liaisons, and other resources designed to enhance each state's ability to meet its P.L. 99-660 state plan goals, including HRD goals. Expected outcomes for families of persons with mental illness in each state include ability to shape professional training on family issues and encourage innovation adoption in this area, as well as to receive training on systems change approaches. The Center's evaluation plan includes measuring actual impact of the Center on services provided to consumers. Consumers provide advisory input to all phases of the Center's activities.

The consultation and technical assistance model utilized in this activity will draw on a number of resources in addition to the Caplanian concepts already presented, all of them required to fit the "survival mode" requirement:

1   Knowledge utilization methods—for identifying, obtaining information, and considering and applying specific innovations related to targeted needs in the six states; and emphasizing inexpensive or free information resources and strategies for cost savings through targeted technical assistance, state-to-state joint ventures, and so forth. (Backer, 1991a, 1991b).

2   Change management methods—for dealing with the human and organizational aspects of change; these strategies involve dealing particularly with the clinical phenomena of anxiety, depression, and paranoia. "Survival mode innovation" begins with the recognition that these psychological dynamics of change are likely to be *increased* when the organization is in turmoil. Thus it is even more important to deal with these changes.

3   Strategic planning—methods for dealing with change that draw on work done in the private sector, both for generic strategic planning and for the use of planning approaches to corporate downsizing and cutback management that fit with the survival mode.

4   HRD strategies—using the existing training and development infrastructure for HRD in each of the six states, but again looking for cost-saving approaches because these HRD state programs all face their own budget and staff cutbacks.

5   HRD leadership from the National Institute of Mental Health—HRD is seen as the "engine" for systems change within NIMH's HRD Program (Salasin & Backer, in press), and this point of view is reinforced by the 1991 NIMH *Services Research Plan*, which states that the "mission of a mental health system is inexorably tied to human resources, its most valued asset" (National Institute of Mental Health, 1991, p. 45).

During the Center's first 3 months of operation, what is being heard from the states without exception is that assistance is greatly needed in dealing with the negative by-products of undesired change (such as budget cutbacks or reorganizations imposed from above), as well as in learning about and adopting innovations. Action-oriented problem solving, rather than academically-based training, is preferred. Technical assistance provided must stay close to the immediate challenges faced by public mental health systems if it is to be supported by staff. Nonetheless, there is a recognition that larger issues of innovation and change can still be dealt with, even in this troubled time, and that remaining responsive is centrally guided by such efforts.

Managing change in the turbulent 1990s also can benefit from the model of "logical incrementalism," first advanced by Quinn (1980). This approach involves planning a change, applying the plan, and then seeing how the environment changes as a result of both the planned change effort and other forces at play, followed by reworking the change program as needed. This is more a process of "managing change that is happening anyway" than planned change in the traditional sense, but it is likeliest to result in real organizational improvement in public mental health agencies for the 1990s.

In sum, "survival mode innovation" draws on each of the Caplanian principles advanced earlier. Both intrapsychic and environmental factors are studied as part of the initial diagnostic stage (using a diagnostic approach similar to that advanced by Levinson [1972]), and the professional disciplines of the mental agency staff are taken into careful consideration (the study team includes members of most of these disciplines to provide appropriate context). The public mental health agencies that receive consultation are encouraged to retain responsibility for the systems change efforts that result, including an emphasis on state-to-state technical assistance and joint venture activities. The consulting process is seen as just one element in a larger matrix of problem-solving approaches, such as legislative efforts or training provided in a classroom teaching environment by public-academic liaisons (Salasin & Backer, in press). It is assumed that most of the intrapsychic forces evaluated will be treated confidentially and will not enter into the process of the consultation overtly, because they cannot be dealt with directly. The focus remains on the problems to be solved. Caplan's four-step model for the consulting process, leading to a report for action, also is being used as part of this system.

Some specific, practical situations, in which technical assistance consultation using "survival mode innovation" approaches can be found, include:

1   A special treatment center was initiated in fall 1991 on the grounds of Las Vegas Medical Center (the state hospital for New Mexico), which specializes in handling treatment-refractory patients using behavioral and psychiatric rehabilitation approaches. Because this represents such a major change in treatment approach, especially within the confines of a state hospital, consultation has been provided both on specific innovations to be adopted and on how to cope with staff resistance and other systems change tensions.

2   In California, major changes are taking place in the organization of the public mental health system. Reorganization within the State Department of Mental Health has occurred recently, and profound changes have been made in the funding authority for community mental health services, putting much more authority into the hands of California's 58 counties. The state also is conducting the first staffing study of its large state hospital system that has occurred in 20 years. Within this context of great systems change, the agency also is conducting what seems to be a successful experiment with integrated services for the mentally ill, using a managed mental health care model. The Center is exploring ways in which this innovation can be adopted more widely, taking account of all the other complexities of change now happening in California.

3   A recent property tax initiative in Oregon resulted in a 15% budget cut for the state's mental health agency. Simultaneously, the state learned that both its adult and children's mental health plans were found to be out of compliance by the National Institute of Mental Health, requiring an all-out effort to improve the plans to avoid further federal budget cuts. In this turbulent, high-anxiety environment, the state remains committed to expanding psychiatric rehabilitation services for the mentally ill population. The Center is collaborating with the state's psychiatric rehabilitation steering committee on development of a strategic plan to guide future efforts in this area.

Many other such challenging situations are expected in all six states of the Center's consortium.

CONCLUSION: SOME CAUTIONS
ABOUT SURVIVAL MODE INNOVATION

Worthy (1992), in a pioneering study of personnel attitudes and organizational changes in Sears Roebuck in the 1940s (studies that are just now receiving wide attention), found that significant differences often exist between the appearance and the operating reality of a business management strategy. The larger implication of this finding is that consultants need to examine thoughtfully both the environments they work in and the strategies they suggest to see if there is a good fit between appearance and reality (Backer, 1992).

Worthy's (1992) results also point out that "desirable change" (reducing the degree of administrative structure, in his example) can sometimes have "undesirable consequences" (e.g., putting managers into work environments not suited to their personalities and styles). Recent reviews of OD and Organizational Transformation work (Beer & Walton, 1987; Porras & Silvers, 1991) also emphasize the limits of these approaches, and the importance for success of a careful fit between goals, strategies, and environments.

Worthy's (1992) study also found that organizational stability (e.g., low staff turnover) was necessary if the management strategy of broadened span of control is to be effective. This suggests that managing change may require a blend of changing some organizational aspects while holding others constant, bringing to mind George Bernard Shaw's dictum, "If it is not necessary to change, it is necessary not to change."

Ending with these three cautions—look for differences between appearances and reality, look for undesirable side effects of change, and examine carefully what needs to be constant for change to work—further underscore the complexity of "survival mode innovation." Public mental health agencies may find that (a) political exigencies press them toward "appearance" solutions, (b) the undesirable side effects of certain changes in a resource-poor system may be unavoidable, and (c) "holding constant" may be easier said than done. Yet Caplan's basic approach to consultation still provides a powerful set of tools for engineering change, even in a hostile environment, so that at least incremental progress can be made toward improving public mental health systems.

REFERENCES

Backer, T. E. (1982). Psychological consultation. In J. R. McNamara & A. G. Barclay (Eds.), *Critical issues in professional psychology* (pp. 227–269). New York: Praeger.

Backer, T. E. (1991a). Knowledge utilization: The third wave. *Knowledge: Creation, Diffusion, Utilization, 12*(3), 225–240.

Backer, T. E. (1991b). *Drug abuse technology transfer*. Rockville, MD: National Institute on Drug Abuse.

Backer, T. E. (1992). Getting management knowledge used. *Journal of Management Inquiry, 1*(1), 39–43.

Backer, T. E., & Grant, M. E. (1981). Getting the most from program consultation: Guidelines for mental health administrators. *Journal of Mental Health Administration, 9*(1), 29–32.

Beer, M., & Walton, A. E. (1987). Organization change and development. *Annual Review of Psychology, 38*, 339–367.

Brown, D., Pryzwansky, W. B., & Schulte, A. C. (1991). *Psychological consultation: Introduction to theory and practice* (2nd ed.). Boston: Allyn & Bacon.

Caplan, G. (1970). *The theory and practice of mental health consultation*. New York: Basic Books.

Caplan-Moskovich, R. B. (1982). Gerald Caplan: The man and his work. In H. C. Schulberg & M. Killilea (Eds.), *The modern practice of community mental health* (pp. 1–39). San Francisco: Jossey-Bass.

Drucker, P. (1985). *Innovation and entrepreneurship*. New York: Harper & Row.

Glaser, E. M., & Backer, T. E. (1979). Organization development in mental health services. *Administration in Mental Health, 6*, 195–215.

Levinson, H. (1972). *Organizational diagnosis*. Cambridge, MA: Harvard University Press.

National Institute of Mental Health. (1991). *Caring for-people with severe mental disorders: A national plan of research to improve services*. Washington DC: U.S. Department of Health and Human Services.

Porras, J. I., & Silvers, R. C. (1991). Organization development and transformation. *Annual Review of Psychology, 42*, 51–78.

Quinn, J. B. (1980). *Strategies for change: Logical incrementalism*. Homewood, IL: Irwin.

Salasin, S. E., & Backer, T. E. (in press). NIMH's Human Resource Development Program: A systems approach for improving community-based mental health services. In J. E. Callan, G. R. Leon, & P. Wohlford (Eds.), *Public-academic linkages for clinical training in psychology*. Washington, DC: American Psychological Association.

Worthy, J. C. (1992). The more things change, the more they stay the same: The original Sears, Roebuck and Company studies. *Journal of Management Inquiry, 1*, 10–32.

Part Three

Assessing the Present and Future Impact of Caplan's Contributions

Chapter 9

Gerald Caplan and the Unfinished Business of Community Psychology: A Comment

Edison J. Trickett
University of Maryland

INTRODUCTION

It is a pleasure and privilege to reflect on the contributions of Gerald Caplan to the field of community psychology. My association with his work began as a graduate student, when my advisor, Jim Kelly, suggested I read *Principles of Preventive Psychiatry* (Caplan, 1964). Kelly had worked with Caplan and Erich Lindemann at Harvard, and was in the process of developing an ecological perspective for the emerging field of community psychology. In an excellent, although rather traditional, clinical program at Ohio State University, I was captured by the vision of the community-oriented professional found in that book.

In 1965, the year after the book's publication, a group of clinical psychologists gathered in Swampscott, Massachusetts, to initiate what would become the field of community psychology. The Swampscott Conference (Bennett et al., 1966) articulated a variety of commitments on which this new field would be based: a concern with underserved populations, a person-in-environment level of analysis, an avoidance of a "blaming the victim" ideology, and, most generally, an attempt to link the concept of psychology with the concept of community. It signaled a new perspective or paradigm for research and service within the helping professions. As Rappaport (1977) wrote, "the defining aspects of the perspective are cultural relativity, diversity, and ecology: the fit between persons and environments" (p. 2). The concept of community was intended to designate not only a site where research and intervention should occur, but also a level of analysis and intervention in its own right.

The intent of this chapter is not only to trace some of the influences that Caplan has had on the field of community psychology, but also to speculate on how his rich store of ideas may continue to influence the field in the future. Caplan's direct mentoring influence on the field included work with three of the early presidents of the Division of Community Psychology—Don Klein, Jim Kelly, and Ira Iscoe. Beyond those individuals, Caplan had little direct mentoring influence on those who would later become leaders of the field. Indeed, many "second-generation" community psychologists, such as myself, seemed to be only incidentally grounded in his early works. However, my association with Kelly, and his enthusiasm about his time with Caplan and Lindemann, made Caplan's work more central to me as a heuristic for community psychology research and practice.

In preparing this chapter, I reread four of Caplan's books: *Principles of Preventive Psychiatry* (1964), *The Theory and Practice of Mental Health Consultation* (1970), *Support Systems and Community Mental Health (1974)*, and *Population-Oriented Psychiatry* (1989). Considerable time had elapsed since I had read the first three of these, and as my own professional experience has grown, I felt a freshness about the books that comes from seeing them in a new light.

Two aspects of these books were particularly striking, and they form the framework for this chapter. First is the degree to which Caplan anticipated the varying directions that others in the field of community psychology would later take. Often these ideas were woven into a web of speculative ideas about, for example, social support systems that would later be put to empirical test by others. Second is the degree to which Caplan embedded his specific contributions, such as mental health consultation practice, in a larger population-oriented approach to preventing mental health problems in a community. This integrative aspect of Caplan's work has not been acknowledged as widely as some of his more specific contributions. Together, these aspects represent both his impact on the field thus far and the potential for his continuing influence in the future.

First, let me briefly describe my assessment of Caplan's vision of what he initially called preventive psychiatry (1964), and later called population-oriented psychiatry (1989). This larger vision provides the context for his more specific investigations of such preventive interventions as mental health consultation and support system enhancement.

The Community Vision of Caplan

The Population Focus   Although Caplan may be most immediately associated with specific typologies such as primary, secondary, and tertiary prevention, or specific helping modalities such as mental health consultation, it is the population focus that provides his clearest conceptual identification with the origins of community psychology. Although various conceptual models for preventive interventions are possible within the larger population emphasis, the community as level of analysis has been a recurrent image for Caplan. This point is sometimes overshadowed by his better-known specific contributions. To quote Caplan (1964), "Primary prevention is a community concept" (p. 26), and "Preventive psychiatry must continually take into account the multifactorial nature of the forces which may provoke or ameliorate mental disorders" (p. 11). Thus, for Caplan, the population emphasis was an integrative one that was intended to incorporate varied approaches to primary, secondary, and tertiary prevention as part of a coordinated set of services.

The Integration of Multiple and Varied Services Flow from a Knowledge of the Community   Central to this integrative approach was the importance of spending time getting to know the community and allowing the community (particularly the professional help givers) to get to know the psychiatrist. As Caplan (1989) emphasized, implementing this idea required a paradigm shift in the field of psychiatry. It required an understanding of community structure, community resources, and community culture. This community knowledge would allow the psychiatrist to avoid fixating on a particular type of intervention. Rather, it would promote interventions that arise out of an analysis of what the population needs.

> We must be prepared to deal with *all* members of the population at risk, and to tailor our services to their idiosyncratic needs, rather than perfecting a method and then recruiting clients for whom the method is appropriate, while rejecting those for whom it is unsuitable. This involves us in developing a wide range of methods and techniques, and in constantly innovating additions in order to cater to the needs of individuals, families, subcultural, and socioeconomic groups. (Caplan, 1989, p. 29).

A Contextualized Perspective on Behavior   Understanding the community represents one aspect of Caplan's (1964) commitment to a context-bound understanding of behavior.

> We have come to realize that the disorder of the individual patient must usually be regarded as a presenting manifestation of a maladjustment in the social system of which he (sic) is a part and that its causes and expectable progress cannot be properly understood without a first-hand appraisal of the other elements of the

system. Our diagnostic focus must often be enlarged, therefore, to include the patient's family and the social institutions in which he is involved. (p. 92).

This ecological perspective cuts across a variety of levels of analysis, from comments on how population movement and urbanization place new stresses on families to mother–child interactions (Caplan, 1989): "We can no longer think without discomfort of isolating the mother-child relationship in a static way as we did then (in 1949)" (p. 55). Furthermore,

> We cannot expect to make lists of those signs and symptoms which occur univer-sally in children as the early manifestation of certain mental disturbances; any particular item of disturbed behavior will have a different meaning from one child to the next, and must be understood not in relation to a circumscribed disease process but in relation to the adaptive responses of a particular individual person in a particular situation. (p. 67)

New Paradigms Require New Professional Roles Paradigm shifts in ways of thinking are accompanied by the creation of new and distinct profes-sional roles. Caplan (1964) has emphasized, on many occasions, the importance of developing a clear and coherent professional role to carry out the work of the population-oriented psychiatrist:

> A fundamental issue which must be dealt with by all clinicians when they leave the confines of their offices, clinics, and hospitals and move into the community is the change in professional role which this entails and the consequent change in their style of thinking and behavior. . . . The challenge for the clinician is to retain his (sic) professional objectivity, self-awareness, self-control, and sensitivity to the nu-ances of personal interaction and, at the same time, to give up the relative aloofness and superiority of the physician role and replace it by the egalitarian role of the consultant or by the subordinate role of the community servant. The other challenge of community functioning is that the psychiatrist must move freely in an unstruc-tured situation which is usually not under his own control, instead of operating in a structured situation which he controls and with patients who usually "know their place" (p. 275)

Caplan (1964, 1989) has envisioned a multiplicity of potential roles for the population-oriented psychiatrist, including consulting to policymakers, collabo-ration with other professionals to stimulate their proactive efforts, and collabo-rating with community planners. As always, these efforts are surrounded by a contextual analysis of appropriate role-related behavior.

> An effective local service for the prevention and control of mental disorder must be integrated with community life. Its workers must be able to build up relationships with the key authority and influence figures of the community and also with the care-giving professionals. This is likely only if the majority of these people are in

favor of the type of service that is being offered and preferably if they have had a hand in molding the pattern to fit their own needs and to avoid infringement on their vested interests. (Caplan, 1964, pp. 135–136).

Although this approach may seem more evolutionary than revolutionary, more oriented to status quo politics and vested interests than to empowering the disenfranchised, Caplan (1989) also discussed the value of collaborating with those members of the legal professions who served advocate roles for the disenfranchised:

> To a population-oriented psychiatrist, the legal profession provides personal advocates to help individuals confront the establishment, and to amplify the voice of dissent, which, emerging as it often does from the weak and disregarded, may otherwise go unheard in the halls and offices of high-status planners and administrators. (p. 53).

Collaboration as a Value Within Caplan's writings, the relationship of the professional to the community is one of respect, involvement, ongoing commitment, and, quintessentially, collaboration. The commitment to collaboration derived, in part, from a belief that a population-oriented problem-solving approach needed to draw on the distinctive contributions of many different types of professionals in many different community systems. "Professionals . . . must be trained to recognize that theirs is only one of a variety of possible approaches" (Caplan, 1974, p. 255). Only through collaboration could optimal resources be brought to bear on the varied issues facing the community.

Collaboration also provided access to learning about how the community functioned, not only in terms of its formal resources, but its indigenous culture. When designing preventive interventions, knowledge and understanding of the potential differences between profession and local knowledge was recognized as important for the population-oriented professional. For example, natural or spontaneous support systems are important to understand, "because support systems are not a professional modality and they differ in essential aspects of their operation from the helping process that we are used to seeing when a caregiving professional deals individually or in a group with lay clients" (Caplan, 1974, p. 8).

Collaboration was seen as necessary to mobilize relevant resources and gather local knowledge; it was also critical in understanding other areas of scholarly inquiry relevant to community dynamics and change. "We will be helped (in understanding the relationship between the individual and the larger social context) if we maintain active collaboration with social scientists, planners, and other specialists in social policy development . . . ." (Caplan, 1964, p. 268). Yet Caplan (1964) was careful not to advocate spreading oneself too thin:

However much we widen our focus, we retain the sick individual as our primary frame of reference; the questions we ask, whether in research or practice, deal with issues that relate directly to him (sic). If we were to make too sudden a jump into social science, we might lose interest in such questions. (p. 268)

Summary

Caplan's community vision, largely articulated in his 1964 book *Principles of Preventive Psychiatry*, predated the nominal origin of organized community psychology at the Swampscott conference the following year. The paradigmatic thrust of his work, however, was reflected closely in the themes of the Swampscott conference. The contextual understanding of populations and individuals in context, the importance of creating new professional roles with respect to the client, and the emphasis on commitment to the community of interest all resonated with the social values of those shaping the emerging field of community psychology.

To be sure, the early history of community psychology adopted a somewhat more populist stance on certain values than did Caplan: the explicit commitment to underserved populations, the value of citizens' empowerment in interactions with professionals, the emphasis on the positive value of cultural pluralism, and the promotion of a wider range of potential advocacy and policy roles for mental health professionals. The initial energy of the field was fueled by a stronger explicit social critique than is evident in Caplan's writings. Still, there were broad areas of common cause. For example, Caplan's plea to involve citizens in defining appropriate services was consistent with the emerging empowerment ideology of the community psychology field.

Before commenting on Caplan's overall contribution to community psychology, and what the field can still learn and build on from his work, it is useful to briefly mention some of the more discrete areas of work that Caplan embedded in his community vision. These areas have made, are making, and will continue to make contributions to community psychology in the years ahead.

Specific Components of the Community Vision: Prevention, Crisis Theory, Mental Health Consultation, and Support Systems

Since its inception in 1965, community psychology has drawn from four primary areas of Caplan's writings: prevention, crisis intervention, mental health consultation, and the role of support systems in promoting adaptive responses to stress. In Caplan's writings, these areas are portrayed as additive and emerging aspects of a population-oriented approach to mental health. Although these concepts and their elaboration represented the work of many psychiatrists and psychologists during their formative years (e.g., Albee, 1959; Cassel, 1974; Klein & Lindemann, 1961; Ojemann, 1961; Silverman, 1969), Caplan deserves undeniable credit for providing integrative heuristics and case examples for the field of community psychology. In each of the areas of work, his writings were among the first to clarify the concepts and provide a framework for further elaboration and, of course, critique.

Prevention   Although the concept of prevention in mental health had been advocated previously by Adolf Meyer (see Rappaport, 1977) and, with respect to crisis theory, by Erich Lindemann (Klein & Lindemann, 1961), Caplan's *Principles of Preventive Psychiatry* (1964) is credited aptly with providing mental health professionals with a public health-oriented taxonomy for varied new approaches to dealing with the resource crisis earlier articulated by Albee (1959). Not only have books in community psychology focused on prevention (e.g., Felner, Jason, Moritsugu, & Farber, 1983), but a recent annotated bibliography on work in primary prevention cites over 1,300 articles in the last 8 years in many fields of mental health scholarship and practice (Trickett, Dahiyat, & Selby, in press). The concepts of primary, secondary, and tertiary prevention clearly continue to serve an organizing function in the prevention field.

In adopting this taxonomy, community psychology has tended to focus on primary prevention over secondary and tertiary. Further, it has contrasted prevention with empowerment as a guiding metaphor for the field (Rappaport, 1981). One reason for the emergence of the empowerment concept has been the concern that the imagery of prevention still implies an expert-client relationship rather than the collaborative role advocated by Caplan. Within Caplan's community vision, collaboration with other professionals and, indeed, citizens was not contrasted with a population-oriented preventive stance, but was seen as an integrative aspect of it.

Thus, the preventive emphasis in mental health has remained central in community psychology, although the field has expanded its focus of both professional roles and intervention strategies over those discussed by Caplan. This expanded definition is found in the recent change in the name of Division 27 of the American Psychological Association from the Division of Community Psychology to the Society for Community Research and Action.

Crisis Theory   Caplan's early books (1961, 1964) closely linked the concept of prevention with the onset of crisis. Crises were seen as times of disequilibrium, during which maximum impact of both professionals and naturally occurring support networks could be expected. The notion that crisis represents opportunity is embedded firmly in the paradigms of community psychology (e.g., Danish & D'Augelli, 1980; Slaikeu, 1984). Delineating these times has provided community psychologists with many different approaches to primary prevention, including the transitions of school children from one school to the next (e.g., Felner, Farber, & Primavera, 1983), bereavement following the death of a spouse (Silverman, 1969), and community reactions to terrorist attacks (Klingman & Ben Eli, 1981). Although the focus has broadened from crises to transitions, which have enduring sequelae over a period of time (e.g., divorce not as an event but as an initiator of multiple events or crises occurring at different points in time), crises represent one salient emphasis for preventive activities in community psychology.

Importantly, in terms of influence, many of the topics presented in Caplan's *Prevention of Mental Disorders in Children* (1961) and *Principles of Preventive Psychiatry* (1964) have been pursued in subsequent years by community psychologists. For example, Ojemann's (1961) paper in the volume on the training of "causal thinking" in children and the development of a training program for teachers to instill such thinking provides the early basis for the immensely popular social problem-solving approach to competency development (Spivack & Shure, 1974). As Caplan (1964) wrote, "Resistance to mental disorder can be increased by helping the individual extend his (sic) repertoire of effective problem-solving skills, so that he will not need to use the regressive, non-reality based, or socially unacceptable ways of dealing with predicaments" (p. 37). In like manner, Brim's (1961) chapter on "Methods of Educating Parents and Their Evaluation" provided early guidance for many of the later early childhood intervention programs for parents. Caplan's (1961) concluding chapter likewise foreshadowed many topics later addressed in prevention research and intervention, such as the programmatic implications of the distinction between disease prevention and health promotion.

Mental Health Consultation   As Mannino and Shore (1986) have pointed out, consultation as a professional role for mental health professionals had been sporadically practiced since Witmer's psychological clinic, which started in 1896. Indeed, the resurgence of consultation in the 1960s produced increasingly sophisticated accounts of this activity (e.g., Newman, 1967; Sarason, Levine, Goldenberg, Cherlin, & Bennett, 1966). However, Caplan's *The Theory and Practice of Mental Health Consultation* (1970) created a defining moment with respect to this professional role. The elaboration of the role's defining characteristics, its limits, and the description of the now well-known four types of consultation provided a perspective for reflection and critique that had not been available before.

Community psychologists were attracted to consultation as a means for radiating change (e.g., Kelly, 1970). As Caplan (1970) wrote, "Consultation provides an opportunity for a relatively small number of consultants to exert a widespread effect through the intermediation of a large group of consultees, each of whom is in contact with many clients" (p. 21). The potential for systemic impact was energizing, and a large literature across many disciplines was generated in the 1970s and early 1980s (see Grady, Gibson, & Trickett, 1981; Kidder, Tinker, Mannino, & Trickett, 1986). Among its most sobering lessons was the difficulty of demonstrating the radiating effect of consultation (see

Mannino & Shore, 1975, 1979; Medway & Updyke, 1985). Although the process clearly affected consultees, change in the clients of the consultees was more slippery to document.

What remains intriguing in Caplan's consultation model for community psychology is the manner in which consultation fits into an overall plan for population-oriented interventions. Consultation should be embedded in an

> [O]verall mission of promoting the mental health of the population and reducing the rates of community disorder. A mental health consultant in this setting is not an independent practitioner who responds to ad hoc invitations by other professionals to help them by using the skills he happens to possess. (Caplan, 1970, p. 35)

Rather, consultation represents one of several potential additive strategies for aiding a community.

Within several areas of professional psychology, such as school, counseling, and organizational psychology, consultation developed into and remains a major role function. Within community psychology, however, after an initial outburst of enthusiasm (e.g., Mannino et al., 1986; O'Neill & Trickett, 1983), consultation has waned as a specific role for radiating change. The most interesting work reflecting Caplan's population-oriented approach is perhaps Kelly and Hess' (1986) book entitled *The Ecology of Prevention: Illustrating Mental Health Consultation*. Here, several case studies of consultation in contrasting ecological settings are used to demonstrate how the consultative role must be defined differently in different ecologies. Further, the potential of the role for creating population-oriented, additive interventions is highlighted. Just as Caplan has cited the influence of Lindemann on his approach to consultation, so have Kelly and Hess (1986) acknowledged Lindemann and Caplan as mentors.

Social Support Systems It is useful to recall that the title of Caplan's (1974) book on this topic is *Support Systems and Community Mental Health*. This title emphasizes the role of naturally occurring and professionally developed support efforts in the context of a larger population-oriented enterprise. Further, his chapter "The Contribution of the School to Personality Development" serves as a reminder that support systems transcend the concept of "personal community," which currently predominates in the community psychology literature and includes organized settings of socialization or remediation. His final chapter "Conceptual Models in Community Mental Health" underscores the notion that in providing preventive services to a population, a variety of approaches is useful.

One of the striking aspects of Caplan's (1974) support systems book is the degree to which it foreshadows research initiatives still current in community psychology. The important role of self-help groups and religious organizations as structures of support is discussed, as is the potential role of "generalists," such as bartenders and hairdressers, who "are likely to be people who are widely recognized in their neighborhood to have wisdom in matters of human relations or to be knowledgeable about the community caregiving system'' (p. 12). Caplan (1974), like many community psychologists, asserted that fostering support systems should be a central role for the mental health professional committed to prevention of pathology and promotion of health in a population.

Within community psychology, the topic of social networks and social support has become central. Indeed, the field's primary journal, the *American Journal of Community Psychology*, is sometimes referred to informally as the *American Journal of Social Support*. As a stimulator of ideas about the role of social support, Caplan has been a critical resource. Unlike most writing in the social support field, he has carefully linked the role of consultant to the enhancement or development of support systems. His attention to this process is consistent with his belief that professionally initiated programs should be incorporated in the host environment after they have been initiated (see Caplan, 1974, Ch. 1).

Caplan and the Unfinished Business of Community Psychology

In enumerating the various substantive areas of Caplan's contribution to community psychology, it seems readily apparent that his influence has cut across several bedrock areas of the field. Preventive interventions, particularly those focusing on responses to crises and the development of social support, build on his early writings, although a much more solid empirical base now forms the specific foundations of this work than was available when Caplan first discussed these topics. Mental health consultation as a preventive intervention has been less fully developed and has proved to be elusive as a means of radiating change. The dimensions of crises form the conceptual base for many ongoing preventive interventions. Thus, Caplan's work has had an important heuristic impact on the field, with some areas more influential than others over time.

Yet, as time has passed, many of the topics that Caplan discussed as part of an integrated program of population-oriented intervention have been atomized by the research and intervention processes of the community psychology field. Specialization and fragmentation are likely to dominate over integration and synthesis. Caplan, for example, remained steadfast in linking the content of social support interventions to the process of generating community data and creating collaborative relationships with relevant community caregivers. Process was linked with content, and individual interventions were to be integrated into larger community efforts. Most social support interventions reported in the community psychology literature do not clearly integrate the process of developing the actual support program with its content, nor is consideration generally given to how any discrete support intervention can contribute to the well-being of the larger population.

Similar comments can be made about the ways in which mental health consultation research and practice has evolved. Caplan's initial conception of consultation was as one aspect of an additive intervention program for a population. Understanding the nature of the community and its caregivers was a prerequisite for an informed choice about consultation strategy. However, mental health consultation research and practice has tended to focus on techniques more than how context affects the selection or usefulness of techniques. Further, consultation is seldom portrayed as one step in a larger plan for the improvement of the well-being of a population (see Mannino et al., 1986).

The most important aspect of Caplan's work for the future of community psychology involves not only the elaboration of specific preventive interventions or consultations; it also focuses on how an understanding of the needs of a population provides the basis for generating multiple and additive community-appropriate preventive interventions. This approach can be achieved only when a priority is placed on understanding the community context, and when the mental health professional is committed to the long haul in that community. This perspective highlights the *community* in community psychology, and is Caplan's most enduring conceptual gift to the field. His community vision, not his specific areas of interest, represents his contribution to community psychology's unfinished business.

REFERENCES

Albee, G. W. (1959). *Mental health manpower trends*. New York: Basic Books.

Bennett, C. C., Anderson, L. S., Cooper, S., Hassol, L., Klein, D. C., and Rosenblum, G. (Eds.). (1966). *Community psychology: A report of the Boston conference on the education of psychologists for community mental health*. Boston: Boston University Press.

Brim, O. G., Jr. (1961). Methods of educating parents and their evaluation. In G. Caplan (Ed.), *Prevention of mental disorders in children* (pp. 122–141). New York: Basic Books.

Caplan, G. (Ed.) (1961). *Prevention of mental disorders in children*. New York: Basic Books.

Caplan, G. (1964). *Principles of preventive psychiatry*. New York: Basic Books.

Caplan, G. (1970). *The theory and practice of mental health consultation*. New York: Basic Books.

Caplan, G. (1974). *Support systems and community mental health*. New York: Behavioral Publications.

Caplan, G. (1989). *Population-oriented psychiatry*. New York: Human Sciences Press.

Cassel, J. C. (1974). Psychiatric epidimiology. In G. Caplan (Ed.), *American handbook of psychiatry, Vol. II* (pp. 401–411). New York: Basic Books.

Danish, S., & D'Augelli, A. (1980). Promoting competence and enhancing development through life development intervention. In L. A. Bond & J. C. Rosen (Eds.), *Competence and coping during adulthood*. Hanover, NH: University Press of New England.

Felner, R., Farber, S., and Primavera, J. (1983). Transitions and stressful life events: A model for primary prevention. In R. D. Felner, L. A. Jason, J. N. Moritsugu, and S. Farber (Eds.), *Preventive psychology: Theory, research, and prevention* (pp. 191–215). New York: Pergamon.

Felner, R., Jason, L., Moritsugu, J., & Farber, S. (1983). *Preventive psychology: Theory, research, and prevention*. New York: Pergamon.

Grady, M. A., Gibson, M. S., & Trickett, E. J. (1981). *Mental health consultation theory, practice, and research 1973–1978: An annotated reference guide* (DHHS Publication No. ADM 81-948). Washington, DC: U.S. Government Printing Office.

Kelly, J. G. (1970). The quest for valid preventive interventions. In J. Carter (Ed.), *Current topics in clinical and community psychology*. New York: Academic Press.

Kelly, J. G., & Hess, R. E. (Eds.). (1986). *The ecology of prevention: Illustrating mental health consultation*. New York: Haworth Press.

Kidder, M. G., Tinker, M. B., Mannino, F. V., & Trickett, E. J. (1986). An annotated reference guide to the consultation literature: 1978–1984. In F. V. Mannino, E. J. Trickett, M. Shore, M. C. Kidder, & G. Levin (Eds.), *Handbook of mental health consultation* (DHHS Publication No. ADM 86-1446) (pp. 523–796). Washington, DC: U.S. Government Printing Office.

Klein, D. C., & Lindemann, E. (1961). Preventive intervention in individual and family crisis situations. In G. Caplan (Ed.), Prevention of mental disorders in children (pp. 283–306). New York: Basic Books.

Klingman, A., & Ben Eli, Z. (1981). A school community in disaster: Primary and secondary prevention in situational crisis. *Professional Psychology, 12*, 523–533.

Mannino, F. V., & Shore, M. F. (1975). The effects of consultation: A review of empirical studies. *American Journal of Community Psychology, 3*, 1–21.

Mannino, F. V., & Shore, M. F. (1979). Evaluation of consultation: Problems and prospects. In A. S. Rogawski (Ed.), *Mental health consultation in community settings: New directions for mental health services*. San Francisco: Jossey-Bass.

Mannino, F. V., & Shore, M. (1986). History and development of mental health consultation. In F. V. Mannino, E. J. Trickett, M. Shore, M. G. Kidder, and G. Levin (Eds.), *Handbook of mental health consultation*, DHHS Publication No. ADM 86-1446, pp. 3–28). Washington DC: U.S. Government Printing Office.

Mannino, F. V., Trickett, E. J., Shore, M., Kidder, M. G., & Levin, G. (1986). *Handbook of mental health consultation* (DHHS Publication No. ADM 86-1446). Washington, DC: U.S. Government Printing Office.

Medway, F., & Updyke, J. (1985). Meta-analysis of consultation outcome studies. *American Journal of Community Psychology, 13*, 489–506.

Newman, R. (1967). *Psychological consultation in the schools*. New York: Basic Books.

Ojemann, R. H. (1961). Investigating the effects of teaching an understanding and appreciation of behavior dynamics. In G. Caplan (Ed.), *Prevention of mental disorders in children* (pp. 378–397). New York: Basic Books.

O'Neill, P., & Trickett, E. J. (1983). *Community consultation*. San Francisco: Jossey-Bass.

Rappaport, J. (1977). *Community psychology: Values, research, and action*. New York: Holt, Rinehart and Winston.

Rappaport, J. (1981). In praise of paradox: A social policy of empowerment over pre-vention. *American Journal of Community Psychology, 9*, 1–26.

Sarason, S. B., Levine, M., Goldenberg, I. I., Cherlin, D. L., & Bennett, E. M. (1966). *Psychology in community settings: Clinical educational, vocational, social aspects*. New York: Wiley.

Silverman, P. (1969). The widow to widow program: An experiment in preventive intervention. *Mental Hygiene, 53*, 333–337.

Slaikeu, K. (1984). *Crisis intervention: A handbook for practice and research*. Boston: Allyn and Bacon.

Spivack, G., & Shure, M. (1974). *Social adjustment of young children*. San Francisco: Jossey-Bass.

Trickett, E. J., Dahiyat, C., & Selby, P. (in press). *Primary prevention in mental health 1983–1991: An annotated bibliography*. Washington, DC: U.S. Government Print-ing Office.

Chapter 10

Caplan's Ideas and the Future of Psychology in the Schools

Jane Close Conoley and Carolyn Wright
University of Nebraska-Lincoln

INTRODUCTION

Schools offer organized settings of well-trained professionals who accept the responsibility of providing services to children and youth. Although educators are competent in various content areas, their training may be deficient in the mental health and related behavioral concerns of children and youth. Teachers, administrators, and other personnel are an attractive audience for the implementation of school consultation programs aimed at increasing the academic, behavioral, and emotional adjustment of children. It is within the context of American public education that Caplan's (1970) pioneering work in mental health consultation may have received its most extensive research and practice attention.

No serious student of consultation in the schools would argue that the model espoused by Caplan (1970) has been incorporated wholesale into the basic regularities of school life, but most would point out undeniable evidence that aspects of Caplanian thinking are pervasive in the training and practice of many school professionals, especially school psychologists. Meyers, Brent, Faherty, and Modafferi, in Chapter 6 of this volume, summarize Caplan's particu-

177

lar contribution to the practice of school-based consultation. They note how often his writing; his model of primary, secondary, and tertiary prevention; and his conceptualization of consultee-centered consultation, with accompanying attention to relationship issues, have been cited by school researchers. In addition, in Chapter 7 Knoff and Batsche provide a comprehensive description of how Caplan's notions of prevention and social support, as well as consultation, may be implemented in an elementary school setting.

To set the stage for a discussion of future directions, a brief overview of mental health consultation is presented below, with special emphasis on the practical implications of Caplan's theory building and research on school-based practice (Conoley & Conoley, 1992). The relationship of mental health consultation to entry issues, choices of targets, particular strategies, and evaluation concerns is highlighted.

MENTAL HEALTH CONSULTATION

Caplan's model of mental health consultation is the prototypic consultation approach. It has the longest history and is based on the most traditional psychological understandings of human behavior. In 1970, mental health consultation was a revolutionary step away from classical Freudian or psychodynamic psychology. Caplan (1970) proposed that caregiver consultees' (e.g., teachers, nurses, probation officers, ministers) job effectiveness could be enhanced through a coordinate process of case discussion and problem solving with a consultant. He also suggested that consultants pay close attention to the organizational realities of their consultation settings and concentrate on the relationships among people rather than on the intrapsychic difficulties that might be uncovered.

Caplan (1970) conceptualized caregivers' difficulties as stemming from lack of skills, knowledge, self-esteem, or professional objectivity. Although Caplan was a revolutionary in the 1960s and 1970s, he was and still is somewhat dynamically oriented. In 1970, he hypothesized and presented supportive evaluative evidence that most consultees had work difficulties due to problems in professional objectivity. He asserted that such difficulties must be handled through delicate and covert verbal strategies.

Subsequent research has cast doubt on Caplan's insistence on indirect strategies (Meyers, 1975; Meyers, Freidman, & Gaughan, 1975; Meyers, Parsons, & Martin, 1979) and his predictions of the primary source of consultee difficulties (Gutkin, 1981). However, in consultation, as in any other endeavor, people tend to find that for which they are looking (Salmon & Lehrer, 1989). For example, the belief of Meyers et al. (1975, 1979) in teachers' emotional strength led them to see direct confrontation as appropriate. Gutkin's (1981) student consultants, trained in behavioral consultation, were likely to see consultees' lack of overt skills and behaviors, whereas Caplan's (1970) psychiatrists tended to emphasize unconscious dynamics in their case reports. In Chapter 3 of this volume, Caplan suggests a modification in his historical emphasis on lack of objectivity as the preeminent consultee problem. He, like Gutkin's (1981) consultants, suggests that a lack of skills and knowledge should be carefully acknowledged before lack of objectivity is hypothesized.

Because Caplan (1970) considered losses in professional objectivity to be the most common causes of consultee difficulty, his most important mental health consultation intervention was aimed at reducing just that problem. *Theme interference* was the term he used to describe consultees' unconscious link with a particular case. This link or irrational connection is seen by Caplan as causing unusual ineffectiveness in the consultee's professional functioning. Theme-interference reduction is the major strategy to help consultees break loose of constricting thoughts or feelings about a particular client or issue.

Entry Issues

A major contribution of Caplan's perspective is the recognition that not all consultee behavior is rationally or consciously motivated. Consultees become overly identified with their constituencies (e.g., children, principals, colleagues, work problems, parents), they become angry while denying anger as a possibility, and, at times, they need emotional support as much, or more, than they need answers.

Introducing mental health consultation to a school may be difficult. The techniques used by the consultant may seem rather vague to an administrator (indirect confrontation, support, theme-interference reduction), the timeframes associated with noticeable improvement in consultee or client performance are impossible to specify, and explaining mental health consultation to teachers can be problematic. Sarason's (Sarason, Levine, Goldenberg, Cherlin, & Bennett, 1966) entry speech is still quite applicable to these entry concerns:

> When we say we want to be helpful in . . . the school, we mean that in addition to talking with the teacher about a child, *we have to be able to observe that child in the context of the classroom in which the problem manifests itself.* For help to be meaningful and practical it must be based on what actually goes on in the classroom setting. . . . We do not view ourselves in the schools as people to whom questions are directed and from whom answers will be forthcoming. . . . We have no easy answers, but we have a way of functioning that involves us in a relationship with the teacher and the classroom and that together we can come up with concrete ideas and plans that we feel will be helpful to a particular child. . . . I hope I have made clear that when we say we want to help it means that we want to talk to the teacher, observe in the classroom, talk again to the teacher, and together come up with a plan of action that with persistence, patience, and consistency gives promise of bringing about change. It is not a quick process and it is certainly not an easy one. (pp. 58–62)

School administrators often understand that some of their staff's problems with children and youth are due to staff difficulties. For example, teachers may lack knowledge of particular teaching strategies. Administrators may be befuddled, however, by the suggestion that a relationship process like consultation is necessary to improve teachers' skills. They are more likely to believe that inservice training, supervision, and more effort on the part of the teachers are the predictors of improvement.

Most consultees accept that they make some contribution to the failures they experience in their professional functioning, but admitting such contributions is very threatening (Friend, 1984, 1985). Therefore, they must have consultation explained to them in such a way that the threat of having another adult involved with them in their difficulties is reduced.

> I cannot state too strongly that we are not coming into the schools with the intent of criticizing or passing judgment on anyone. We are nobody's private FBI or counter-intelligence service. We are not the agent of the principal or some other administrative office. (Sarason et al., 1966, p. 61)

Targets

Although mental health consultants have diverse goals, they primarily work to improve client gains. To accomplish such an improvement, however, mental health consultants most often work solely with the consultees (e.g., teachers, therapists, ministers). Given the assumption that at least some of a student's difficulties are exacerbated by teachers' characteristics (or characteristics of other significant relationships), consultants target working with teachers and other educators. Their direct work with students is done only to model more appropriate styles or strategies, or to accomplish some diagnostic procedures. This caregiver-focused service is clearly the most reasonable approach (see Conoley & Gutkin, 1986; Gutkin & Conoley, 1990), but it creates difficulties with consultees who would like consultants to take clients away, fix them, and then (and only then) send them back.

Consultants can choose among four variants of mental health consultation (i.e., client-centered, consultee-centered, program, and administrative consultation). Further, consultants must decide if the program or administrative work will be mainly client- or consultee-centered. These distinctions refer to goals and major targets for change. Client-centered approaches are used when a consultee lacks (mainly) information. The focus is on the case as defined by the consultee and consultant. However, in the consultee-centered approaches the consultant determines that consultee skills, objectivity, or self-esteem are interfering with work performance, and so emphasizes working with the consultee. The case, administrative issue, or program is used merely as a vehicle to assist the consultee.

The consultant must retain the flexibility of moving among the four types of mental health consultation as the situation demands. However, this presupposes that the consultant is constantly conceptualizing and testing hypotheses about the sources of the problem between the teacher and the student.

Strategies

The key strategies used by mental health consultants include sophisticated diagnostic formulations, theme-interference reduction, relationship building, and "one-downsmanship." Because mental health consultants view their consultees' emotional lives as crucial in explaining the consultee's work effectiveness, consultants must be very talented in discerning what is blocking the consultee's problem-solving skills. Is it simply a lack of knowledge or skills? If this is the case, the consultant can supply information or model skills, but must do so while maintaining the coordinate, nonhierarchical relationship. Is the problem due to poor confidence or self-esteem? If so, the accepting, egalitarian relationship offered to the consultee will improve the situation.

Are the problems due to theme interference? A theme is an unconscious formulation by the consultee that inhibits problem solving. For example, a teacher who is having serious trouble disciplining his or her adolescent daughter may experience difficulty in managing a student who resembles the daughter. The teacher may be unaware of the connection, or aware but unable to change the situation. The consultant can show respect for the consultee's ideas and opinions, thus increasing the consultee's self-confidence. In addition, the consultant can point out all the other young female students being taught successfully by the teacher, thus disputing the teacher's unconscious belief that he or she is bound to fail with hard-to-manage girls. Finally, the consultant can share incidents with the teacher (stories or parables) that illustrate other teachers gaining control over difficult situations, doing well at work despite stressful home environments, overcoming certain behavioral "blocks," and so on.

Parables were seen by Caplan (1970) as a way to tell consultees very important information without directly confronting them about their own behaviors. Direct confrontation was deemed unacceptable by Caplan because such confrontation might arouse unconscious material that would then require therapeutic support.

Evaluation Issues

Mental health consultation is successful when teachers seek out the consultant for information and support, feel more self-confident and skillful in their work, and use problem-solving approaches with new problems. Students' situations also should improve from the work of a mental health consultant. Child and adolescent change may come a while after teacher change, however, so early evaluation strategies may focus on consultee attitudes and behaviors more than on clients (see Fuchs & Fuchs, 1989, for an analogous situation using behavioral consultation). After a consultant has worked in an organization for 2 or 3 years, client-focused evaluation is an important priority.

CURRENT AND FUTURE CHALLENGES

In Chapter 2 of this volume, Caplan reiterates his belief in the basic concepts explicated in 1970, and describes his thinking regarding prevention, population-oriented psychiatry, and mutual support groups (1974, 1989; Caplan & Killilea, 1976). It is interesting that these developments in Caplan's thinking are related to current challenges and attempted solutions in public schools.

For example, increasing attention is being paid to the problem of establishing supportive linkages between homes and schools (Christenson & Cleary, 1990; Fine, 1990; Sheridan, 1989; Sheridan & Elliott, 1991; Sheridan, Kratochwill, & Elliott, 1990), using consultation principles as a model. These particular attempts have elements of both sophisticated population approaches (e.g., interventions aimed at parents of troubled children within a particular school area) and social support groups (e.g., parent groups related to single parenting).

Within the school, intervention assistance teams and notions of collaborative professional development are appearing to maximize the help that educational professionals can offer to each other in small, problem-solving groups and/or as members of transformed organizations (Gelzheiser & Meyers, in press; Gelzheiser, Meyers, & Pruzek, 1990; Glatthorn, 1990; Graden, Casey, & Bonstrom, 1985b; Graden, Casey, & Christenson, 1985a; Graden, Zins, & Curtis, 1988; Meyers, Gelzheiser, & Yelich, 1990; Rappaport, 1981; Villa, Thousand, Paolucci-Whitcomb, & Nevin, 1990; Witt & Martens, 1988; Zins & Ponti, 1990).

The array of developments alluded to in the previous two paragraphs gives a glimpse of the enduring impact that Caplan continues to have in the conceptualization of strategies to improve the experience of clients and consultees in school organizations. It is clear that many treatment and preventive opportunities exist in the implementation of Caplan's concepts.

Psychology in the Schools

The body of Caplan's work is particularly relevant to the future of psychology in the schools. Faced with increasing challenges ranging from students entering school without the necessary academic and behavioral readiness (Gettinger, 1987) to serious violence in school buildings (Goldstein, Apter, & Harootunian, 1984), educators and psychologists must turn away from individualistic notions that rely on treatment or remediation only. Further, they must conceptualize ways of increasing the resources made available to children in an era of shrinking public financial and moral support.

Caplan's (1970) description of mental health consultation requires some updates (e.g., sexist attributions, fuller explication of strategies to meet consultee lack of knowledge and skills), but his subsequent approaches to link important groups in providing and supporting prevention and treatment are critically important to the future of psychology in the schools (Caplan, 1989; Caplan & Killilea, 1976).

Clearly, a new kind of psychology in the schools is called for when prevention and resource linking are the important school system goals. Cowen et al. (1975) have called for a "quarterback"—a psychologist who manages people and programs that anticipate and meet the needs of children. This psychologist is an expert about children: who they are, where they live, what they need, and what can go wrong. He or she is a family and school systems expert, because to not know families and schools is to not know children. In line with this notion, Caplan has called for an understanding of systems before attempting intervention. Current conditions require a knowledge of how to intervene at system levels (Henning-Stout & Conoley, 1988; Norris, Burke, & Speer, 1990) across many problem areas facing children, staff, and families.

The quarterback psychologist can assist all facets of the system to work in concert. Comer and his colleagues (1980, 1984, 1987; Comer & Haynes, 1991; Haynes, Comer, & Hamilton-Lee, 1988, 1989) used teams of teachers, administrators, parents, social services, and mental health workers to affect school reform. Only when all groups were engaged in promoting positive school experiences did the system begin to change. Comer and his associates' work is an interesting parallel to Caplan's notions of prevention, consultation, social support, and collaboration.

Psychologists who would practice this future brand of intervention would require flexibility in actual roles and functions, and in operational levels. The schools must have clinicians who can work from micro- to macro-systems levels, piecing together comprehensive, coordinated service packages for children and families. Psychologists must be important members of many teams and plan interventions for children based on children's particular needs and their special potentials. Children identified as vulnerable or at risk in the school environment absorb a good portion of psychologists' time, but the future of psychology in the schools depends on the development of prevention and enhancement programs for all children, their teachers, and their parents.

A comprehensive school psychology informed by Caplanian ideas would involve the deployment of enough psychologists to keep ahead of the unrelenting press of clinical cases. However, some service providers must be assigned to find out how to stop the casualties, rather than waiting for the next victim to be identified or crisis situation to explode.

The impact of a Caplanian school psychology would likely be profound, indeed, on the activities and priorities of the school psychologist. Traditional norm-referenced testing would become an optional and perhaps infrequently seen activity. Children would be known by their strengths and weaknesses, not by shorthand descriptions of their problems. Psychologists' recommendations would be tied to the daily behavior of teachers and parents, and would be based on well-tested cognitive-behavioral principles.

Psychologists also would become far more active in teacher and parent consultation. Overall, Stallings (1975) reported that about 40% of children's achievement can be accounted for by classroom instructional procedures (and 30% by their entry abilities). If 40% of children's achievement is explained by teacher instructional behavior, then teachers and psychologists belong together to produce optimal instructional environments for children (Ysseldyke & Christenson, 1986). If another 30% of children's achievement is explained by entry skills, then parents are prime targets for intervention as well (Conoley, 1987; Hansen, 1986).

A Caplanian Research Perspective for the Schools

A broadened focus, from children alone to the significant others who surround them, is particularly important if Caplan's legacy is to be developed in the schools. Children are undoubtedly active agents in creating their environments, but they are also vulnerable to the influence of other people and their physical, social, and emotional contexts.

Detailed analyses of causes of dysfunction and health reveal a complex, multivariable situation, which suggests a need for prevention and treatment programs that target children, their caregivers, and their environments. Cowen's (1984) call for the construction of a generative base (i.e., identification of the causal links involved in specific disorders, early manifestations of the disorder, and potentially helpful intervention approaches) prior to prevention efforts is a necessary precursor to deciding intervention targets and timetables. Experience has shown prevention efforts must be built on solid research bases concerning specific causal links related to specific behaviors to be prevented. Common sense notions about what people need to be invulnerable to mental health problems have not always proved true. For example, the idea that people act rationally (i.e., if given correct information they will make good decisions) has been a disappointingly incomplete understanding of human behavior (Chassin, Presson, & Sherman, 1985; Cowen, 1984).

By the 1970s, the importance of "lifestyle" on physical health was recognized widely (i.e., 7 out of 10 leading causes of death in the United States have critical behavioral determinants). The analogy to mental health, however, was not accepted widely (Goldston, 1986; Heffernan & Albee, 1985). The Vermont Conferences on Primary Prevention (Albee & Joffe, 1977; Bond & Rosen, 1980; Forgays, 1978; Kent & Rolf, 1979) have provided consistent prods to mental health agencies and researchers to include preventive initiatives in their agendas. Although important and supportive research has been accomplished in many fields (e.g., competence and competency building, learned helplessness, maternal self-concept and perception of the newborn, the preventive potential of mutual-help groups, environmental influences on behavior, marital disruption as a psychopathological stress, community dysfunctions or disintegration as factors in mental disorder, promotion of self-esteem, and the measurement and assessment of the effects of critical life events and life transitions), a coordinated policy to both study and implement preventive interventions has been elusive (Goldston, 1986).

Caplan (1970, 1974, 1989) is not a sophisticated researcher by today's standards. However, the results of child-focused interventions done by other researchers clearly challenge school practitioners to continue refinement of techniques that are consistent with Caplanian thought. A meta-analysis of 40 strategies, which appear to be influenced by preventive and population-based thinking, indicates the approaches differ in their effectiveness (Baker, Swisher, Nadenichek, & Popowicz, 1984). The overall effect size of studies using cognitive coping skills as the intervention was only about .26 (a small effect, according to Cohen, 1969). In contrast, communication-skills training had an effect size of about 3.90 (.93 with outliers removed; a large effect). The overall effect size for primary prevention studies was about .55 (medium effect). This .55 effect size suggests that a person receiving certain preventive interventions, whose score on a variable was that of the mean of the control group, would improve on that variable .55 standard deviations above the mean. This would translate into a change from the 50th percentile on some hypothetical variable to the 73rd percentile.

Obviously, however, the improvements vary according to the type of intervention received. Career maturity enhancement, communication-skills training, deliberate psychological education programs, and a combination of deliberate psychological education and moral education programs show large effect sizes. Values clarification programs have medium effect sizes. Cognitive coping skills training programs, moral education programs (alone), substance abuse prevention programs, and programs blending values clarification with other strategies are viewed as showing low effect sizes (see Baker et al., 1984, for the list of studies and specific effect sizes).

This review is highlighted because of the obvious link between these kinds of intervention with children to Caplan's (1970) call for strategies that improve the success of clients in various organizations.

Implementation

Intervention programs that are conceptualized with consultation, prevention, and a population orientation in mind are targeted at groups that may or may not be known to be at risk for particular dysfunctions. The interventions have a before-the-fact quality (i.e., some of the programs are initiated before any problems are noted).

School psychological services must support programs aimed at both reducing the possibility of dysfunction and at enhancing the quality of life. For example, when considering the options for prevention with children, Rosenberg and Reppucci (1985) identified four ecological target levels with examples of known dysfunctional events. At the *individual* level, children are born with different temperaments, physical strengths, and vulnerabilities. These differences make children more or less likely to be well parented, easy to manage, and teachable. Children may suffer a history of abuse, parental rejection, or inappropriate expectations from their parents and teachers. At the *familial* level (or other small-group level), children may be a part of ineffective interactions among family members, conflictual spousal relationships, poorly managed classrooms, or emit behaviors that increase the probability of abuse from their parents. At the *community* level, children may experience isolation from helpful supports, family unemployment, and other examples of unmanageable stress. Finally, at the *societal* level, children are embedded in cultures that may sanction physical punishment in homes and schools, be unsupportive of education, or be uninvolved in facilitating family functioning.

These already well-known stresses can be chosen as intervention targets, as can activities that are competency enhancing or remedial. For example, teaching parenting skills and social problem solving, providing child development information, and training in coping strategies useful in reducing and managing stress, as well as in skills for finding employment, are additional possibilities for preventive or remedial programs, which involve the important systems that influence child adjustment.

Programs in schools that can benefit from consultation support are quite varied. They might be both child focused and more broadly ecologically based (Durlak, 1985). Examples of child-focused programs include affective education, social problem solving/coping skills, and prevention of academic problems (Baskin & Hess, 1980; Blechman, Kotanchick, & Taylor, 1981; Blechman, Taylor, & Schrader, 1981; Boike, 1986; Durlak, 1983; Hansford & Hattie, 1982; Jason, Durlak, & Holton-Walker, 1984; Medway & Smith, 1978; Rickel, Eshelman, & Loigman, 1983; Sharp, 1981).

Ecological interventions with children in schools include classroom organization, interdependent learning, peer tutoring, parent programs, teacher programs, and program implementation research. These last three areas are badly neglected in terms of research, whereas the first three seem neglected by practitioners (Allen, 1976; Gump, 1980; Harris & Sherman, 1973; Jason, Frasure, & Ferone, 1981; Stallings, 1975; Turk, Meeks, & Turk, 1982).

Ecological interventions appear very promising. For example, interventions involving interdependent learning or peer tutoring have been associated with improved attitudes toward school, better peer relations, and other social and academic gains for both tutors and their students (Hightower & Avery, 1986). Classroom structures have been described prescriptively with open classrooms facilitating the achievement of high-socioeconomic status and high-IQ students, while worsening the achievement of low-IQ students. Increased structure has been associated with gains in math and reading, whereas less structure has facilitated growth in independence, cooperation, initiation, and reduced absenteeism.

If Caplan's ideas were to permeate educational intervention, significantly more work would be done in the area of teacher and parent interventions (Durlak, 1985). There is increasing evidence that work with parents helps children adjust. In fact, some research suggests that direct work with parents may be more effective than direct interventions with maladapting children (Epstein, Wing, Koeske, Andrasik, & Ossip, 1981; Griest et al., 1982). It may be that working directly with teachers would be as fruitful in improving the coping abilities of children. Caplan's early focus on consultee-centered approaches, and more recent focus on collaboration, would certainly suggest that possibility.

An additional improvement that Caplanian thinking might evidence in school work would be an increased attention to implementation realities. It is disheartening to consider that carefully conceptualized intervention programs may never be correctly implemented at classroom or building levels. However, such may be the case, indicating a critical need to identify elements that affect the implementation process (Berman & McLaughlin, 1976; Fullan & Pomfret, 1977). Caplan's emphasis on consultee and organizational variables provides a useful model of checking for implementation realities.

CONCLUSIONS

A school psychology based on Caplan's ideas seems very promising. In discussing primary prevention, Cowen (1980) wrote that it was "something to be approached with massive giant steps" (p. 1). A similar entreaty might be made for a transformation of our current form of school psychological services toward one more congruent with Caplan's writings and clinical work.

A critical analysis of what is occurring in schools suggests both hopeful beginnings of programs and strategies and the enormity of the challenge. *A school psychology that is primarily preventive sounds perfect.* It is clearly what most of psychology should be about. Unfortunately, prevention is harder than most thought it would be, and most psychologists (despite some frustration with diagnosis that is not linked to treatment and available remedial technologies) are socialized as healers, not preventers.

Preventing problems is not only a massive logistical problem (i.e., getting services to people), but a difficult theoretical problem (i.e., developing the generative base—the causal links involved in dysfunctions). But some problems are already well understood and others can be dissected. The school remains the place to access children. Schools are not perfect platforms for consultation programs, but, along with day-care centers, could be sites for a revolution in psychological service delivery if psychologists would have the will to continue a refinement of Caplan's ideas in an educational arena.

REFERENCES

Albee, G. W., Joffe, J. M. (Eds.). (1977). *The issues: An overview of primary prevention.* Hanover, NH: University Press of New England.

Allen, V. L. (1976). *Children as teachers: Theory and research on tutoring.* New York: Academic Press.

Baker, S. B., Swisher, J. D., Nadenichek, P. E., & Popowicz, C. L. (1984). Measured effects of primary prevention strategies. *The Personnel and Guidance Journal, 63,* 459–463.

Baskin, E. J., & Hess, R. D. (1980). Does affective education work? A review of seven programs. *Journal of School Psychology, 18,* 40–50.

Berman, P., & McLaughlin, M. W. (1976). Implementation of educational innovation. *Educational Forum, 40,* 345–370.

Blechman, E. A., Kotanchick, N. L., & Taylor, C. J. (1981). Families and school together: Early behavioral intervention with high-risk children. *Behavior Therapy, 12,* 308–319.

Blechman, E. A., Taylor, C. J., & Schrader, S. M. (1981). Family problem solving versus home notes as early intervention for high-risk children. *Journal of Consulting and Clinical Psychology, 49,* 919–926.

Boike, M. F. (1986, August) *Classroom coping skills program.* Paper presented at the annual meeting of the American Psychological Association, Washington, DC.

Bond, L. A., & Rosen, J. C. (Eds.). (1990). *Competence and coping during adulthood.* Hanover, NH: University Press of New England.

Caplan, G. (1970). *The theory and practice of mental health consultation.* New York: Basic Books.

Caplan, G. (1974). *Support systems and community mental health: Lectures in concept development.* New York: Behavioral Publications.

Caplan, G. (1989). *Population-oriented psychiatry.* New York: Human Science Press.

Caplan, G., & Killilea, M. (Eds.). (1976). *Support systems and mutual help: Multidisciplinary explorations.* New York: Grune and Stratton.

Chassin, L. A., Presson, C. C., & Sherman, S. J. (1985). Stepping backward in order to step forward. *Journal of Consulting and Clinical Psychology, 53,* 612–622.

Christenson, S. L., & Cleary, M. (1990). Consultation and the parent-educator partnership: A perspective. *Journal of Educational and Psychological Consultation, 1,* 219–241.

Cohen, J. (1969). *Statistical power analysis for the behavioral sciences.* New York: Academic Press.

Comer, J. P. (1980). Child development and education. *Journal of Negro Education, 58,* 125–139.

Comer, J. P. (1984). Home-school relationships as they affect the academic success of children. *Educational and Urban Society, 16,* 323–337.

Comer, J. P. (1987). New Haven's school-community connection. *Educational Leadership, 44,* 13–16.

Comer, J. P., & Haynes, N. M. (1991). Parent involvement in schools: An ecological approach. [Special Issues.] Educational partnerships. *Elementary School Journal, 91*, 271–277.

Conoley, J. C. (1987). Families and schools: Theoretical and practical bridges. *Professional School Psychology, 2*, 191–203.

Conoley, J. C., & Conoley, C. W. (1992). *School consultation: Practice and training.* Boston, MA: Allyn and Bacon.

Cowen, E. L. (1980). The wooing of primary prevention. *American Journal of Community Psychology, 8*, 258–284.

Cowen, E. (1984). Training for primary prevention in mental health. *American Journal of Community Psychology, 12*, 253–259.

Cowen, E. L., Trost, M. A., Lorion, R. P., Dorr, D., Izzo, L. D., & Isaacson, R. V. (1975). *New ways in school mental health: Early detection and prevention of school maladaption.* New York: Human Science Press.

Durlak, J. A. (1983). Social problem-solving as a primary prevention strategy. In R. D. Felner, L. A. Jason, J. N. Moritsugu, & S. S. Farber (Eds.), *Preventive psychology: Theory, research, and practice* (pp. 31–48). New York: Pergamon.

Durlak, J. A. (1985). Primary prevention of school adjustment problems. *Journal of Consulting and Clinical Psychology, 53*, 623–630.

Epstein, L. H., Wing, R. R., Koeske, R., Andrasik, F., & Ossip, D. J. (1981). Child and parent weight loss in family-based behavior modification programs. *Journal of Consulting and Clinical Psychology, 49*, 674–685.

Fine, M. J. (1990). Facilitating home-school relationships: A family-oriented approach to collaborative consultation. *Journal of Educational and Psychological Consultation, 1*, 169–187.

Forgays, D. G. (Ed.). (1978). *Environmental influences and strategies in primary prevention.* Hanover, NH: University Press of New England.

Friend, M. (1984). Consultation skills for resource teachers. *Learning Disability Quarterly, 7*, 246–250.

Friend, M. (1985). Training special educators to be consultants: Considerations for developing programs. *Teacher Education and Special Education, 8*, 115–120.

Fuchs, D., & Fuchs, L. S. (1989). Exploring effective and efficient prereferral interventions: A component analysis of behavioral consultation. *School Psychology Review, 18*, 260–279.

Fullan, M., & Pomfret, A. (1977). Research on curriculum and instruction implementation. *Review of Educational Research, 47*, 335–397.

Gelzheiser, L. M., & Meyers, J. (in press). Special and remedial education in the classroom: Theme and variations. *Journal of Reading, Writing, and Learning Disabilities International.*

Gelzheiser, L. M., Meyers, J., & Pruzek, R. M. (1990, April). *Effects of pull-in and pull-out approaches to reading instruction for special education and remedial reading students.* Paper presented at the annual meeting of the American Educational Research Association, Boston, MA.

Gettinger, M. (Ed.). (1987). Research in effective teaching: Implications for school psychologists. [Special issue.] *Professional School Psychology, 2*(1).

Glatthorn, A. A. (1990). Cooperative professional development: Facilitating the growth of the special education teacher and the classroom teacher. *Remedial and Special Education, 11*, 29–34.

Goldstein, A. P., Apter, S. J., & Harootunian, B. (1984). *School violence.* Englewood Cliffs, NJ: Prentice-Hall.

Goldston, S. E. (1986). Primary prevention: Historical perspectives and a blueprint for action. *American Psychologist, 41*, 453–460.

Graden, J. L., Casey, A., & Bonstrom, O. (1985b). Implementing a prereferral intervention system: Part II. The data. *Exceptional Children, 51*, 487–496.

Graden, J. L., Casey, A., & Christenson, S. L. (1985a). Implementing a prereferral intervention system: Part I. The model. *Exceptional Children, 51*, 377–384.

Graden, J. L., Zins, J. E., & Curtis, M. J. (1988). *Alternative educational delivery systems: Enhancing instructional options for all students.* Washington, DC: National Association of School Psychologists.

Griest, D. L., Forehand, R., Rogers, T., Breiner, J., Furey, W., & Williams, C. A. (1982). The effects of parent enhancement therapy on the treatment outcome and generalization of a parent training program. *Behavior Research and Therapy, 20*, 429–436.

Gump, P. V. (1980). The school as a social situation. *Annual Review of Psychology, 31*, 553–582.

Gutkin, T. B. (1981). Relative frequency of consultee lack of knowledge, skill, confidence, and objectivity in school settings. *Journal of School Psychology, 19*, 57–61.

Gutkin, T. B., & Conoley, J. C. (1990). Reconceptualizing school psychology from a service delivery perspective: Implications for practice, training, and research. *Journal of School Psychology, 28*, 203–223.

Hansen, D. A. (1986). Family-school articulations: The effects of interaction rule mismatch. *American Educational Research Journal, 23*, 643–659.

Hansford, B. C., & Hattie, J. A. (1982). The relationship between self and achievement/performance measures. *Review of Educational Research, 52*, 123–142.

Harris, V. W., & Sherman, J. A. (1973). Effects of peer tutoring and consequences on the math performance of elementary school classroom students. *Journal of Applied Behavior Analysis, 6*, 587–597.

Haynes, N. M., Comer, J. P., & Hamilton-Lee, M. (1989). School climate enhancement through parental involvement. *Journal of School Psychology, 27*, 87–90.

Haynes, N. M., Comer, J. P., & Hamilton-Lee, M. (1988). The school development program: A model for school improvement. *Journal of Negro Education, 57*, 11–21.

Heffernan, J. A., & Albee, G. W. (1985). Prevention perspectives from Vermont to Washington. *American Psychologist, 40*, 202–204.

Henning-Stout, M., & Conoley, J. C. (1988). Influencing program change at the district level. In J. Graden, J. Zins, & M. Curtis (Eds.), *Alternative educational service delivery systems* (pp. 471–490). Washington, DC: National Association of School Psychologists.

Hightower, A. D., & Avery, R. R. (1986, August) *The study buddy program.* Paper presented at the annual meeting of the American Psychological Association, Washington, DC.

Jason, L. A., Durlak, J. A., & Holton-Walker, E. (1984). Prevention of child problems in the schools. In M. C. Roberts & L. Peterson (Eds.), *Prevention of problems in childhood: Psychological research and applications* (pp. 311–341). New York: Wiley.

Jason, L. A., Frasure, S., & Ferone, L. (1981). Establishing supervising behaviors in eighth graders and peer-tutoring behaviors in first graders. *Child Study Journal, 11,* 201–219.

Kent, M. W., & Rolf, J. E. (Eds.). (1979). *Social competence in children.* Hanover, NH: University Press of New England.

Medway, F. J., & Smith, R. C., Jr. (1978). An examination of contemporary elementary school affective education programs. *Psychology in the Schools, 15,* 260–269.

Meyers, J. (1975). Consultee-centered consultation with a teacher as a technique in behavior management. *American Journal of Community Psychology, 3,* 111–121.

Meyers, J., Freidman, M. P., & Gaughan, E. J., Jr. (1975). The effects of consultee-centered consultation on teacher behavior. *Psychology in the Schools, 12,* 288–295.

Meyers, J., Gelzheiser, L. M., & Yelich, G. (1990, April). *Do pull-in programs foster teacher collaboration?* Paper presented at the annual meeting of the American Educational Research Association, Boston, MA.

Meyers, J., Parsons, R. D., & Martin, R. P. (1979). *Mental health consultation in the schools.* San Francisco: Jossey-Bass.

Norris, D. A., Burke, J. P., & Speer, A. L. (1990). Tri-level service delivery: An alternative consultation model. *School Psychology Quarterly, 5,* 89–110.

Rappaport, J. (1981). In praise of paradox: A social policy of empowerment over prevention. *American Journal of Community Psychology, 9,* 1–25.

Rickel, A. U., Eshelman, A. K., & Loigman, G. A. (1983). Social problem-solving training: A follow-up study of cognitive and behavioral effects. *American Journal of Community Psychology, 11,* 15–28.

Rosenberg, M. S., & Reppucci, N. D. (1985). Primary prevention of child abuse. *Journal of Consulting and Clinical Psychology, 53,* 576–585.

Salmon, S., & Lehrer, R. (1989). School consultant's implicit theories of action. *Professional School Psychology, 4,* 173–187.

Sarason, S. B., Levine, M., Goldenberg, I. I., Cherlin, D. L., & Bennett, E. M. (1966). *Psychology in community settings: Clinical, educational, vocational, social aspects.* New York: Wiley.

Sharp, K. C. (1981). Impact of interpersonal problem-solving training on preschoolers' social competency. *Journal of Applied Developmental Psychology, 2,* 129–143.

Sheridan, S. M. (1989, March). *Conjoint behavioral consultation: A link between home and school settings.* Paper presented at the annual meeting of the National Association of School Psychologists, Boston, MA.

Sheridan, S. M., & Elliott, S. N. (1991). Behavioral consultation as a process for linking the assessment and treatment of social skills. *Journal of Educational and Psychological Consultation, 2,* 151–173.

Sheridan, S. M., Kratochwill, T. R., & Elliott, S. N. (1990). Behavioral consultation with parents and teachers: Delivering treatments for socially withdrawn children at home and school. *School Psychology Review, 19,* 33–52.

Stallings, J. (1975). Implementation and child effects of teaching practices in follow through classroom. *Monograph of the Society for Research in Child Development, 40*(7-8, Serial No. 163).

Turk, D. C., Meeks, S., & Turk, L. M. (1982). Factors contributing to teacher stress: Implications for research, prevention, and remediation. *Behavioral Counseling Quarterly, 2,* 2–25.

Villa, R. A., Thousand, J. S., Paolucci-Whitcomb, P., & Nevin, A. (1990). In search of new paradigms for collaborative consultation. *Journal of Educational and Psychological Consultation, 1,* 279–292.

Witt, J. C., & Martens, B. K. (1988). Problems with problem-solving consultation: A re-analysis of assumptions, methods, and goals. *School Psychology Review, 17,* 211–226.

Ysseldyke, J., & Christenson, S. (1986). *The instructional environment scale.* Austin, TX: Pro-Ed.

Zins, J. E., & Ponti, C. R. (1990). Strategies to facilitate the implementation, organization, and operation of system-wide consultation programs. *Journal of Educational and Psychological Consultation, 1,* 205–218.

Chapter 11

Looking Ahead: Caplan's Ideas and the Future of Organizational Consultation

Harry Levinson
The Levinson Institute

INTRODUCTION

Organizations are growing bigger. They also are growing smaller. Those two statements do not necessarily contradict each other. They describe what is happening in the organizational world. Large business organizations refer to their strategic positions as taking a global view, but having a local orientation. That means that, although a business organization may have operations in many parts of the world, it must deal with those individual units in keeping with the cultural and political requirements of the sites in which they are located. Chinese people, for example, are uncomfortable with American overt individual competitiveness. Filipino women cannot tolerate group discussion of interpersonal problems that arise in their work with each other (Proehl, 1989). Men almost everywhere have difficulty accepting women as their peers, let alone their managers.

Although business organizations are becoming larger through merger, acquisition, and internal growth, the age of the conglomerate is over. Large business organizations now tend to concentrate more heavily on what they know and do best. Although they are narrowing their focus, rapid scientific and technical evolution requires that many large firms undertake joint ventures with other companies to combine disparate technologies for innovative products and processes. These joint ventures usually are small, start-up operations, many of them requiring the participation of managers and employees from different cultures.

The structural patterns in business and industry are replicated in other social institutions. Business organizations are not alone in their pursuit of bigness. In the United States, the mega-church has arisen. Its thousands of members utilize the church for a wide variety of personal, social, and physical, as well as religious, activities. In the last, they eschew the traditional symbols of religion. Such a church becomes a psychologically supportive community center with many outreach functions. Concomitantly, in education there is a trend toward school-based management—smaller units, which, like self-managed work teams in industry, conduct their own affairs within the requirements of budget and goal.

In most of the large business operations, except those that are capital intensive such as mines, railroads, and electric power generation, the planning purview is relatively short—usually about 5 years. Technical and cultural changes quickly make many manufacturing processes obsolete. Consumer preferences are notably fickle. Work groups increasingly are transitory as a product of repetitive down-sizing, reorganization, and acquisitions.

Time was, when many people counted it an achievement to get a job in a good company, meaning one where people stayed working a lifetime with a fine pension at retirement. But these contemporary corporate transitions make it more difficult for people to attach themselves to organizations, despite their wish to be able to do so, because they can no longer depend on organizations. Besides, organizations no longer offer security as a recruiting incentive. Nevertheless, given the fundamental need for attachment (Bowlby, 1969) and the greater involvement with each other in group decision making and occupational interdependence, there is greater attachment to peers and, when people work together, greater mutual support.

In the community at large, mutual-support groups of all kinds have arisen. Their theme is individuals with the same problem helping each other to cope with or surmount it. Bonding occurs on the basis of mutually shared pain. In the business world, there is increased use of psychological services, ranging from employee assistance programs to outplacement activities to a wide range of organization development techniques. These, too, are forms of support.

Thus, we are in an era of greater psychological sensitivity, greater use of people's talents and skills, and greater need to facilitate people's efforts to work with and help each other. This also is an era of increased effort to balance work and family needs, and of rising concern with consumer value and environmental issues.

CAPLAN'S CONTRIBUTIONS
TO ORGANIZATIONAL CONSULTATION

These trends and forces give fresh significance to Caplan's contributions. Caplan (1970) noted that there will never be enough mental health professionals to do the necessary preventive work in the mental health field. Therefore, it is necessary to train people, particularly in other helping professions, to act in ways that enhance mental health and prevent mental illness. Despite refining and teaching techniques to do that, he cautioned that tumultuous change was coming and, therefore, those who have learned from what he wrote and taught should not depend solely on those methods.

Caplan anticipated what Bennis and Slater (1968) later called *The Temporary Society*. Caplan pointed out that his techniques are particularly relevant because, in his form of consultation, one cannot build and sustain long-term relationships. Furthermore, the consultees usually do not have the skills to implement more elaborate psychological conceptions and techniques. In client- and consultee-centered consultation, the consultant has perhaps only two or three consultation periods for his or her helping function. Therefore, the consultant is someone who combines consultation with straightforward teaching, supervision, and collaboration when those methods are appropriate. Such short-term productive interpersonal interactions, he contended, retard the development of social incapacity.

A consultant helps most efficiently by exerting influence on those helping persons whose function is to help other people in those others' own professional arenas. Consultants are therefore active agents for the promotion of techniques that may enable the consultee and his or her client to cope more effectively with crises. Their role is to be ego-supportive—a focus that requires them to trust the competence of their consultees without usurping their roles. In addition, the consultants are in a position to exert significant influence on the leadership of the organizations to which they consult.

According to Caplan, the task of the consultant is to add to the consultee's knowledge and lessen areas of misunderstanding. That task is most effectively accomplished when there is no power differential between the consultant and the consultee. The primary goal is to increase the consultee's effectiveness in his or her own work setting, avoiding uncovering consultees' private problems and interpreting their motivations.

However, when it comes to consulting with organizations (one type of which Caplan calls consultee-centered administrative consultation), the consultant has to evolve a diagnostic formulation. He has noted that organizations ideally develop shared concepts and a common view of immediate and distant goals. They have a history of economic, political, and sociocultural life in their respective communities. Therefore, the consultant needs cumulative statistics and information about demographic and ecological matters, as well as the results of morale studies, attitude surveys, and other organizational information. Still, the fundamental principle is to create proximity with organizational leadership and to establish a reputation for being trustworthy, competent, and eager to help, without infringing on the rights of others or endangering their programs. The posture Caplan has advocated is still one of collaboration without power differential.

Caplan has emphasized the need, in organizational consultation, for the consultant to eschew low-level contacts in favor of contact with authority figures in the consultee organization, although those who are in the most pain are likely to be marginal or deviant, and therefore the ones to have precipitated the consultation. Caplan has pointed out the need to explore the social system, to elucidate its authority and communications networks, and to find key members of those communications networks.

In the course of gathering information, the organizational consultant necessarily provokes fantasies that reflect the anxiety of those who are being interviewed and who, therefore, however unconsciously, seek to block and distort communications. They bring into their relationship with the consultant transference attitudes derived from their experiences with previous authority figures, especially parents. Therefore, the consultant has to be alert to the latent content of communications, which he or she is better able to understand because of his or her psychological training, and be sensitive to his or her own countertransference feelings and behaviors. In Chapter 8 of this volume, Tom Backer points to these same issues.

The consultee's staff should clearly know the role of the consultant and what to expect from the consultation. Together, the consultant and the consultee's staff develop the steps in the process of consultation, working through the layers of the organization, and revising their agreement as it becomes apparent that they should pursue certain directions and not others, but always keeping the top management informed. In such consultation, Caplan has observed, the consultant is always learning from the consultees, particularly about the idiosyncratic features of the various subcultures of the organization. Many of the employees, particularly those who are young and inexperienced, are in no mood to be compliant in the consultation. Besides, as Backer (Chapter 8) notes, it is particularly important that the consultees "own" the solution.

Given enough time and information, Caplan has reported, one can eventually discover the patterns of forces in the organization. Then the consultant can understand the attitudes and behaviors of the people involved as logical manifestations of their interacting motivations and goal-oriented striving, however strange those attitudes and behaviors might appear.

At the same time, if change is to occur, the experienced consultant learns that the most potent intervention is made when his or her consultee is within a range of moderate emotional involvement and has an appropriate level of anxiety. Below this range, messages are ineffective; above this range, emotional upsets are too high and members of the client organization will displace their anger on the consultant or take his or her interventions personally. In short, "no pain, no gain," but calibrated interventions to maximize the positive effects of anxiety are essential. The outcome: The consultee should experience the success of the consultation as his or her own doing, not the result of the consultant's direction, so as not to evade the realization that he or she has personally mastered a previously impossible task. Caplan's thesis is equally valid for groups or an organization as a whole. The consultant then has to be available for further support as necessary.

By Caplan's definition, this kind of consultation is focused ego-support in relationship to highly significant segments of the consultee's ego-functioning, namely improving his or her capacity for reality testing regarding the expected outcome category. Accordingly, the consultee (whether individual, executive, or a whole organization) should develop a feeling of increased mastery and autonomy, and a concomitant relaxation in his or her superego pressures about the experience of organizational conflict. In short, there should be less "ought" and perfectionistic self-criticism and greater satisfaction with self. Similar feelings should prevail in organizations.

Caplan's thesis is supported by others:

> Generally, most of the resistance against change bears little relationship to the soundness of the change advocated, but relates instead to the types of anxieties that change as such produces. Change therefore has to be coupled with a program of anxiety reduction. . . . Anxiety cannot be reduced to zero. Indeed, a certain amount of tension is necessary for continued productivity. (Greenblatt, Sharaf, & Stone, 1971, p. 6).

Edelson (1970) described consultation to an organization as sociotherapy, an orientation to the situation or social system as the object of analysis and intervention. As Caplan pointed out earlier, Edelson (1970) noted that the consultant's work is

> informed by his awareness of group processes, including intergroup relations; and his knowledge of the covert or unconscious, and often shared, meanings groups and organizations or their parts have for the individuals participating in them, and of the covert aims group members share, which determine to some extent their relation to one another, to their leaders, to other groups, and to the tasks that presumably they have joined together to achieve. (p. 312)

CAPLAN AND ORGANIZATION DEVELOPMENT

Much of contemporary organizational consultation goes largely under the rubric of Organization Development. This tradition is derived from the work of Lewin (1947) and evolved out of an early group-process orientation. It places a heavy emphasis on confrontation, communication, survey feedback work, and team-building activities. Many techniques have been invented to bring people to-gether to talk about their common problems, often with an implied or expressed ideology of openness. In the absence of significant clinical psychological train-ing and experience, the Organization Development movement is not character-ized by much psychological depth (Levinson, 1973). The following section documents this phenomenon in the Organizational Development literature.

As a first example, Gibb (1959) touched on the nature and meaning of dependency and counterdependency and their correlates, but offered little psy-chological commentary beyond that, and certainly nothing about diagnosis, prognosis, or the management of transference. Lippitt (1959) stated, "[V]ery frequently in the case of group consultation, the consultant who has the analytic skills for diagnosis does not have the training and therapeutic skills required for a working through of the implications of the diagnosis" (p. 9).

Bennis (1966), an early authoritative writer on the dynamics of change, reported, "Heavy emphasis is placed on the strategy of role model because the main instrument is the change agent himself: his skills, insight, and expertise" (p. 122). He noted that the behavior the consultant encounters from authority figures in the organization is likely to be the same kind of behavior that subordi-nates experience—in short, transference behavior—but he did not elaborate on the meanings of that behavior and how the consultant should cope with it. Bennis (1969) advocated obtaining diagnostic data from what people say and from cognitive confrontation with reality in a collaborative relationship—in short, helping people recognize and face up realistically to their problems. But, unlike Caplan, Bennis (1969) did not discuss the nature of the relationship, nor did he offer an underlying theory of unconscious motivation that would guide the consultant in that effort.

Beckhard (1969), one of the pioneers of Organization Development, agreed (as do most others in that activity) with Caplan's emphasis on the egalitarian relationship between the consultant and the consultee or client system. Organi-zation Development, by Beckhard's (1969) definition, deals with human vari-ables and values. It assumes that the basic building blocks of organizations are groups, not individuals. Beckhard (1969) spoke of diagnosing systems and pro-cesses, but did not spell out how. He assumed conscious motivation and reward-punishment psychology:

> The reward system is such that managers and supervisors are rewarded (and pun-ished) comparably for short-term profit or production performance; growth and development of their subordinates; and creating a viable work group. (p. 10)

Beckhard (1969) apparently did not recognize, and presumably therefore did not suggest, how to deal with the inherent contradiction between this statement and, ". . . power previously invested in bosses is reduced and should be . . .

managers should manage by influence rather than force or the giving or with-holding of financial rewards'' (p. 6).

Dinkmeyer and Carlson (1973) contended that the primary function of the consultant is to develop the capacity for self-renewal within individual groups and the total system. ''In a sense he is a systems analyst in that he helps the members of the system to conceptualize their problems in ways that allow them to ask significant questions and develop problem-solving capacities'' (p. 42). The target is mutual goal alignment among leaders, managers, and organizational participants. Nothing is said about how to understand the systems, nor is there any discussion of different conceptual levels among people in an organization and how the consultant might deal with them, or of ''future shock''—the reaction to the confrontation with the inevitable reality that the organization faces and its impact on organizational participants.

Schaffer (1971) argued that people in organizations seek to escape into structure and system. Unlike Jaques (1955) and Menzies (1960), he did not offer methods for coping with the essentially unconscious motivations to do so. Jaques (1955) and Menzies (1960) hypothesized that organization structure and processes often serve as devices for coping with frightening paranoid and depressive anxieties. Therefore, resistance to changing organizational mechanisms is firmly anchored in the unconscious minds of individuals and groups. The authors described methods of relieving such anxieties that then made it easier to undertake what is likely to be more successful change.

Goodstein (1978) spoke of symptoms in organizations: overt conflict, failure to attract or retain members, frequent absences, and the inability to agree on primary task or priority of goals. He described these as process concerns, as contrasted with product concerns. However, he did not mention organizational structure, sociology, economics, or politics as they might influence behavior in an organization, nor did he provide either a mode of diagnosis or insight into how to understand and deal with a client. Instead, he reported on the Blake-Mouton Managerial Grid™ (Blake & Mouton, 1964) diagnostic process and that of Weisbord (1976). The latter includes analysis of purpose, structure, rewards, relationships, helpful mechanisms, and leadership. It remained for Kotter (1978) to specify a systematic manner of diagnosing organizations, following on my own *Organizational Diagnosis* (Levinson, 1972).

Lippitt, Langseth, and Mossop (1985) described several diagnostic processes. These authors had much to say about interfaces of groups, but little about how one manages the complexity of those relationships.

Greiner and Metzger (1983) spoke about: (a) coopting naysayers, (b) achieving widespread participation in information meetings, (c) avoiding attacking sacred cows, (d) seeking alternate solutions, (e) proposing ''experimentation'' in a few selected segments of the organization, (f) evolving novel and unconventional solutions, and (g) stressing rewards. However, they did not touch on the problems of power, the politics of change, and the experience of "felt fair" (Jaques, 1989).

Kilmann (1984) gave considerable attention to systematic assessment, but said nothing about unconscious motivation or how one might interpret various forms of behavior. He offered nothing about prognosis nor attention to the attachment process and its meaning. He contended that the consultant does not really need to know anything about the content of the organization's problem. He assumed that freeing people up will enable them to act with their own expertise and, like many of those in the Organization Development movement, denied that the consultant does indeed have power.

Meanwhile, another tradition of consultation has grown up out of the Tavistock Institute. Building on the work of Bion (1959), Rice (1958), Trist and Bamforth (1951), and Jaques (1954), the Tavistock perspective does indeed look at unconscious processes and gives theoretical substance to group processes, including dealing with the experience of loss and depression in change. However, these modes of consultation give little attention to systematic diagnosis of organizations and seem to lose sight of the individual in the context of group processes.

In summary, major topics that by and large have been neglected in the Organization Development literature include: unconscious motivation, transference, working through deeper psychological barriers to change, prognosis, vicissitudes of the client–consultant relationship, contradictions between theory and practice, conceptual level differences, the significance of organizational structure, and political problems of power.

CAPLAN'S PRESCIENCE

Caplan (1970) outlined a mode of consultation based, in part, on clinical psychoanalytic knowledge and experience that specifies a relationship between the consultant and the consultee or the consultee organization. That mode also included a method by which the relationship could be effective without establishing a power differential between the consultant and the consultee. His consultation method recognized that the consultant would be likely to have only short-term relationships with the consultee, and that the consultee would be unlikely to have the skills to carry out more sophisticated psychological behavior. Therefore, his focus was on short-term projected interventions that combine teaching, supervision, and collaboration. The goal is to help people cope more effectively with their occupational relationships with others, and with the organizational realities that they face. *Caplan was prescient.* His mode of consultation has become even more appropriate at a time when consultation on psychological issues is evermore widely accepted. Backer (Chapter 8) demonstrates its immediate relevance to consultation with mental health organizations.

The Organization Development movement, which has since evolved, shares many of the same values and practices that Caplan (1970) enunciated. Like Caplan, its practitioners have emphasized the equality of the consultant and the consultee. Their focus, similarly, is on helping their clients adapt to reality more effectively. However, *much of what Caplan has brought to the fore in organizational consultation is neither recognized nor poorly dealt with in the Organization Development movement and by many others who consult on organizational change, but who do not share Caplan's psychoanalytic orientation.*

For example, from his clinical psychoanalytic base, Caplan (1970) has called attention to the importance of transference and countertransference, issues that seem not to arise at all in most of Organization Development consultation. He called for sensitivity to the latent psychological content of communications, which is also significantly missing in most Organization Development activities. His call for calibrated intervention, which required moderate emotional involvement of the consultee or consultee organization, is something that needs to be practiced. In a discipline that leans heavily on intragroup and intraorganizational feedback, reporting information, and confrontation with reality, timing is of the essence. Still, little mention of this crucial issue appears in the Organization Development literature.

Not only is the whole question of timing untouched in Organization Development, but also the issue of what must be expressed. Organization Development practitioners encourage "letting it all hang out" or expressing whatever feelings one has when they arise. Psychological clinicians, however, understand that not everything must be immediately verbalized, nor should people be urged to do so. To vent such expressions is often to destroy oneself or a part of the organization. Yet, the issues of timing, intervention, and management of expression of feelings must be dealt with at some point. That is the task of the sophisticated consultant. Furthermore, the consultant must take diversity into account. Some people do not want to talk; some people cannot express their feelings for personal or cultural reasons; and some people feel that they would just as soon not be involved in any kind of organized discussion, especially those who are threatened with some kind of significant loss in the projected change.

The specific mode and method that could be maintained in Caplan's client- or consultee-centered consultation hardly can be maintained in consultation to an organization where inevitably the consultant has authority whether he or she wishes it or not. The fact that some people can ask questions and other people are expected to answer them defines an authoritative difference between them. Also, because the consultant can decide which information about group process to feed back to a group gives that person authority. Inevitably, the consultant also is making a diagnosis, however unconsciously, each time he or she chooses to intervene into group process, or an organization activity, one way rather than another.

Therefore, following Caplan (1970), all consultants who would become more sophisticated professionals, are encouraged to combine psychoanalytic theory into their traditional practices. That can be done with appropriate training and integrating those activities with those of the Tavistock group tradition. Sophisticated consultants must be aware of individual psychology (an emphasis Backer (Chapter 8) also endorses), the individual in the group, and the latent meanings of behavior. They also must take into consideration the impact of their own behavior on the consultee organization. They also must be particularly alert to the meaning of loss in change and the depression that follows.

Above all, consultants must learn to understand that all change involves loss, and that loss must be mourned. Otherwise, much effort toward change will fail and other types of efforts will cause considerable psychic damage to those who are involved. It is this particular notion, which arises out of basic clinical orientation, that must come into the organizational consultation process. Backer (Chapter 8) elaborates the need for consultants to recognize and deal with the usual prolonged recovery period that follows significant loss.

A formal diagnostic method, too often missing in organizational consultation, also enables consultants to continuously test hypotheses (Levinson, 1972), even if their method is limited to what Caplan (1970) suggested, namely following their intuition. Experienced clinicians or consultants can pick up much about an organization simply by entering its front door. But most consultants require something more systematic, or they simply will be using ad hoc and trial-and-error methods.

The consultant inevitably must use clinical insights and skills to enable him or her to get close to the client and the client system, but not so close as to be overcome by that relationship. That calls for the kind of training that Caplan (1970) advocated: the additional training in group processes. The consultant must not merely speak of consultation to the individual, group, or organization, but must specifically differentiate the kind of consultation he or she is going to practice on any given occasion. Specifically, how does the consultant propose to help this person or this organization to solve this particular problem under these circumstances within what period of time? In short, what is the method of choice for this client system? As Backer (Chapter 8) notes, how will the consultant take into account the specific professional subcultures of the consultee system?

In contemporary consultation literature, there is no discussion of conceptual differences among people at different levels in the organization, and how the consultant should cope with them. In organizational consultation, Caplan (1970) dealt with this issue by focusing on top management and maintaining that relationship to the end of the consultation. Others in organizational consultation will have to deal with that issue, particularly if they are to work at several levels in an organization, and to communicate with people at those levels.

No mention is made in the contemporary organizational consultation literature about rising levels of intelligence in organizations as they become more technically refined, and what implication that may have for the consultation. Nor in the traditional Organization Development literature is much said about the sophisticated management of long-term relationships. Further, little is said about the management of clinical-type problems, which may be a fallout of the character of the leadership (Kets de Vries & Miller, 1988).

CONCLUSION

In sum, Caplan's (1970) consultation methods, particularly consultee- and program-centered administrative consultation, remain prominent professional models for much of organizational consultation practice, which has arisen since he spelled them out. That they have endured for more than three decades, and still remain as successful models, suggests that those principles are timeless. They will comprise a fundamental professional base for a future sophisticated organizational consultation role.

REFERENCES

Beckhard, R. (1969). *Organization development: Strategies and models*. Reading, MA: Addison-Wesley.

Bennis, W. G. (1966). *Changing organizations*. New York: McGraw-Hill.

Bennis, W. G. (1969). *Organizational development: Its nature, origin and prospects*. Reading, MA: Addison-Wesley.

Bennis, W. G., & Slater, P. E. (1968). *The temporary society*. New York: Harper & Row.

Bion, W. R. (1959). *Experiences in groups*. New York: Basic Books.

Blake, R. R., & Mouton, J. S. (1964). *The managerial grid*. Houston, TX: Gulf.

Bowlby, J. (1969). *Attachment and loss. Vol. 1: Attachment*. New York: Basic Books.

Caplan, G. (1970). *The theory and practice of mental health consultation*. New York: Basic Books.

Dinkmeyer, D., & Carlson, J. (1973). *Consulting*. Columbus, OH: Merrill.

Edelson, M. (1970). *The practice of sociotherapy: A case study*. New Haven, CT: Yale University Press.

Gibb, J. R. (1959). The role of the consultant. *Journal of Social Issues, 15*(2), 1–4.

Goodstein, L. D. (1978). *Consulting with human service systems*. Reading, MA: Addison-Wesley.

Greenblatt, M., Sharaf, M. R., & Stone, E. M. (1971). Dynamics of institutional change. Pittsburgh, PA: University of Pittsburgh Press.

Greiner, L. E., Metzger, R. O. (1983). *Consulting to management*. Englewood Cliffs, NJ: Prentice-Hall.

Jaques, E. (1954). *The changing culture of a factory*. London: Heinemann.

Jaques, E. (1955). Social systems as a defense against persecutory and depressive anxiety. In M. Klein, P. Heimann, & R. E. Money-Kyrle (Eds.), *New directions in psychoanalysis*. London: Tavistock.

Jaques, E. (1989). *Requisite organization*. Arlington, VA: Cason Hall.

Kets de Vries, M. F. R., & Miller, D. (1988). *Unstable at the top: Inside the troubled organization*. New York: New American Library.

Kilmann, R. H. (1984). *Beyond the quick fix: Managing five tracks to organizational success*. San Francisco: Jossey-Bass.

Kotter, J. P. (1978). *Organizational dynamics: Diagnosis and intervention*. Reading, MA: Addison-Wesley.

Levinson, H. (1972). *Organizational diagnosis*. Cambridge, MA: Harvard University Press.

Levinson, H. (1973). *The great jackass fallacy*. Boston, MA: Harvard University Graduate School of Business Administration.

Lewin, K. (1947). Frontiers in group dynamics, *Human Relations, 1*, 5–41.

Lippitt, G. L., Langseth, P., & Mossop, J. (1985). *Implementing organizational change*. San Francisco: Jossey-Bass.

Lippitt, R. (1959). Dimensions of the consultant's job. *Journal of Social Issues, 15*(2), 5–12.

Menzies, I. E. P. (1960). A case study in the functioning of social systems as a defense against anxiety. *Human Relations, 13*, 95–121.

Proehl, R. K. (1989, March). When cultures clash. *Vision/Action, 8*(1), pp. 23–26.

Rice, A. K. (1958). *Productivity and social organization: The Ahmedabad experiment*. London: Tavistock.

Schaffer, R. H. (1971, April). The psychological barriers to management effectiveness. *Business Horizons*, pp. 17–30.

Trist, E., & Bamforth, K. W. (1951). Some social and psychological consequences of the long-wall methods of coal-getting. *Human Relations, 4*, 3–38.

Weisbord, M. R. (1976). Organizational diagnosis: Six places to look for trouble with or without a theory. *Organization and Group Studies, 1*(4), 30–47.

Chapter 12

Epilogue

Gerald Caplan

The dominant theme throughout my 50 years as a psychiatrist has been my active search for new concepts, service models, and techniques to prevent psychosocial disorder in a population. In fulfilling this mission, I have become accustomed to crossing boundaries: (a) *spatial boundaries*, when I went out of the mental hospitals, in which I, like most psychiatrists, worked fifty years ago, to establish outpatient clinics in the community, and then to open psychiatric departments in general hospitals—a revolutionary step in those days—and later to offer mental health consultation in schools and public health centers; and (b) *boundaries between the professional disciplines and between professional domains*, involving my reaching out to recruit other professions in carrying out my own professional mission.

In the 1950s and 1960s, as a member of the Executive Committee of the International Association of Child Psychiatry, I became a passionate advocate of opening up our membership to national societies that admitted, as full members, such non-psychiatrists as psychologists and psychiatric social workers. My pressure group of reformers eventually carried the day. We changed our constitution and adopted the title of the International Association of Child and

Adolescent Psychiatry and Allied Professions. It seems strange, looking back from the multidisciplinary egalitarianism of 1992, to realize that it took us many years of acrimonious debates to achieve this constitutional parity of other professions with psychiatrists and of the newer field of adolescent psychiatry with the established subspecialty of child psychiatry.

Some psychologists blamed the exclusiveness of traditional psychiatrists on the latter's adherence to the medical model. I am a staunch supporter of the medical model, when relating to patient management. In accordance with a central tenet of the model, I feel strongly that to achieve effective management it is essential that a particular physician accept responsibility and accountability for a patient and that this responsibility be linked with the physician being granted authority to make immediate decisions on the diagnosis and treatment of that patient. Otherwise, the very life of the patient may be endangered. The physician must act as the leader of the multidisciplinary clinical group that is diagnosing and treating the patient. But when physicians extrapolate from this hierarchical pattern to assume leadership privileges in all professional and administrative matters in which other professions are involved, and when they immodestly claim authority over the others, I have long parted company from them. I do not agree that such attitudes of professional arrogance necessarily follow from the medical model. Nor do I agree that this model implies restricting our focus to intraorganismic biological factors in diagnosis and treatment of a patient. A wider focus, which includes psychological and environmental factors, and especially family and social factors, clearly would lead physicians to recognize that other professional disciplines with greater expertise in appraising such factors must be accepted as potential authority figures, particularly in planning, research, and organizational matters.

Another set of boundaries, which I felt long ago should be crossed, was that of conceptual models. My own basic model was that of psychoanalytic psychology, but I was opposed to squeezing all of my professional thinking into this conceptual framework. I also saw merit in seeking to guide my operations in data collection and action planning by using a variety of models of family groups, social systems, and sociological and cultural forces, as well as making use of epidemiological and public health practice models. I also felt the need to build new conceptual models. These guided my efforts when I explored the territory into which I penetrated after leaving the spatial and conceptual domains of traditional psychiatry, and after entering the unfamiliar world of non-psychiatric institutions and organizations and of normal people in their ecological settings in the community.

Crossing these boundaries did not lead me to abandon my old professional identity, but rather to add new and enriching elements. Using a political analogy, I did not advocate *cosmopolitanism,* but rather *internationalism.* I retained the knowledge, skills, and system of values of a psychoanalytic psychiatrist, but I also became interested in new ideas, intervened in new organizational and social settings, and established relationships with new sets of professionals dealing with issues with which I had no previous experience. It was in this connection that I pioneered the techniques of mental health consultation as a systematic modality of interprofessional communication, through which I might make my contribution to fulfillment of my colleagues' professional mission while influencing them to play an important part in achieving my own goals. At the Harvard Laboratory of Community Psychiatry, I had recruited my fellow workers from many professional disciplines, each of which had something special to contribute to our joint understanding of health-related behavior. When we developed our method of mental health consultation, we agreed that, although the members of our team might use the same techniques of communicating with other professionals, the content of our communications would differ because it would be based on the different professional discipline and background of each of us. There would be some overlap, but there would also be something idiosyncratic in the content of what was communicated by each person.

Every profession has a core of knowledge and skills that is relatively unique. In addition, each profession deals traditionally with clients and problems that also are dealt with by other professions. All of these professions may make use of similar *generic* knowledge and skills. Over and above this, each profession may extend beyond its traditional domain to deal with new problems. In dealing with the latter, generic concepts and skills are most likely to be involved, and these may be shared equally by all workers. When members of different professions work together, and, more significantly, when a worker from one profession teaches members of another profession, there should be no incompatibility as long as the content of the teaching is restricted to shared domains and generic knowledge and skills. However, if what is communicated overlaps the unique core area of the different professions, there may be dissonance.

In a volume devoted to my contributions to American psychology, one may ask whether my being a psychiatrist, identified with the medical model and the ways of thinking and working of a physician, has led to any significant problems in the interactions between me and psychologists. Because my main contributions have been based on ideas I developed after crossing the traditional boundaries of my own profession, and during my penetration of fields in which psychologists were also charting new paths, it might be expected that there would be little dissonance related to differences between the core cognitive base of each. But I believe that, in at least two areas, there has been such dissonance. First, several school psychologists have expressed reservations about the *manipulative* aspects of so-called Caplanian mental health consultation. This led my daughter, Ruth, and me to devote a chapter in our latest book (Caplan & Caplan, 1993) to an analysis of the techniques of *manipulation* and a discussion of its use in mental health consultation. We showed that manipulation may be used unethically (i.e., as a covert way of gaining personal benefit for the manipulator at the expense of an unsuspecting victim, whose rights are thereby subordinated to those of the manipulator). It also may be used, as indeed it is in our method of mental health consultation, to benefit equally both consultant and consultee, and to avoid forcing the consultees to become aware of thoughts and feelings against which they are unconsciously defending themselves. Such an ethical use of manipulation is commonplace in the traditional practice of physicians. Their guild, as well as governmental controls linked with the terms of medical licensure, provide adequate safeguards to prevent unethical misuse of the technique. Physicians rely on these controls, and they usually feel no ambivalence in using manipulation. Nor have any psychiatrists expressed reservations to me about our incorporating a manipulation element in our consultation method. We never considered it a problem until the ethical issue was drawn to our attention by members of other professions, who are not accustomed to using the manipulation technique in their daily work. As long as this issue is clearly recognized, I do not feel that it raises an insurmountable obstacle to psychologists using our mental health consultation techniques. Instead of relying on controls derived from their traditional professional framework and setting, as psychiatrists do, psychologists must pay explicit *personal* attention to not misusing the manipulative element of the techniques to subordinate the interests of their consultee to their own. The nature of the consultation situation, in which the consultants are intent on benefiting the consultees, helps them to accomplish this.

The second area of dissonance is harder to handle. Although most psychologists have no difficulty accepting our formulations of "theme interference" as an adequate way of understanding that subjective involvement in their work may, in some cases, distort the professional functioning of consultees, many of these psychologists have difficulty learning our techniques· of theme-interference reduction. The skills involved in the latter were derived from those of psychoanalytic psychotherapy, which are part of my own pool of skills as a psychoanalytic psychiatrist. These skills are shared by other psychoanalytically oriented psychotherapists, and are not the restricted province of psychiatrists. Clinical psychologists and psychiatric social workers also use similar therapeutic techniques. Professionals with training in these subspecialities have no difficulty learning our method of theme-interference reduction, as long as they can bring themselves to avoid uncovering types of interpretation. But this is often not the case with school psychologists who have not undergone clinical psychology, in addition to educational psychology, training.

Today, I understand this issue better than in the past, and I have tried to reduce this interprofessional dissonance in our latest book on mental health consultation (Caplan & Caplan, 1993). This book is designed to appeal to a wider range of professions than *The Theory and Practice of Mental Health Consultation* (Caplan, 1970), and it specifically addresses the interests of school psychologists. In the new book, we have reduced the centrality of our discussion of theme-interference reduction. In our detailed case examples of consultee-centered consultation, which were recorded and analyzed by Ruth Caplan, who is not a psychoanalytic psychotherapist, we proposed variations of our original technique that are likely to be more acceptable and feasible for use by a broader range of consultants.

I realize now that my original preoccupation with the theme-interference reduction technique (Caplan, 1970) was linked to the excitement its development aroused in me, because it represented a novel variant of my customary psychoanalytic psychotherapy techniques. In consultation, I was exploiting my insights about the unconscious aspects of defense mechanisms and their adaptive value in safeguarding the integrity of the ego, while drastically deviating from the usual psychoanalytic approach of "making the unconscious conscious," which, in those days, was considered the royal road to benefiting patients. I was beginning to appreciate that it was possible to make use of clinical skills in dealing professionally with healthy people, but that these skills had to be modified for use in a nonclinical setting. Although clinical patients and the professional colleagues who asked us for consultation shared basic psychological features because of their common humanity, they also differed in important respects, and techniques for helping them had to be adapted to these differences. I was interested that the nonconfrontational and noninterpretational therapeutic modes, which I had previously learned to use in dealing with sick patients with fragile ego structures, were precisely what seemed most appropriate for use with the mentally healthy professionals who were my consultees.

My book was molded by my salient personal interests in 1970, and I must admit that I paid little attention to the likely professional heterogeneity of my potential readers. I naively took it for granted that most readers would be community mental health workers, who had come into the community field from a background in clinical work with psychiatric patients. It was not until later, when I started training Episcopal bishops as mental health consultants (Caplan & Caplan, 1993), that I realized that our mental health consultation techniques also could be modified for use by nonclinicians, who might be as sensitive as us to psychosocial issues and who might be helped by us to develop potent techniques of interpersonal influence in consultation.

A comparable factor that molded my 1970 book was my oversimplified idea that mental health consultants would, like me and my Harvard colleagues, come into consultee institutions from an outside base, such as a community mental health center or some other psychiatric agency. I did not consider the possibility that mental health consultants might be employed as in-house members of staff of the institution whose non-mental health staff might be asking them for consultation. In my book, I discussed the advantages to be derived from the outsider status of the consultant. It was not until later, when I began working as a member of the regular staff in general hospitals, that I began to appreciate that many of the techniques discussed in the 1970 book were very difficult, or impossible, to use if the mental health consultant was an insider. In our 1993 book, we devoted three chapters to techniques of "mental health collaboration," which must replace mental health consultation as the most frequent mode of interprofessional communication to be used by mental health specialists who are staff members of an institution. We also discussed how the specialist may use mental health consultation techniques within this framework, and we analyzed the modifications in technique that are demanded if the consultant is an insider. School psychologists and other insider specialists who attempted to use, without modification, the techniques of consultation advocated in my 1970 book encountered great difficulties. Therefore, it is perhaps strange that this book became so popular among them, especially when we add these difficulties to those associated with manipulation and theme-interference reduction.

I believe that the attractiveness of the 1970 book, which succeeded in overcoming these obstacles, was that readers were able to appreciate that, although I described in specific detail a number of techniques, I did so as a vehicle for postulating a series of general principles, the understanding of which had enabled me to guide my actions and develop useful methods of interprofessional cooperation in unfamiliar settings. These principles are of a generic nature and may be used to guide workers of other professions. Most of the contributors to the present volume perceived my contribution to professional psychology along these lines. The fact that some of the techniques I advocated proved inappropriate for use by school psychologists was of lesser importance than the benefits that were derived from their accepting the general principles, which provide a conceptual framework for understanding the process of transactions between mental health specialists and their non-mental health colleagues. Acceptance of these basic principles equipped school psychologists to work out their own techniques for data collection and remedial intervention, rather than feeling that they had to copy those that I had used in my work settings.

Through the medium of my 1970 book, I similarly communicated with my readers what I was advocating they should do with their consultees. I did so by asking questions and adding to understanding, rather than issuing directives or offering advice. Thus, I fostered a process through which other persons would feel free to choose what seemed sensible and useful to them, which they might actively incorporate within their personal system of ideas and practices.

The fact that I was a member of a different profession from these readers, and that the settings in which I was working were far removed from their own, helped readers to actively draw out what made sense to them, much as a mental health consultant uses a parable to communicate potent messages to his or her consultees. Like the parable maker, I was careful to describe my case examples in vivid details, which made them come alive for the readers. However, many readers must have realized that, to preserve professional confidentiality, my examples had to be carefully disguised and, to some extent, fictionalized. The power of the communication in my book, as in a parable, lies not in the artistry of description, important as that must be in holding the attention of the reader or consultee, but in the potency of the covert message. In the case of my book, I would like to think that the basic principles I was communicating were recognized as particularly significant by my readers.

I also felt it was important that the principles I proposed were not drawn by me from a systematic theory, but were accumulated, one at a time, as a result of analyzing my transactions in various practice settings, as I grappled with problems raised by my consultees and tried to support their professional development within the constraints and assets of their personal and institutional realities. Formulation of each principle emerged from what seemed to have worked for me and for members of my team, as we struggled to make sense of complicated constellations of individual, interpersonal, and organizational forces, and as we tailored our intercessions in accordance with this understanding. The principles were those that appeared to guide us effectively as practitioners, and therefore that might be expected to guide other practitioners in different settings. Our approach was different from deriving hypotheses from a scientific theory and then systematically testing these hypotheses through the use of a research design. It was akin to the process whereby an experienced clinician acquires wisdom as a result of intuitively perceiving significant patterns across many case histories. We tried to shorten this process by explicitly analyzing the patterns in our practical experience, but we relied on intuition and subjective impressions to arrive at hunches, which we then accepted, modified, or discarded by seeing whether they held up in our future practice.

I believe that our basic principles must eventually be tested scientifically. Meanwhile, the fact that colleagues so different from us (e.g., school psychologists) have continued to use them over a period of years perhaps indicates that they do have intrinsic merit.

I regard the thinking that underlay the writing of our 1993 book, as well as my contribution to the present volume, to be an opportunity to review some of my basic principles and assumptions, and to modify and enrich them in the light of confrontation with the discrepant needs of psychologists and the characteristics of their work settings. I am most grateful to Bill Erchul and his colleagues for affording me this opportunity. I am also grateful for their emphasizing, in several chapters in this volume, that important as has been my development of a particular style of consultation and of the underlying basic principles, psychologists also should pay attention to my other conceptual and technical innovations. These include models of prevention, models of service delivery, ''crisis theory'' and techniques of crisis intervention, and support systems methods. I have described and analyzed these concepts and skills, which originally were used in community mental health centers, but which also proved valuable in other types of settings, in my recent book *Population-Oriented Psychiatry* (Caplan, 1989). In contrast to the popularity, among American psychologists, of my book on mental health consultation (Caplan, 1970), my 1989 book has aroused little interest in this country, whereas in Europe it already has been translated into German and Spanish, and may shortly be published in Portuguese. Perhaps the widespread utilization of my ideas over a period of 30 years in the community mental health field in the United States has reduced their novelty, as well as having stimulated a large number of competing publications by other specialists. Another influence may be the current recurrence of the pendulum swing of popularity away from psychosocial interests toward psychobiological preoccupations in American psychiatry (Caplan, 1969), and the fact that, in the United States, leadership in the field of community mental health has traditionally been in the hands of psychiatrists, in contrast to leadership in such fields as primary prevention, family mental health, and organizational and industrial mental health, which has been exercised by psychologists. This pattern has been different in Europe. For instance, in the Scandinavian countries, particularly in Denmark, the community mental health movement was initiated 40 years ago, largely by psychologists; and currently in Spain, this pattern also is being repeated. I am presently planning to teach a second series of seminars in a Spanish university department of psychology (University of Salamanca), which seeks to develop to cadre a leaders for a new governmental program of community mental health services. When I gave the first series of lectures in this program 2 years ago, I found that most of the participants were psychologists, and that the postgraduate students included a few psychiatrists—a pattern similar to what I had experienced when I participated in the annual conference on primary prevention (Kessler & Goldston, 1986) at the University of Vermont. In my Spanish seminars, I was asked to focus my lectures on those concepts and techniques of population-oriented psychiatry that I listed previously, and the interest in mental health consultation expressed by the course organizers was only secondary. This mirrors the organizational demands of developments in the service delivery field in a country where psychiatrists are still mainly working inside mental hospitals, as they did in the United States 50 years ago.

This brief reference to national historical trends appears to reveal a counterpoint between the operations of psychiatrists and psychologists. I end this chapter with the hope that American psychologists will take over leadership roles in community mental health services being vacated at present by psychiatrists, as the latter transfer their interests and activities from the psychosocial to the psychobiological spheres. If psychologists take over this field in the United States, as their colleagues are doing in Spain, I would like my writings to influence population-oriented practice development among them, as appears to have happened in the field of mental health consultation.

REFERENCES

Caplan, G. (1970). *The theory and practice of mental health consultation.* New York: Basic Books.

Caplan, G. (1989). *Population-oriented psychiatry.* New York: Human Sciences Press.

Caplan, G., & Caplan, R. B. (1993). *Mental health consultation and collaboration.* San Francisco: Jossey-Bass.

Caplan, R. B. (1969). *Psychiatry and the community in nineteenth-century America.* New York: Basic Books.

Kessler, M., & Goldston, S. E. (Eds.). (1986). *A decade of progress in primary prevention.* Hanover and London: University Press of New England.

Author Index

Subject Index